indonesia

1991

No. 52 (October)

Submissions: Submit manuscripts in a typewritten or computer-keyed, *double-spaced* format with footnotes and other stylistic conventions in accordance with *The Chicago Manual of Style,* 13th ed. Double space footnotes and group them at the end of the article. Include a short statement of your institutional affiliation and status to be used in the "List of Contributors" if the article is published.

Address: Please address all correspondence and manuscripts to *Indonesia,* Cornell Modern Indonesia Project, 102 West Avenue, Ithaca, NY 14850.

Computer submissions: Submissions on disk facilitate and accelerate the publication process. The editors will request disk copies and FAX, telex, and telephone numbers when your manuscript is accepted for publication.

Reprints: Contributors will receive ten complimentary reprints of their articles and one complimentary copy of the issues in which their articles appear. They may order additional reprints at cost *at the time the manuscript is accepted for publication.*

Abstracts: Abstracts of articles published in *Indonesia* appear in *Excerpta Indonesica,* which is published semiannually by the Centre for Documentation on Modern Indonesia, Royal Institute of Linguistics and Anthropology, Leiden.

Subscription rates: US $18.00 per year or $9.50 per issue. For mailings outside the United States, add US $5.00 per year postage. Order from Southeast Asia Program Publications, East Hill Plaza, Ithaca, NY 14850.

ISBN: 978-0-87727-853-5

Cover: Prabu Kresnå: Part god, Kresnå is an incarnation of the mighty Wisnu. Consummate politician, diplomat, and strategist of war, Kresnå is the most intellectually brilliant of the Pendåwå faction and it is he who makes their final victory possible.

Contents

EARLY STATE FORMATION

Introduction 1

K. W. Taylor

Epigraphical References to the "City" and the "State" in Early Indonesia 3

Hermann Kulke

States without Cities: Demographic Trends in Early Java 23

Jan Wisseman Christie

The Merchant and the King: Political Myths of Southeast Asian Coastal Polities 41

Pierre-Yves Manguin

Competing Hierarchies: Javanese Merchants and the *Priyayi* Elite in Solo, Central Java 55

Suzanne A. Brenner

Javanese Mysticism and Art: A Case of Iconography and Healing 85

Astri Wright

Vivere Pericolosamente 105

Tjalie Robinson, Translated by Winniefred Anthonio

Why I Didn't Set Up My Own Business 119

Idrus, Translated by A. L. Reber

Malay Manuscripts and Early Printed Books at the Library of Congress 123

A. Kohar Rony

INTRODUCTION

The three articles by Hermann Kulke, Jan Wisseman Christie, and Pierre-Yves Manguin published in this volume are revised versions of papers presented at a panel on early Indonesian state formation during the Association for Asian Studies Meeting at Washington, DC, in 1989. Using different kinds of evidence and different methodologies, these authors share a common interest in how new structures of authority were conceptualized and formalized in early Java and Sumatra and how these structures may have responded to pre-existing patterns of hierarchy. These papers reveal possibilities for analyzing early state formation that suggest diversity both in the Indonesian past and in the epistemological and methodological potentialities of various kinds of evidence. They are published here not out of an antiquarian interest in the distant past but more with the conviction that efforts to analyze the past into coherent narratives or models reveal important aspects of contemporary academic and political culture.

K. W. Taylor.

EPIGRAPHICAL REFERENCES TO THE "CITY" AND THE "STATE" IN EARLY INDONESIA

Hermann Kulke

I.

As explained elsewhere in a more theoretical context, state formation in Southeast Asia took place in three consecutive phases, which correspond with chiefdom (or local principality), the early kingdom, and finally the imperial kingdom.[1] The present article organizes and analyzes the epigraphical references to the "city" and the "state" according to these three developmental phases. Part I deals with Indonesia's earliest inscriptions of Mūlavarman and Pūrṇavarman of the fifth century C.E., which depict the transformation of a chiefdom into an early kingdom. Parts II to IV analyze various developmental stages and structural problems of early kingdoms as exemplified by the inscriptions of early Śrīvijaya and of Central and Eastern Java from the late seventh to twelfth centuries. The final part deals with the growth of the imperial kingdom under Singasari and Majapahit. The emphasis of the paper is the descriptive analysis of the epigraphical evidence rather than an evaluation of its theoretical implications.[2]

This study was undertaken at the Institute of Southeast Asian Studies, Singapore, with a Southeast Asia Fellowship for German Scholars of the Stiftung Volkswagenwerk. I am grateful to both institutions for providing me their unfailing hospitality and financial support from March to September 1987. Furthermore I wish to express my thanks to Prof. J.G. de Casparis, Prof. Boechari, Dr. J. Wisseman-Christie, Dr. P.-Y. Manguin, and Dr. J. Miksic for their help and comments.

[1] H. Kulke, "The Early and the Imperial Kingdom in Southeast Asian History," in: *Southeast Asia in the 9th to 14th Centuries*, ed. D.G. Marr and A.C. Milne (Singapore: Institute of Southeast Asian Studies, 1986), pp. 1–22; also "Indian Colonies, Indianization or Cultural Convergence? Reflections on the Changing Image of India's Role in South-East Asia," in: *Onderzoek in Zuidoost-Azië. Agenda's voor de Jaren Negentig*, ed. H. Schulte Nordholt (= *Semaian*, 3), Rijksuniversiteit te Leiden 1990, pp. 8–32.

[2] For further theoretical discussions, see D. Lombard, "Le concept d'empire en Asie du Sud-Est," in: *Le Concept d'Empire*, ed. M. Duverger (Paris, 1980), pp. 433–41; see O.W. Wolters, *History, Culture, and Region in Southeast Asian Perspectives* (Singapore: Institute of Southeast Asian Studies, 1982); L. Gessick, ed., *Centers, Symbols and Hierarchies: Essays on the Classical States of Southeast Asia* (New Haven: Yale University Southeast Asian Studies

The first step towards state formation that is discernible in inscriptions is the transition from chieftaincy to early kingdom. In Indonesia this transition is illustrated very instructively by the famous Kutei inscriptions of Mūlavarman who ruled about 400 C.E. in East Kalimantan.[3] These earliest inscriptions of Indonesia, incised on seven yupa or sacrificial stone posts that bear a strong resemblance to menhirs, contain the unique story of the rise of a local chieftaincy and its transformation into an early kingdom within three generations.[4] The story begins with a local leader, perhaps a lineage elder, with the name Kundunga. His Sanskrit title "Lord of Men" (*narendra*) may have been conferred upon him only posthumously by his son or grandson. Under his son something important apparently took place, as one of the inscriptions reports that he became the founder of a lineage or "dynasty" (*vaṃśa-karta*) and assumed the Sanskrit name Asvavarman. Whatever that may have meant in detail, it appears that Asvavarman was able to raise considerably the status of his lineage (*vaṃśa*) within his own clan.

The decisive steps towards the establishment of an early kingdom took place in the third generation under Mūlavarman. He assumed the royal title *rājā*, defeated neighboring chiefs (*pārthiva*), and made them his tributaries (*karadā*). Furthermore, he invited Brahmins "who came hither" (*ihāgata*) and celebrated grand rituals at a "most sacred place" (*puṇyatama kṣetra*) called Vaprakeśvara, and had a series of impressive inscriptions incised.[5] The meaning of the unusual name of "Lord (Śiva) of the Vapra(ka)" is unclear. But the fact that the place is explicitily described as "most sacred" allows us to infer that it had something to do with Mūlavarman's rise to power. Sanskrit *vapra* has the meaning of either "rampart" and "earth raised as the foundation of a building" or "mound" and "hillock." Thus this "Lord of the Vapra(ka)" may have been associated either with the foundation of Mūlavarman's own "town" (*pura*), which is mentioned in one of the inscriptions, or with a ritual on a hillock. Although the first meaning cannot be ruled out, the latter is more likely in view of other examples known from Southeast Asia where liṅgas of Śiva (*isvara*) were consecrated on a hillock (*vapra*) in connection with the foundation ritual of a polity. The most famous example is, of course, the establishment of a Śivaliṅga as Devarāja on the Mahendra mountain in 802 C.E. by Jayavarman II, the founder of the kingdom of Angkor.[6] More important in the context of early Javanese history, however, is the consecration of a Śivaliṅga by Sañjaya on a hillock in Central Java in 732 C.E.[7] In regard to Mūlavarman's Vaprakeśvara, we may even go a step further and infer that the deity Vaprakeśvara may have also been associated with the cult of a deified ancestor, the very "root" of the "dynasty" established by Mūlavarman's father. At least Mūlavarman's name, "protegé (*varman*) of the root (*mūla*)," makes such an

---

Monographs, 1983); P. Wheatley, *Nagara and Commandery: Origins of Southeast Asian Urban Traditions* (Chicago: The University of Chicago Department of Geography Research Paper Nos. 207–208, 1983); K. R. Hall, *Maritime Trade and State Development in Early Southeast Asia* (Honolulu: University of Hawaii Press, 1985); Marr and Milner, eds., *Southeast Asia;* S. Subrahmanyam, "Aspects of State Formation in South India and Southeast Asia, 1550–1650, in: *Indian Economic and Social History Review*, 23 (1986): 358ff; for Mainland Southeast Asia see C. Higham, *The Archaeology of Mainland Southeast Asia* (Cambridge: Cambridge University Press, 1989; R. Hagensteijn, *Circles of Kings. Political Dynamics in Early Continental Southeast Asia* (Dordrecht, 1989).

[3] B. Ch. Chhabra, *Expansion of Indo-Aryan Culture During Pallava Rule* (New Delhi, 1965) pp. 85–92.

[4] See also F. H. van Naerssen, *The Economic and Administrative History of Early Indonesia* (Leiden/Köln, 1977), pp. 18–23.

[5] See also J. G. de Casparis, "Some Notes on the Oldest Inscriptions of Indonesia," in: *A Man of Indonesian Letters. Essays in Honour of Professor A. Teeuw*, ed. C.M.S. Hellwig and S. O. Robson (Leiden, 1986), pp. 242–55 (= VKI, 121).

[6] H. Kulke, *The Devaraja Cult* (Ithaca: Cornell University Southeast Asia Program Data Paper 108, 1979).

[7] H. B. Sarkar, *Corpus of Inscriptions of Java*, vol. I (Calcutta: Mukhopadhyay, 1971), pp. 15–24.

inference quite likely. Finally, it should be emphasized that the making and establishment of the monumental *yūpa* stone inscription by the Brahmins (their authorship is mentioned twice in the inscriptions) in a tribal surrounding must have been particularly impressive and successful in raising the status of Mūlavarman. The Brahmins "who had come hither" were generously rewarded by Mūlavarman with land (*bhūmi*) and thousands of cows.

The analysis of the epigraphical evidence of these earliest inscriptions of Indonesia allows us to draw the following tentative picture of Mūlavarman's new polity. At its center was the *pura*, which, however, certainly did not yet represent a truly urban settlement. The statement that it was "his own (*svaka*) pura" makes it more likely that, as in later cases, here, too, *pura* meant the "residence" or kraton of Mūlavarman. Not very far away from the *pura* was the "most sacred place" (perhaps on the "sacred mountain") of Mūlavarman's polity, which might have been associated with a Hinduized ancestor cult. The *pura* may have been surrounded by the dwelling places and lands of the Brahmins "who came here" and by the places of other members of Mūlavarman's lineage (*vaṃśa*). Beyond this nuclear area and its adjoining jungle, similar, though most likely smaller, places of other "landlords" (*pārthiva*) and lineage elders and their family members were situated. Some of these little chiefs had been defeated by Mūlavarman and thus become his tributaries. This is all we know about Mūlavarman's polity from his inscription. Apart from the *pura*, the holy *kṣetra*, the land (*bhūmi*) donated to the Brahmins, and the surrounding "landlords" (*pārthiva*) donated to the Brahmins, no other evidence is known that allows us to define the polity spatially. Furthermore, it is significant that no "officers" of any political function are mentioned in these inscriptions. In Weberian terminology, Mūlavarman's authority was thus a purely patriarchal rule based, most likely, on his patriarchal household and its *oikos* economy. But there was one significent difference. Mūlavarman's court was able to attract Brahmins who certainly acted not only as ritual specialists but also as advisers, thus fulfilling a role that comes already near to Weber's extra-patrimonial staff. The fact that Mūlavarman managed to invite (and feed!) Brahmins and to have them perform grand rituals and to compose and incise seven impressive yūpa inscriptions distinguishes Mūlavarman's polity from the many little chieftaincies that surrounded him. However, although he claimed to have defeated them, he still remained one of them, though as primus inter pares; whereas these chiefs were called "Landlord" (*pārthiva*) Rājā Mūlavarman was praised in his inscriptions as the "Lord of the Landlords" (*pārthiva-indra*).

In this connection a small hint from the earliest inscription of mainland Southeast Asia, the famous Vo-Canh inscription from Central Vietnam, is very instructive.[8] It reports an announcement "beneficial to the people" (*prajā*) by King Śrī Māra that he was willing to share all his property with those dear to him. Among these were his sons, brothers, and relatives explicitly mentioned as having been satisfied by Śrī Māra while he sat on the throne in the midst of his kinsmen (*svajana*). Much has been written about this inscription. On palaeographical grounds, its date is usually given as the second or third centuries C.E. G. Coedès and others assumed an identity of Śrī Māra with Fan Shih man, the great king of Funan in the third century C.E.[9] But to my understanding it is absolutely impossible to interpret this inscription as a document of a great Funanese king who, in this case, would have been ruling over a large kingdom that spread from Funan's center in the Mekong Delta up the Annamite coast where the Vo-Canh inscription was found. Instead, the Vo-Canh inscription appears to represent a "state" that has to be equated evolutionarily with Mūlavarman's polity. In the Vo-Canh inscription we meet only the king, his relatives, and

8 R. C. Majumdar, *The Inscriptions of Champa* (Lahore, 1927), pp. 1–3.

9 G. Coedès, *The Indianized States of Southeast Asia* (Honolulu: University of Hawaii Press, 1968), p. 40.

the people. He sat amidst his own kinsmen and promised to share his property with them. As in the case of Mūlavarman's inscription, there were no officers of any kind present during the ceremony. Some Brahmins must have been around to compose and to incise the inscription, but they seem to have been even less influential than under Mūlavarman as they are not referred to at all. Śrī Māra's "state affairs" were therefore clearly the affairs of the "royal family" (*rājakula*) which is mentioned in the inscription.

There is yet another fact that brings the Vo-Canh inscription typologically even nearer to the Kutei inscriptions. In its (otherwise very mutilated) introduction, the Vo-Canh inscription, too, mentions a "first conquest" (*prathama vijaya*). As in the case of Mūlavarman in Kalimantan, Śrī Māra's family (*kula*) or clan obviously had just undertaken some successful raids against neighboring chiefs. In order to ascertain the loyalty of his (envious?) relatives (in this regard the explicit mention of his brothers is noteworthy), Śrī Māra felt obliged to assure them of his willingness to share the spoils, and he appealed to future kings to do the same. From a structural point of view, we have thus the same situation as we came across in Eastern Kalimantan after Mūlavarman had undertaken his first conquests. In this regard it is important that D. C. Sircar, the renowned Indian epigraphist, stated that "the date (of the Vo-Canh inscription) is not much earlier than the 5th century AD."[10] Śrī Māra thus would have been a contemporary of Mūlavarman, facing obviously quite similar problems while extending his authority beyond his own family or clan territory.

Pūrṇavarman's nearly contemporary inscriptions of mid-fifth century West Java depict a picture of a slightly more developed early statehood.[11] Pūrṇavarman is praised as the "Lord (*īśvara*) of the city (*nagara*) of Tārumā" whose predecessor Pīnabāhu already bore the truly royal title "Foremost King of Kings" (*rājādhirājā*). Whereas Pīnabāhu had dug a canal passing beside the "famous city" (*purī*), Pūrṇavarman dug another canal that cut across the "cantonment" (*śibira*) of his grandfather, who might have been identical with Pīnabāhu. In any case, here, too, three generations are mentioned, although in this case already the grandfather seems to have been able to impose his authority upon other chiefs. Pūrṇavarman continued this policy as he is explicitly praised as conquerer of the "towns of his enemies" (*arinagara*). In this connection, too, it is interesting to note that Pūrṇavarman, in spite of his conquest, remained a primus inter pares, ruling over his own *nagara* as did his enemies (*ari*) in their own *nagara*. As in the case of Mūlavarman's (and Śrī Māra's) inscriptions, we find no mention of officers or any references pertaining to the spatial aspect of his authority. Therefore we have no idea about the character of Pūrṇavarman's relations with the "cities" (*nagara*) of the enemies that he claims to have conquered. There was, however, a remarkable difference between these early kings. Pūrṇavarman's association with the Hindu deities Viṣṇu and Indra[12] clearly indicates that his court has already come under much stronger Indian influence, perhaps over several generations, than those of Mūlavarman and Śrī Māra. But in Java, too, this influence had not yet fundamentally changed the nature of the state of Tārumānagara.

However, one aspect of the epigraphical evidence of Pūrṇavarman's inscription deserves our attention. Whereas Mūlavarman's inscription mentions only once a *pura* (there is no

---

[10] D. C. Sircar, *Select Inscriptions*, vol. I (Delhi: Motilal Banarsidass, 1965), p. 54, note 1.

[11] Chhabra, *Expansion*, pp. 93–97.

[12] In his Ci-arutan Rock Inscription, a pair of human footprints "which belongs to the illustrious Pūrṇavarman, the Lord of Tārumānagara" are compared with Viṣṇu's footprints, whereas in the Kebon-Kopi Rock Inscription the footprints of his royal elephant are compared with those of Indra's elephant Airavata. (Chhabra, *Expansion*, pp. 93 and 95.)

such mention at all in Śrī Māra's inscription), Pūrṇavarman's four inscriptions refer to *nagara, purī,* and *śibira.* The so-called Ci-Arutan inscription clearly praises Pūrṇavarman as the "Lord of Tārumānagara"; the Jambu Rock inscription mentions Tārumā and the defeated *arinagara;* the Kebon-Kopi Rock inscription praises the "Lord of Tārumā" (without mentioning *nagara*); and the Tugu Stone inscription describes the two canals in connection with the "famous *purī*" and the *śibira..* The meager epigraphical evidence does not allow a clear distinction between these three terms. But we may infer that *śibira.* meant a fortified place, perhaps the kraton of Pūrṇavarman or his grandfather, which was situated within the *purī.* This expression then would refer to Tārumā as a semi-urban or urban-like settlement.

Already at this early time, the third term, *nagara,* might have had a wider connotation, referring to the city and the hinterland controlled by it. The question as to whether the epigraphical evidence allows such a terminological distinction between the kraton, the town, and its politically controlled hinterland will remain a crucial problem throughout this article. One point, however, is worth mentioning in connection with the *nagara* of Pūrṇavarman's inscription. The fact that only the term *nagara* occurs in connection with Tārumā and the polities of its defeated enemies may be understood as an indication that the spatial concept of the "state" in fifth-century Java was primarily "city"-centered. The earliest epigraphical evidence of Indonesia from the fifth century thus confirms Wheatley's definition of early political units on the Malay peninsula which he derived mainly from Chinese sources: "a polity in which a focally situated settlement exercised direct control over a restricted peripheral territory and exacted whatever tribute it could from an indefinite region beyond."[13]

II.

The next evidence of early urbanism and state formation in Indonesia comes from the most interesting corpus of inscriptions of the early Malay world, i.e. the inscriptions of early Śrīvijaya which can be dated around 682 to 686 C.E. The spatial distribution of the seven major inscriptions indicates an interesting pattern. Three have been found at Śrīvijaya's center around Palembang[14] and four were discovered in outer regions (*maṇḍala*)[15] that encircled the center at a distance of several hundered kilometers. Furthermore, some fragmentary inscriptions have come to light in the center.[16] This distribution pattern foreshadows a major problem of Śrīvijaya's statehood, the control of its outer regions. The most important inscription is the Telaga Batu or Sabokingking (Skk) inscription of Eastern Palembang, which contains dreadful curses against disloyal members of the royal family and local chiefs. The author of all these inscriptions seems to have been king Jaynāśa under whom

13 Wheatley, *Nagara and Commandery,* p. 233.

14 P.-Y. Manguin, "Palembang et Sriwijaya: anciennes hypotheses, recherches nouvelles," *BEFEO* 76 (1987): 337–402.

15 From Palembang, the Kedukan Bukit and Talang Tuwo inscriptions were published by G. Coedès, "Les inscriptions malaises de Çrivijaya," *BEFEO* 30 (1930): 29–80; for the Telaga Batu [Sabokingking] inscription see J.G. de Casparis, *Prasasti Indonesia,* vol. II, (Bandung: Masa Baru, 1956), pp. 15–46; The more or less identical "*maṇḍala* inscriptions" are known from Karang Brahi (Jambi) and Kota Kapur (Bangka), see Coedès, "Les inscriptions," and from Palas Pasemah (South Lampung), see Boechari, "An Old Malay Inscription of Srivijaya at Palas Pasemah," *Pra Seminar Penelitian Sriwijaya* (Jakarta, 1979), pp. 19–40; another badly weathered version of the *maṇḍala* inscription was also found in the Lampung district and has been dealt with by Boechari in his article "New Investigations on the Kedukan Bukit Inscription" *Untuk Bapak Guru (Bernet Kempers Festschrift)* (Jakarta, 1986), pp. 33–56.

16 de Casparis, *Prasasti Indonesia,* vol II, pp. 1–15.

Śrīvijaya experienced a period of breath-taking expansionism, conquering Malayu-Jambi and Kedah and attacking Java with a naval expedition.[17]

The Skk inscription begins with "an almost entirely unintelligible oath formula,"[18] which is followed by a peculiar list of officers and occupational groups.[19] It includes princes (*rājaputra*), landlords (*bhūpati*), army leaders (*senāpati*), local magnates (*nāyaka*), confidants (*pratyaya*), royal confidants (*hāji pratyaya*),[20] judges (*daṇḍanāyaka*), surveyors of groups of workmen (*tuhā an vatak = vuruḥ*), surveyors of low castes (*addhyāksi nījavarna*), cutlers (*vāṣīkarana*), ministers of princely status (*kumārāmātya*), regular and irregular troops (*cāṭabhata*), administrators (*adhikaraṇa*), clerks (*kāyastha*), architects (?, *sthāpaka*), naval captains (*puhāvaṃ*), merchants (*vaṇiyāga*), royal washermen (*marsī hāji*), and royal slaves (*hulun hāji*). De Casparis is certainly right to assume that this heterogeneous list contains those "categories of people that might constitute a possible danger"[21] to the security of the king and his court and who had therefore to swear the oath. The inscription furthermore refers to three categories of princes: the crown prince (*yuvarāja*), second crown prince (*prātiyuvarāja*), and other princes (*rājakumāra*).

These lists seemingly depict a well-organized hierarchy of princes, court officers, and servants at Śrīvijaya. As no identical lists are known from contemporary India or Southeast Asia it is likely that they reflect a fairly true picture of an already quite advanced society at the court of Śrīvijaya. However, it may have been differentiated more horizontally than hierarchically structured. This assumption is based on the fact that the many Sanskrit titles of court officers are known only from the introductory list of the Skk inscription, which, later on, also thrice mentions the three categories of princes. Otherwise two other Malay terms were apparently considered much more important than these "foreign" names. These were *dātu* and *huluntuhān*. *Dātu* appears to be the traditional Malay title of a chief and occurs frequently in all Malay inscriptions of early Śrīvijaya. In the maṇḍala inscriptions even the "King" of Śrīvijaya is referred to by this traditional title.[22] *Huluntuhān*, the "slaves [*hulun*] and lords [*tuhan*]," occur seven times in the Skk inscription. This term obviously denotes the members of the traditional patriarchal household of the *dātu* of Śrīvijaya and therefore would have included all sorts of family members and retainers who acted on behalf of the *dātu* of Śrīvijaya. These *huluntuhān* most likely were identical with those officers mentioned in the introductory list.

As regards the spatial dimension of Śrīvijaya's political authority these Malay inscriptions contain several new pieces of important information that can be derived from several key-words in these inscriptions, in particular *kadātuan*, *vanua*, *samaryyāda*, *maṇḍala*, and

---

[17] Coedès, "Les inscriptions," note 7 pp. 81–85; O. W. Wolters, *Early Indonesian Commerce. A Study of the Origins of Śrivijaya* (Ithaca: Cornell University Press, 1967), pp. 15–29.

[18] de Casparis, *Prasasti Indonesia*, vol.II, p. 36, note 1.

[19] The translation follows, in most cases, ibid., pp. 36ff.

[20] J. G. de Casparis (ibid., p.37, n.7) calls his translation of *hāji pratyaya* as "confidents of the king" as conjectural ("but we do not see another alternative"). Perhaps one could also think of the group of officers who are so frequently mentioned in later Javanese inscriptions as *mangilala drawya haji* ("persons who collect the lord's property"); *pratyaya* has the meaning of "revenue, income or tax"; D. C. Sircar, *Indian Epigraphical Glossary* (Delhi, 1966), p. 262.

[21] de Casparis, *Prasasti Indonesia*, vol II, p. 21.

[22] In the Talang Tuwo inscription of 684 C.E. king Jayanāśa is also addressed with the priestly (?) title *(da)punta hiyam*.

bhūmi. In a recent paper[23] I have tried to show that these terms allow us to draw some conclusions on the early process of concentric state formation in seventh-century Sumatra. The center of this process was the kadātuan Śrīvijaya, "the place of the dātu" of Śrīvijaya, which had thus the same meaning as Javanese *kĕraton*, "the place of the ratu."[24] According to the Skk inscription the *kadātuan* contained the inner apartments of the residence (*tnaḥ rumaḥ*) of the dātu where his women folk (*bini hāji*) lived and where gold (*mas*) and tribute (*drawya*) were kept. Most likely the kadātuan also housed the dewata, or tutelary deity (a deified ancestor?), which, according to the *maṇḍala* inscriptions, protected the *kadātuan* of Śrīvijaya.

The *kadātuan* was surrounded by the *vanua Śrīvijaya*, the semi-urban area of Śrīvijaya.[25] Fragments of inscriptions refer to citizens (*paura*) and to a "*vihara* in this *vanua*."[26] This monastery may have housed some of the one thousand Buddhist monks whom the Chinese monk I-ching mentioned as being in Śrīvijaya during these years. Furthermore, the Buddhist park Śrīkṣetra established by King Jayanāśa and Bukit Senguntang, Śrīvijaya's "sacred center"[27] where a number of Buddhist remains have been unearthed, may have been situated within this *vanua Śrīvijaya*. Morever, we may assume that it contained several truly agricultural villages, and, in particular, the markets frequented by the foreign merchants (*vaṇiyāga*) and sailors (*puhāvam*) who are mentioned in the Skk inscription. The *kadātuan* and the *vanua* formed the nucleus of Śrīvijaya. Only these two terms occur in connection with the name Śrīvijaya[28] and, what is perhaps equally revealing, only these two central spheres are known by their Malay terms. The other more distant surrounding "circles" of this nuclear area are referred to in the inscriptions only by the Sanskrit names *samaryyāda*, *maṇḍala*, and *bhūmi*.

The term *samaryyāda* is very unusual; in fact, it is unknown in Indian[29] or Southeast Asian epigraphy. De Casparis translates the term as "frontier province" whereas I prefer its literal meaning "having the same boundaries" (*maryyāda*). The *samaryyāda* thus would have referred to the neighboring region beyond the *vanua* Śrīvijaya. According to the Skk inscription the *samaryyāda* was connected with the central *vanua* by special roads (*samaryyāda-patha*). This hinterland was populated by an obviously large number of *dātu* who resided—according to the Skk inscription—in their own places (*sthāna*) on their own land (*deśa*). But these local *dātu* have come under the control of the *dātu* of Śrīvijaya and his *huluntuhān* who appear to have been particularly active in the *samaryyāda* hinterland. The endeavor of these *dātu* to again become "independent" (*swasthā*) must have posed one of the greatest dangers to the security of the *dātu* of Śrīvijaya and the *kadātuan* as these *dātu* are threatened several times by the imprecations of the Skk inscription.

---

23 H. Kulke, "*Kadātuan Śrīvijaya*—Empire or Kraton of Srivijaya? A Reassessment of the Epigraphical Evidence," in: *The Ancient Southeast Asian City and State*, ed. J. Stargardt (in press).

24 J. G. de Casparis and Coedès translate *kadatuan* as "Empire" and "province" respectively. Boechari prefers "kingdom," although he admits that, strictly speaking, *kadatuan* is the equivalent of *kĕraton*, "Old Malay Inscription," p. 23.

25 J. G. de Casparis (*Prasasti Indonesia, Vol II*, p. 14) and Boechari ("Old Malay Inscription, p. 22) translate *vanua* as "country" and Coedès as "le pays" ("Les Inscriptions," p. 35, n. 12).

26 de Casparis, *Prasasti Indonesia*, Vol. II, p. 14.

27 O. W. Wolters, "Restudying Some Chinese Writings on Sriwijaya," *Indonesia* 42 (1986): 1–41.

28 *dātu Śrīvijaya* is mentioned in all *maṇḍala* inscriptions, whereas *vanua Śrīvijaya* is known from the Kedukan Bukit inscription.

29 Thus *samaryyāda* is not mentioned in D. C. Sircar's *Glossary*.

The fourth important term for our consideration about the spatial dimension of Śrīvijaya's statehood is *maṇḍala*. It occurs only once in the Skk inscription in the famous passage *maṃrakṣāña sakalamaṇḍala kadātuanku*, which de Casparis translates "you who protect all the provinces of my empire."[30] I have tried to show that, in the context of early Śrīvijaya, the term *maṇḍala* most likely did not refer to centrally administered provinces in the extended core area of an empire, as such provinces did not yet exist in early kingdoms; they became a typical feature only of the later imperial kingdoms.[31] In the context of early kingdoms, the term *maṇḍala* usually referred to autonomous or semi-autonomous principalities and chiefdoms at their periphery. Several such *maṇḍala* are known from contemporary Southern and Eastern India.[32] In the case of late seventh-century Śrīvijaya "all the maṇḍalas" therefore appears to have meant those outlying regions where the above-mentioned "*maṇḍala* inscriptions" have been found. The exact nature of Śrīvijaya's control over its *maṇḍala* is unknown. They had certainly been conquered by Śrīvijaya's army (*bala*), which is mentioned several times in Śrīvijaya's inscriptions. However we have no evidence at all that they had come under the direct political control of Śrīvijaya as no *huluntuhān* or royal princes of Śrīvijaya are mentioned in these *maṇḍala* inscriptions. They were obviously still ruled by the local *dātu* who lived in their own *vanua*, as is known from these inscriptions. They had been recognized (*sanyāsa*) in their position by Śrīvijaya. But their precarious loyalty obviously had to be improved by the *maṇḍala* inscriptions and their peculiar mixture of imprecations and taking of the oath of allegiance. However, military coercion and imprecations alone would not have sufficed to establish an enduring relation. Of equal importance must have been the incentive to participate in Śrīvijaya's international trade.

Apart from providing us with a conceivable model of an early concentric state, Śrīvijaya also provides us with the first generic term of such a state. As mentioned above, Coedès, de Casparis, and Boechari regarded *vanua*, *kadātuan*, and *huluntuhān* as just such a comprehensive term and translated them accordingly as "le pays," "empire," or "kingdom." But, according to my interpretation, none of these expressions had such a comprehensive spatial connotation in the context of early Śrīvijaya. The word *bhūmi*, however, appears to have been such a generic term for Śrīvijaya's statehood. In Sanskrit, *bhūmi* means primarily "earth" or "soil" but also "realm" and "country." It occurs twice in Śrīvijaya's inscription. One instance is in a more or less identical passage found in all the *maṇḍala* inscriptions, which threatened the disloyal "people inside the land [that is] under the order of *kadātuan*" (*uraṅ di dalaṅña bhūmi ājñāña kadātuanku*).[33] As this passage occurs only in the *maṇḍala* inscriptions it has to be inferred that the places where they have been found either constituted a *bhūmi* or formed part of a larger polity which was called *bhūmi* . Although the first meaning cannot be excluded, two other references make the latter connotation of *bhūmi* more likely in the context of early Indonesian history. The first of these references comes from the important passage of the Kota Kapur inscription of the year 686 which announces the departure of an army expedition against *bhūmi jāwa*, which had not yet become submissive to Śrīvijaya. Obviously, Java was not regarded just as one of the many *vanua* or *maṇḍala* surrounding Śrīvijaya but as an equally matched opponent of Śrīvijaya. The other evidence of a *bhūmi* polity comes from several inscriptions of late ninth and early tenth-century Java that

[30] de Casparis, *Prasasti Indonesia*, Vol II, p. 43.

[31] Kulke, "The Early and the Imperial Kingdom."

[32] Thus, in the early Middle Ages, Tosali, the center of coastal Orissa in Eastern India, was surrounded by more than half a dozen such semi-autonomous *maṇḍala*-principalities; see S.N. Rajaguru, *Inscriptions of Orissa*, vol. I, 2. [300–700 A.D.] (Bhubaneswar, 1958); and B. Misra, *Dynasties of Medieval Orissa* (Calcutta, 1933).

[33] Boechari, "Old Malay Inscription," p. 38 and Coedès, "Les inscriptions," p. 47.

refer to *bhūmi* Matarām (infra). As in the case of *bhūmi* Java and *bhūmi* Matarām, the Śrīvijayan concept of "the *bhūmi* under the control of my *kadātuan*" apparently referred to the whole sphere that had come under the control of Śrīvijaya.

Comparing Mūlavarman's and Pūrṇavarman's fifth-century polities with Śrīvijaya in the late seventh century we are able to recognize several important structural changes. The "first victories" (*prathama vijiya*) of these earliest kings certainly had led to the defeat of neighboring "landlords" (*pārthiva*) and "hostile towns" (*arinagara*). And in some cases a victorious "lord of the landlords" (*pārthiva-indra*) may have been able to collect (most likely irregular!) tribute (*kara*). But none of their earliest inscriptions allow us to infer that this pristine political development presupposed or led to far-reaching structural changes. The courts of these early rulers still remained patriarchal households. Their rule was the affair of the chief's family (*kula*) or lineage/"dynasty" (*vaṃśa*). It is this background that explains the frequent mention of these two kinship terms in these early inscriptions, that is, *kula* and, particularly, *vaṃśa*. However, it is worth mentioning that these Sanskrit terms only occur whenever the foundation of a "dynasty" is reported in inscriptions. As no equivalent Malay or Javanese word ever occurs in inscriptions written in these languages, it is likely that these Sanskrit terms were required for the definition of an apparently new social institution, that is, a "ruling lineage" in a hitherto rather unstratified tribal society.

This situation had already changed considerably in late seventh-century Sumatra around present-day Palembang. Whether international trade by the "sailors and traders" (*puhavaṃ vaṇiyaga*) mentioned in the Skk inscription was the main cause of this change is still an open question. But it is evident that the inscriptions of Śrīvijaya which have been discovered around Palembang depict an already fairly well-developed society. But in this regard, too, we have to distinguish between different spatial zones of social change. Social differentiation and stratification was strongest in the *vanua*, center from where its influence spread into its *samaryyāda* hinterland. But we have no evidence of such a development in the outer *maṇḍala*, even though we may conjecture that the *dātu* of these regions had their own *huluntuhān*. But particularly in these cases they would have been patriarchal "servants and lords" rather than administrative officers.

Apart from new social stratification in *vanua* Śrīvijaya, the other decisive difference between the epigraphical evidence of fifth-century Kalimantan and Java on the one side and late seventh century Śrīvijaya on the other side is an incipient change in the center-periphery relations. Śrīvijaya seems to have been the first Indonesian state that succeeded in extending its direct political authority beyond its own *vanua* into the *samaryyāda* hinterland and to conquer even far-off powerful chieftaincies and trade emporia (e.g. Malayu and Kedah) and to establish some sort of hegemony over these outer *maṇḍala*. Śrīvijaya's rapid expansion was due to two new factors which had different spatial significances. First, Śrīvijaya's direct rule in the *samaryyāda* hinterland was based primarily on its disposal of a fairly well-developed staff of "administrators," the *huluntuhān* of the Skk inscription. However, these "officers" still had to face various types of difficulties at the center and in its hinterland that are vividly accursed in the Skk inscription. As shown by J.G. de Casparis in his analysis of the fragmentary inscriptions, *vanua* Śrīvijaya was still afflicted by dangerous rebellions of internal insurgents.[34] Second, Śrīvijaya's control over the far-off *maṇḍala* presupposed the existence or at least the temporary availability of a strong army (*vala*). Its inscriptions show that the main cause of Śrīvijaya's hold over the outer *maṇḍala* was the ability to muster an army of apparently uncontested strength. Nevertheless, Śrīvijaya's

[34] de Casparis, *Prasasti Indonesia*, Vol. II, pp. 4ff (particularly inscriptions *a* and *b*).

authority still remained very precarious in these *maṇḍala*. Śrīvijaya's major problem at this point appears to have been its "failure" either to integrate at least some of the more powerful *dātu* chiefs of the *maṇḍala* into its own central court or to obliterate and replace them with loyal members of its own court. In fact, the solution of these center-periphery relations remained the crucial problem of all pre-modern states. As we will see, the Matarām-Śailendra dynasties chose the first and Majapahit the second method to solve this problem.

In regard to the main concern of this article, the epigraphical evidence for the "city" and the "state" in early Indonesia, Śrīvijaya provides for the first time a rather clear picture of an already well-developed concentric state in early Indonesia. Mūlavarman's polity had comprised only two such spatial spheres. These were a still rather undifferentiated center consisting of a *pura* (= kraton?), a "most holy place" (*kṣetra),* and the living places of the "royal" *vaṃsa* and the Brahmins. Beyond this center a group of unspecified defeated chiefs (*pārthiva)* existed whom Mūlavarman claims to have made his "tribute-givers" (*karadā). Pūrṇavarman's* inscriptions from West Java offer a slightly more-developed stage of an early polity. As all three epigraphical terms that occur in these inscriptions and that are relevant for our study, that is, *śibira, purī,* and *nagara,* have a clear urban connotation, Tārumānagara appears to have been a typical early "city state." But we have to keep in mind that in the context of early Indonesia these Sanskrit terms may have referred to kratons of strong chiefdoms and Hinduized "little kings" rather than to an urban "city."

The major contribution of Śrīvijaya's inscriptions to our study is the fact that they indicate several spatial spheres of its political authority. And moreover, for the first time in early Indonesia, a generic term, *bhūmi* , for the "state" is given. This *bhūmi* realm was divided into three zones, that is, the *vanua* center, its *samaryyāda* hinterland, and the outer *maṇḍala.* The center, too, consisted of two distinct zones, the *kadātuan* (or kraton) of the ruling *dātu* and its surrounding *vanua. Vanua* Śrīvijaya seems to have comprised a densely populated area at present-day Palembang with urbanized "pockets." However, it is astonishing that we only once hear of Śrīvijaya's "citizens" (*paura*) whereas the terms *pura* or *nagara* never occur in Śrīvijaya's inscriptions. Whether this evidence is sufficient to infer that no "city" outside the *kadātuan Śrīvijaya* existed in the late seventh century is difficult to decide. But the epigraphical evidence makes such an inference quite likely.[35] A possible reason why we may search in vain for the epigraphical terms *pura* and *nagara* in the context of early Śrīvijaya may be the fact that much of its urban life took place in the many houseboats on the Musi river.

III.

The two earliest dated inscriptions of the middle period of early Indonesia, the Canggal inscription of Sañjaya of the year 732 C.E.[36] and the Dinaya inscription of 760 C.E.,[37] belong to Central and Eastern Java, respectively. Their date is only about two generations later than Śrīvijaya's early inscriptions. But in regard to Java itself, there is a wide gap of three centuries between Pūrṇavarman and Sañjaya. Both inscriptions of the eighth century provide some new evidence of a conceptual and structural development of the "city" and the "state" in early Indonesia. Sañjaya's inscription reports the consecration of "a liṅga on a mountain" *(prātiṣṭhipat parvate liṅgaṃ)* in a place or "country" *(deśa)* called Kuñjarakuñja in the island *(dvīpa)* of Java. Sañjaya is praised for protecting the "royal highways" *(rājapathi),* defeating

[35] In this connection further excavations at the newly discovered sites at Karanganyar in western Palembang will be most important. See P.-Y. Manguin, "Palembang et Sriwijaya."

[36] Sarkar, *Corpus*, pp. 15–24.

[37] Ibid., pp. 25–33.

"numerous circles of neighboring chiefs" *(aneka-sāmanta-cakra-rāja),* and for ruling justly his kingdom *(rājya).* From later inscriptions we know that the Matarām dynasty praised him as "king" *(ratu)* and founder of their dynasty.[38] Furthermore it is worth mentioning that Sañjaya's Canggal inscription provides the first epigraphical evidence for agrarian extension when it mentions that Java was "rich in rice and other seeds."

The evidence of Sañjaya's inscriptions as well as that of later inscriptions leaves no doubt that Sañjaya established a genuine early kingdom, in fact the first known in Javanese history. It is of particular interest for our study that the concept of his state and the *praśasti* eulogy of the inscription were much nearer to contemporary Indian models than the earlier cases that so far have been discussed. For the first time, the "ṣtate" is called *rājya.* It comprised, most likely, several *deśa* which were linked by "royal highways." It was surrounded by a *sāmantacakra,* the common term of Indian and future Javanese inscriptions referring to the "circle of (originally independent) neighboring rulers *(sāmanta).*"[39] According to the Indian concept they had to be subjugated to the central king. Another indicator of Indian influence is the consecration of a purely Hindu temple, dedicated to Śiva.

But despite this evidently strong Indian influence, Sañjaya's inscription lacks several important indicators of contemporary Indian statehood and kingship. This is most evident in regard to the complete absence of officers usually mentioned in connection with such a grand ceremony as the establishment of Sañjaya's "royal" Śivaliṅgaṃ. Whether this evidence allows the *argumentum ex silentio* that Sañjaya's court still consisted only of his extended family *(kula),* which in fact is mentioned twice in the inscription, is a matter of conjecture. But in this regard it has to be remembered that Sañjaya's "dynasty" was not yet an old-established one. He traced his genealogy back only to his father Sanna, and he himself is praised in a later inscription by the Malay title *ratu* whereas his successors are glorified as *mahārāja.*[40] In this regard it is significant that his father is reported to have ruled his people by the traditional method of "conciliation and gifts" *(sāma-dāna).* Another interesting point is the fact that Sañjaya's inscription does not contain any term that can be associated with an urbanized settlement. This again does not automatically mean that no such settlement existed in his *rājya* in Central Java. But at least this evidence shows that he did not regard it necessary (or important enough) to mention such a settlement in his inscription.

A rather different picture of an early kingdom is depicted in the Dinaya inscription of the year 760 C.E., the earliest one known from East Java. Much has been written about it because of several uncertainties about its contents, which, however, need not bother us here.[41] It reports the consecration of a temple and a stone image of the divine seer Agastya by king *(rāja)* Gajayāna who protected a *pura,* called Kañjuruha. King Gajayāna urged his relatives *(bāndhava),* sons *(nṛpasuta),* and his principal ministers *(mantri mukhya)* not to act against this gift. He appealed to the members of the "royal dynasty" *(vaṃśa nṛpa)* to follow his example and to perform meritorious acts and thus to protect the kingdom *(rājya).*

---

[38] Ibid., vol. II, p. 68 (Mantyasih I copper-plates, B, 8).

[39] L. L. Gopal, "Samanta—Its Varying Significance in Ancient India," *Journal of the Royal Asiatic Society of Great Britain and Ireland* (1963): 21–37.

[40] See above note 38.

[41] F.D.K. Bosch, "Het Lingga-Heiligdom van Dinaja," *Tijdschrift voor Indische Taal-, Land-, en Volkenkunde* 64 (1924): 225–91; J.G. de Casparis, "Nogmals de Sanskrit-inscriptie op den steen van Dinojo," *Ibid.* 81 (1941) 499–513; W.J. van der Meulen, "The Purī Pūtikeśvarapāvita and the Pura Kāñjuruhan," in *Bijdragen tot de Taal-, Land-, en Volkenkunde van Nederlandsch-Indie* 132 (1976): 445–62.

The interesting evidence in regard to the "city" of Kañjuruha is the fact that the first verse mentions that the *purī* was protected by Gajayāna's deceased father Devasiṃha, whereas the next verse reports that Gajayāna protected the *pura* Kañjuruha after his father had died. Furthermore we are told about "citizens" *(paura)* who, together with the "groups of leaders" *(nāyaka-gaṇa)*, constructed the temple. The juxtaposition of *purī* and *pura* in the first two verses, which were protected by the deceased father and his ruling son respectively, allows us to infer that in this case *purī* may have referred to the *kraton* and *pura* to the "city" of Kañjuruhan. The *purī* thus appears to have been protected by the (deified) ancestor (as was *kadātuan* Śrīvijaya by its *devatā)*, whereas King Gajayāna protected the *pura* "capital" of his *rājya*. It was inhabited by *paura*, groups of *nāyaka*, ministers *(mantri)*, and Brahmins who, too, are mentioned in the inscription.

In contrast to Sañjaya's inscription from Central Java, the Dinaya inscription from East Java thus reveals an urban center comprising the *purī* -kraton and the *pura*. The latter was inhabited by members of the royal family, by "citizens," officers, and priests. However, although Gajayāna's "state" is called a "kingdom" *(rājya)*, the inscription does not contain a single piece of evidence that would allow us to assume the existence of administrative units. This fact reminds us of Sañjaya's nearly contemporary *rājya* where we came to know about the existence of at least one *deśa*. Despite the mention of "principal ministers" and "groups of leaders," and "citizens," the strong emphasis of the responsibility of "royal relatives," princes, and members of the "royal dynasty" for the welfare of the *rājya* makes it likely that Gajayāna's "state," too, consisted mainly of an urbanized center that may have had strong relations with, but only little or even no political control over, its surrounding hinterland. The major difference between Mūlavarman's polity in the fifth century and Gajayāna's eighth-century "kingdom" thus appears to pertain to the degree of urbanization of its center rather than to the development of its territorial dimension.

IV

The late eighth century bears witness to the rise of the Buddhist Śailendras, one of Southeast Asia's most important dynasties to which the world owes one of its greatest religious monuments, the Borobudur. But despite its importance in early Indonesian history and its historically established links with Sumatra, the Malay Peninsula, Śrī Lanka, Bengal, and South India till the eleventh century, its genealogical history and, even more, the structure and extent of its kingdom, particularly during its most important period in Central Java in the eighth and ninth centuries, is only partly known.[42]

The major reason for our lack of knowledge is, no doubt, the relatively small number of inscriptions. But in the same way as the international relations of the Śailendras and their masterpieces of art and architecture indicate a new stage of cultural, societal, and political development, the dynasty's few inscriptions, too, reflect a new type of full-fledged kingdom. Already the earliest-dated Sanskrit inscriptions of the eighth century speak of a *rājya* state, ruled by a *mahārāja* who had defeated the neighboring *sāmanta-rāja*. Ministers *(mantri)*, (local?) lords *(pati)*, and superintendents of *deśa* areas *(deśādhyakṣa)* were in charge of the administration.

In this connection it is of particular importance that the Kalasan Sanskrit inscription of the year 778 C.E. mentions for the first time the local *deśa* officers *paṅgkura, tavān*, and *tīrip* which belong to the large number of different Javanese titles of officers that occur frequently

[42] Coedès, "Les inscriptions," pp. 87–93, 107–9; J. G. de Casparis, *Prasasti Indonesia* II, pp. 288ff.

in Javanese inscriptions of the ninth century and later. The obviously well-established hierarchy of officers, linking the central court with intermediary, territorially defined, administrative units and villages, is certainly the most important new epigraphical evidence of the classical age of central Javanese history under the Śailendra and Matarām dynasties. This is not the place to discuss in detail this complicated administrative set-up of Central Javanese kingdoms.[43] Suffice it to say that it appears to have been the outcome of a double process that must have been operating for a much longer time than evidenced in the inscriptions. On the local level of the *vanua,* agrarian expansion, translocal trade, and social differentiation had created a vast number of village elders and authorities. The early history of this process is unknown to us as we come across its result only when these *vanua* authorities were already fully existing in Central Javanese inscriptions in the early ninth century. The other aspect of this process is of equal relevance for our study as it pertains to the political expansion of supra-local authority. Mūlavarman's and Śrī Māra's inscriptions illustrated the incipient stage of this process. The inscriptions of Pūrṇavarman, Sañjaya, and Gajayāna depicted further stages of this development. But in their cases, too, no political authority appears to have as yet been established permanently beyond the chiefly "Stammland" and its immediate hinterland. This decisive step of early state formation was made by Śrīvijaya which extended its political control into distant *maṇḍala.* However, Śrīvijaya's authority in these *maṇḍala* continued to be precarious, as their local *dātu* leaders remained a threat to Śrīvijaya's *dātu* rather than being integrated into the political structure of the *bhūmi* state.

According to our epigraphical evidence, political expansion through integration occurred only with the rise of the Śailendra dynasty and reached its first culmination towards the end of the central Javanese period in the late ninth century.[44] It is worth noticing that in contrast to the Sanskrit inscriptions of the early period of Java, this ninth-century process of intensive state formation in Central and, from the tenth century onwards, East Java is documented nearly exclusively by Javanese-language inscriptions with but little Sanskrit terminology. The basis of this expansion of royal authority was the stepwise integration of neighboring areas. Even though they remained "under the jurisdiction" *(watĕk)* of local chiefs *(raka),* some of these chiefs slowly rose to high administrative or even "ministerial" positions in the patriarchal central court. In the same way as these chiefs retained their "Stammland" as their own *watĕk,* the king *(mahārāja, ratu)* kept his own *watĕk* land under his direct control. Although having thus, at least theoretically, the same territorial basis of authority, the "Stammland" of the future *ratu* may have been larger, perhaps more fertile, and linked to translocal trade routes. Certain "material" factors must have given the family/lineage of the future *ratu* an advantage over his neighboring chiefs *(raka)* during this process of early state formation in Central Java.

As already mentioned, the early history of this process of territorial and political integration of the *raka* into a central court of a *ratu* is largely unknown, as these *raka* are usually referred to only in the inscriptions of a central *ratu* when a certain degree of their integration had already occurred. However, among the early inscriptions of classical Central Java several inscriptions are known to have been edited by local chiefs without referring to a *ratu* or

---

43 See for instance de Casparis' detailed epigraphical study of the Tjaṇḍi Perot inscriptions of 850 C.E. in ibid., pp. 211–43 or W. F. Stutterheim's study of the Cunggrang II inscription of the year 929 C.E. in *Tijdschrift voor Indische Taal-, Land-, en Volkenkunde* 65 (1925): 208–81.

44 van Naerssen, *Economic and Administrative History,* pp. 46ff; Boechari, "Some Considerations of the Problem of the Shift of Mataram's Centre of Government from Central to East Java in the 10th Century A.D.," *Bulletin of Research Centre of Archaeology of Indonesia* 10 (Jakarta, 1976); J. Wisseman-Christie, "Raja and Rama: The Classical

rājā. A rare case even allows some conclusions about the process of political integration when the Central Javanese court was just moving to the east. In 891 C.E. the *rakryan* of Kanuruhan (a locality most likely identical with Kañjuruhan of the Dinaya inscription of 760 C.E.) established a freehold by his own "favor" *(anugraha)*.[45] But only twenty-four years later, in 915 C.E., it was the central "Great King" *(mahārāja)* Dakṣa who did the favor *(anugraha)* to allow the *rakai* of Kanuruhan to establish another freehold in his own *watĕk* Kanuruhan.[46] Between 891 and 915, under circumstances still unknown, the Lord of Kanuruhan thus had come under the authority of the Mahārāja Dakṣa.[47] During the next century the *rakryan* of Kanuruhan rose to the highest administrative position at the central court, a position which they held for several centuries.

The stepwise integration of local magnates into the central court and the encroachment of the royal "persons who collect the lord's property" (*mangilala drawya hāji*) upon the *watĕk* and *vanua* is perhaps the least known aspect of state formation in early classical Javanese history. But it seems to have been an extremely protracted process that finally worked in favor of the central dynasty only temporarily in the fourteenth century, when Majapahit was able to exchange the local *raka* in the extended core area of its kingdom with members of its own dynasty.

The structure of the Javanese kingdoms of the ninth through early thirteenth centuries is fairly well reflected in the epigraphical evidence and may be summarized as follows. The unique feature of the Javanese kingdom during this period is the highly elaborated and strictly fixed hierarchy of state officers and local authorities as listed in these inscriptions. The establishment and continuous maintainance of this hierarchy appears to have been one of the main means of authority for the center. This hierarchy of patrimonial officers, however, should not be automatically equated with a hierarchy of administrative officers and administrative territorial units. Apart from "personal" *watĕk* and from *vanua* with their village authorities, which are frequently mentioned in inscriptions, we still find nearly no terms that hint at a more sophisticated spatial structure of the kingdom. Very rarely does the term *deśa* occur, which refers to a territorial unit of a larger size than *vanua*. An inscription of the year 824 C.E. appears to indicate that the *rājya* constituted of many *deśa*.[48] The Sanskrit term *deśa* may thus have to be equated with *watĕk*.[49] This inference perhaps may be corroborated by another early Central Javanese inscription of the year 782 C.E. It reports the consecration of a Mañjuśrī image by a Śailendra king and his *guru* who had come from Bengal *(gauḍidvīpa)*. The image was installed by the king in order to protect "his *deśa*" *(deśasya tasya)*.[50] Here *deśa* apparently refers to the land of the king, that is, his *Stammland* or *watĕk*.

Important information about the structural concept of the Javanese state during this period can be derived from a passage which is repeated more or less identically in a few inscriptions of the late ninth and early tenth centuries. It occurs for the first time in an inscription of King Lokāpala of the year 880 C.E.[51] At the end of an extremely long list of

---

State in Early Java," in: *Symbols and Hierarchies*, ed. Gessick; J.G. Casparis, "Some Notes on Relations between Central and Local Government in Ancient Java," in: *Southeast Asia*, ed. Marr and Milner, pp. 49–63.

45 Inscription of Belingavan (Singasari), Sarkar, *Corpus*, vol. I, pp. 295–303.

46 Inscription of Sugih Manek (Singasari), Sarkar, *Corpus*, vol. II, pp. 145–60.

47 van Naerssen, *Economic and Administrative History*, pp. 53ff.

48 Inscription of Gandasuli, line 8D; de Casparis, *Prasasti Indonesia*, vol. I, p. 61.

49 J. G. de Casparis suggests "landstreek" (ibid., p. 68).

50 Inscription of Kelurak, Sarkar, *Corpus*, vol. II, pp. 41–48.

51 Copper-plates of Vuatan Tija (Manggung), Sarkar, *Corpus*, vol. I, pp. 250–61.

Hindu deities who are called upon for protection of a newly established freehold, the tutelary deities are invoked: "Also all you deities who are known to protect the kraton of the illustrious Great King in the country of Matarām" *(devatā prasiddha mangrakṣa kadātuan śrī mahārāja i bhūmi i matarām)*. Nearly exactly the same text is repeated in the same epigraphical context in the stone inscription of Sugih Manek near Singasari of the year 915 C.E[52] Thirteen years later this invocation occurs again in the so-called Minto Stone from the region of Malang, however with an important addition.[53] The tutelary deities are invoked "who are known to protect the kraton of the Great King **in Medang** in the country of Matarām." For the first time, Medang, the capital of the central Javanese kingdom of Matarām, is explicitly mentioned in this context. This latter version of the invocation is then again repeated twice in inscriptions of the years 942 and 944 C.E.[54]

In the context of our study, the most relevant aspect of these inscriptions is the fact that they reveal, at least partly, a repetition of the Śrīvijaya model. As in Śrīvijaya, the center was the kraton *(or kadātuan)* of the Mahārāja, which was protected by ancestor deities. It was situated in (the "capital") Madang which may have been identical with *vanua Matarām*, a resident of which is mentioned in an inscription of the year 919 C.E. *(anak vanua i matarām)*.[55] This center was surrounded, as we know from other contemporary inscriptions, by the *deśa* or *watĕk* of other *raka* or *rakryan*. The state that comprised these "segments" was called *bhūmi*, a term we came to know for the first time in Śrīvijaya's inscriptions. The most important and, in contrast to early Śrīvijaya, new political element of state formation in pre-Majapahit Java is the obviously very successful integration of allodial chiefs and "lords" into the patrimonial hierarchy of the central court without, however, uprooting them in their own *Stammland*.[56] No such attempts to integrate the *dātu* into the court hierarchy are known from the inscriptions of Śrīvijaya. In contrast to *bhūmi Śrīvijaya*, however, *bhūmi Matarām* appears not to have included outlying *maṇḍala*.

Furthermore, the territorial administration of *bhūmi* Matarām in Central Java and its successor kingdoms in East Java may have been structured even less than Śrīvijaya in the late seventh century. At least, we have no inscriptional evidence, for instance, of the kingdom *(bhūmi)* of Keḍiri from the late eleventh to early thirteenth centuries which would allow us to come to a different estimation of its statehood. There seem to have been only two exceptions to this "rule," that is, king Siṇḍok in the early tenth century and Airlangga in the early eleventh century. They obviously had tried to extend their political control even beyond those *watĕk* or *deśa* that had already come under their hegemony. But their personal, most likely military, success did not survive their demise. Airlangga's inability to perpetuate his temporary success was later on transformed into the famous myth of the division of the "empire" by the king himself. However, Airlangga's striving for "imperial" hegemony (he was the first Javanese king who assumed the imperial title *ratu cakravartin*[57]) became a major prop of the imperial ideology of later Singasari and Majapahit rulers.

---

52 Sarkar, *Corpus*, vol. II, pp. 144–60.

53 Ibid., pp. 227–48.

54 OJO, XLVIII and LI; see also W. J. van der Meulen, "King Sanjaya and his Successors," in: *Indonesia* 28 (1979): 17–54 (esp. pp. 24ff).

55 Sarkar, *Corpus*, vol. II, p. 165.

56 Boechari, "Rakryan Mahamantri i Hino. A Study on the Highest Court Dignitary of Ancient Java up to the 13th Century A.D.," *Beberapa Karya Dalam Ilmu-Ilmu Sastra* (Publikasi Ilmiah, No. 2), Universitas Indonesia 1975/76, pp. 61–114.

57 OJO, LXI.

During the Matarām and Keḍiri period, the "*bhūmi* state" of East Java thus remained the classical concentric "Early Kingdom."[58] It comprised the central nuclear area, consisting of the kraton and the *Stammland* or *watĕk* of the central dynasty, and the surrounding *watĕk* whose *rakryan* and *rakai* had been integrated into the patrimonial staff of the central court. The local administration in the royal and allodial *watĕk* remained in the hands of the traditional village authorities.

Finally it should be pointed out that throughout the period of the Śailendra dynasty and the kingdom of Matarām and Keḍiri, no epigraphical evidence exists about the existence of "cities" except those of the "capitals" of these kingdoms, e.g. Madang and Keḍiri. But neither are they called *pura* or *nagara* nor are urban settlements known in the *watĕk* of the *rakryan*. According to the epigraphical evidence, state formation in Java in the eighth to early thirteenth centuries appears to have operated largely without urbanization.

V.

The most dramatic changes in the process of state formation and urbanization in pre-Islamic Indonesia took place in the late thirteenth and fourteenth centuries under Singasari and Majapahit. For nearly two centuries after Airlangga, the history of Java had retreated to the middle Brantas valley. However, the small but obviously prospering kingdom of Keḍiri preserved faithfully the structural concept of the administrative set-up of the Matarām kingdom and the imperial ideology of Airlangga's short-lived East Javanese kingdom. This ideology was based on the (under Airlangga only partly achieved[59]) unification of the two East Javanese nuclear areas Janggala and Pañjalu and the (never-realized) hegemony over the whole of Javadvīpa. The myth of a unified kingdom of Janggala and Pañjalu (and its alleged partition by Airlangga) and East Java's imperial claim over the whole of Java served as legitimation of the imperial expansionism of late Singasari which Coedès summarized as follows:

> The reign of Kṛtanagara [the last king of Singasari] was marked by a considerable expansion of Javanese power in all directions. In 1275, taking advantage of the decline of Śrīvijaya, he sent a military expedition to the west which established Javanese suzerainty over Malayu and probably also over Sunda, Madura and part of the Malay peninsula. After establishing his authority in Sumatra, Kṛtanagara turned toward Bali, whose king he brought back as a prisoner in 1284.[60]

In East Java itself, the most important change was the subjugation of Keḍiri under Singasari's hegemony, which had already been finally established under Viṣṇuvardhana, Kṛtanagara's father. However, Keḍiri still retained an autonomous status as a *sāmantarājya*.[61] King Jayakatwang of Keḍiri still felt strong enough to attack and defeat Singasari in 1292 C.E. During the occupation of the royal residence of Singasari, King Kṛtanagara died. Keḍiri's new hegemony over the whole of eastern Java however came to an abrupt end when Kṛtanagara's son-in-law, Raden Vijaya, with the help of a Chinese expeditionary army, defeated Jayakatwang's army and established himself as the first ruler in the newly founded city of Majapahit.

---

[58] Kulke, "The Early and the Imperial Kingdom."

[59] See Boechari, "Sri Maharaja Mapanji Garasakan," *Madjalah Ilmu-Ilmu Sastra Indonesia* 4, 1/2 (1968): 1–26.

[60] Coedès, *Indianized States*, p. 198.

[61] Nāgara-Kĕrtāgama, 44,1; in Th. G. Pigeaud, *Java in the 14th Century. A Study in Cultural History. The Nāgara-Kĕrtāgama by Rakawi Prapañca of Majapahit, 1365 A.D.*, 5 vols. (The Hague: Nijhoff, 1960).

The kingdom of Majapahit was truly a successor state of Singasari, both in its "internal" policy in eastern Java and in its expansionistic "external" policy in the outer regions. But in both aspects the state of Majapahit represents the culmination of state formation in pre-modern Indonesia. As regards the "internal" policy in eastern Java, the most decisive new development under Majapahit was the systematic replacement of the allodial local *raka* and *rakryan* in East Java by members of the royal family and, in a few cases, by deserving members of the court. It was more than a mere symbolic act that, already in 1295, Raden Vijaya crowned the eldest son of one of his wives (he was married to four daughters of Kṛtanagara) as Prince of Keḍiri. His new policy of systematic annexation or "provincialization" of all neighboring *watĕk* or *deśa* and their many "little kings" led to a series of revolts, which, however, appear to have been successfully supressed by Majapahit. According to our epigraphical evidence, Majapahit succeeded for the first time (after Śrīvijaya's similar attempts) to extend its political control considerably beyond its own *Stammland*, this time, however, by a ruthless policy of annexation and "dynastification" of its hinterland.

In this regard it is significant that the Nāgara-Kĕrtāgama, the famous court chronicle of Majapahit composed by Prapañca in the year 1365 C.E., begins with a descriptive list of the various towns *(nagara)* held by members of the royal family as demesne in the hinterland of Majapahit. Summarizing this chapter, the Nāgara-Kĕrtāgama concludes "All Illustrious Javanese Kings and Queens, the honoured ones who equally are distinguished by their towns *(nagara)*, each having one for his or her own, in one place *(eka sthāna)*, in Wilwa Tikta (= Majaphit) they hold in their lap the honoured Prince-Overlord." [62]

As is known from other Southeast and South Asian kingdoms of this age, too, (e.g. Angkor and the Cōḷas), the establishment of an "Imperial Kingdom" required a considerable enlargement of the original **nuclear area** or *Stammland* of the ruling dynasty.[63] In this extended **core region** the ruling dynasty had to strive for uncontested access to the agrarian surplus and, wherever possible, for some sort of control over, and sharing of, the long-distance trade. However, even in these "Imperial Kingdoms" of pre-modern South and Southeast Asia, the central dynasties still had to share the revenue from these sources with their own local representatives, whether they were princely members of the dynasty or members of the patrimonial staff. The transfer of resources from the local and intermediate levels to the imperial center thus remained a crucial problem even within the core region of these large imperial kingdoms. Although the imperial kings had succeeded in extending their uncontested political authority by eliminating all sorts of potential putschists in their extended core region, actual political control remained fragmented. The "segments" still existed even though they had come under members of the central dynasty.[64] But in contrast to the earlier cases (e.g. in 760 C.E. in Kañjuruhan in East Java) where a "family dynasty" *(kula-vaṃśa)* depended mainly on its own *Stammland*, the imperial dynasty of Majaphit was able to extend its patrimonial control far beyond these pristine boundaries. It systematically distributed its hinterland to members of the dynasty who thus became "share holders" of the state. The central core region of Majapahit had come under a "family regime."

The very center of this family enterprise was the royal compound *(pura)* or kraton. Accordingly the second chapter of the Nāgara-Kĕrtāgama contains a detailed description of this compound and the surrounding *nagara*, that is, the capital of Majapahit. The Nāgara-

[62] Nāgara-Kĕrtāgama, 6,4.

[63] Kulke, "The Early and the Imperial Kingdom," p. 8ff.

Kĕrtāgama again pays special attention to the residences of all the principal ministers and the princely family members whom we have already met in their own *nagara*. According to their status, their residences were distributed in a clear hierarchical order around the royal *pura* or kraton, adjacent to temples, monasteries, markets, and places of the commoners. The Nawanatya, a most-likely much later text, contains a nice definition of the *nagara*. "What is called nagara? All where one can go out (of his house) without passing through paddy fields."[65] Archaeological surveys at present-day Trowulan and literary evidence confirm that Majapahit was a truly urban settlement, in fact the earliest in Java so far known both from archaeological and literary sources.

In regard to the spatial concept of statehood the Nāgara-Kĕrtāgama and an inscription of 1323 C.E. from Tuhañaru contains an interesting piece of information.[66] In this inscription the kingdom (*rājya*) of Majapahit is compared with a temple (*prasāda*) in which the king is worshipped as an incarnation (*avatāra*) of Viṣṇu. The *maṇḍala* of the island (*dvīpa*) of Jawa is equated with the temple land (*punpunan*) whereas the islands (*nūṣa*) of Madhura, Tañjunpura, etc. are compared with *aṃśa* land or dependencies which were only partly (*aṃśa*) under the control of Majapahit. The interesting point is the fact that this inscription clearly distinguishes between the *rājya* Majapahit and the (surrounding) *maṇḍala* of Jawadvīpa. It therefore appears that only the core region, comprising the kraton, the capital, and the *nagara* of the princes, constituted the *rājya* of Majapahit. We are used to translating this term as "kingship" or "kingdom" as in the literal sense it means "belonging to the king." Therefore it should be no surprise that in the context of South and Southeast Asian concentric states, *rājya* actually referred only to the inner core region under the direct authority of the *rājā*.

Beyond this *rājya* of Majapahit in eastern Java was *bhūmi* (or *dvīpa*) *jawā*, which, for the first time in its history, has come under the hegemony of a single dynasty. No sources, however, are available that would allow us to infer that here in *Jawadvīpa-Maṇḍala*, too, members of the central dynasty or court have been imposed "from above" as local rulers. Outside the *rājya* of Majapahit, *bhūmi jawā* apparently was still under the *watĕk* of its autonomous local *raka*. Moreover we have no idea as to whether Majapahit was able to establish any sort of provincial administration in these autonomous *watĕk* of *bhūmi jawā* outside the *rājya* of Majapahit and to collect regular taxes in these regions. But militarily, Java was certainly fully under the control of Majapahit. Furthermore, we may assume that military expeditions and visiting officers of the central court had to be supplied by local authorities.

Beyond *bhūmi jawā* were the "other islands" *(nusāntara* or *dvīpāntara)*. The Nāgara-Kĕrtāgama, 13-16, contains a long list of these islands, which include most of present-day Indonesia's islands as well as parts of the Malay peninsula. Most important among these islands was Sumatra with Malayu, the successor state of Palembang/Śrīvijaya. It was the only polity on these outer islands to which the Nāgara-Kĕrtāgama concedes the important term *bhūmi*. This reminds us of the fact that in Śrīvijaya's early inscriptions, too, the term *bhūmi* was reserved for Śrīvijaya and Java. The outer islands were regarded as tributary states of Majapahit. The Nāgara-Kĕrtāgama claims that "already the other islands *(dvīpāntara)* are getting ready to show obedience to the Illustrious Prince, without exception

---

[64] For the concept of the segmentary state see B. Stein, "The Segmentary State in South Indian History," in *Realm and Region in Traditional India*, ed. R. G. Fox (New Delhi, 1977), pp. 3–51; see also Subrahmanyam, "Aspects of State Formation."

[65] *Nawanatya*, 9a, in Pigeaud, *Java in the 14th Century*., vol. III, p. 121.

they bring in order all kinds of products every ordained season. As an instance of the honoured Prabhu's [King's] exertion for all the good that is in his care, ecclesiastical officers *(bhujaṅga)* and mandarins *(mantri)* are sent to fetch the produce regularly."[67]

The last concentric circle of Majapahit's statehood was constituted by the "other countries" *(deśāntara)*. According to the Nāgara-Kĕrtāgama, Siam, Ayuthaya, Ligor, Martaban, Rajburi, Singhanagarī (=Satingpra), Campā, and Kamboja belonged to this category; Yavana (= Vietnam) "is different, it is a friend *(mitra)*."[68] The *deśāntara* countries most likely were identical with "all the *maṇḍalita rāṣṭra* (which are) looking for support, numerous, entering into the Presence."[69] This description obviously refers to mere diplomatic relations between these countries and Majapahit.

The imperial kingdom of Majapahit thus represents the final stage of a continuous process of state formation in pre-modern Indonesia. The state consisted of a series of concentric circles of authority. Its political control was strongest in its center, that is, the *rājya* of Majapahit. It decreased stepwise in *bhūmi jawā* and the *nusāntara* and ended up in mere diplomatic relations with the *maṇḍalita rāṣṭra* or the "other countries" *(deśāntara)* on Mainland Southeast Asia.

Despite the structural weakness of all pre-modern states of South and Southeast Asia, viz., the lack of actual political control outside the royal core region *(rājya)*, under Majapahit two decisive structural changes had taken place. First, it was able to annex completely the neighboring kingdoms and little chieftaincies which usually still had surrounded the *Stammland* of the "Early Kingdoms" as autonomous *watĕk* or *sāmantacakra*. Majapahit thus created a considerably extended core region *(rājya)*. Second, Majapahit succeeded in extending its uncontested hegemony over Java, to enforce tributary relations with a large number of outer islands and to establish diplomatic relations with kingdoms in Mainland Southeast Asia. Majapahit thus became Indonesia's first truly "Imperial Kingdom."

The concentric structure of the "empire" of Majapahit has indeed a strong resemblance to the conceptual model of the *maṇḍala* state as described by O. W. Wolters and more recently by C. Higham in the context of Mainland Southeast Asia.[70] Derived from the ancient Indian Arthaśāstra, this concept is very suggestive and thus may be applied even more frequently to the pre-modern state in Southeast Asia. But while employing it in this context, one has to keep in mind that we have very little evidence that the term *maṇḍala* was ever used in contemporary Southeast Asian sources in such a comprehensive way. As we have observed in the early Malay inscriptions of Śrīvijaya and in the Nāgara-Kĕrtāgama, the political connotation of *maṇḍala* always referred to a portion rather than to state as a whole. Particularly in the context of early kingdoms it denoted autonomous or semi-autonomous chieftaincies and principalities at the periphery of these states. As they were slowly integrated some of the *maṇḍala* became provinces of the imperial kingdoms. In this later context, particularly in some of the great regional or imperial kingdoms of India (e.g. the Cōḷas in South India and the Gaṅgas in eastern India),[71] the term *maṇḍala* was also used for provinces

---

66 Boechari, "Epigraphic Evidence on Kingship in Ancient Java," *Madjalah Ilmu-Ilmu Sastra Indonesia*, 5,1 (1973): 119–26.

67 Nāgara-Kĕrtāgama, 15,3.

68 Ibid., 15,1.

69 Ibid., 12,6.

70 See above note 2.

71 R. Subbarayalu, "The Cōḷa State," *Studies in History* (New Delhi) 4 (1982): 265–306; S.K. Panda, *Herrschaft und Verwaltung im östlichen Indien unter den späten Gangas (ca. 1030–1434)* (Wiesbaden, 1986).

in the extended central core region. In order to avoid terminological misunderstandings, we have, therefore, to distinguish clearly between the ancient Indian concept of a *maṇḍala* state system and the—rather different—medieval epigraphical meaning of the term *maṇḍala*, denoting peripheral principalities or provinces. Moreover, as shown elsewhere, "the *maṇḍala* concept does not give sufficient scope to structural changes which constitute the difference between the Early and the Imperial Kingdoms."[72]

[72] Kulke, "The Early and the Imperial Kingdom," p. 13.

STATES WITHOUT CITIES: DEMOGRAPHIC TRENDS IN EARLY JAVA

Jan Wisseman Christie

Introduction

Java's place in the demographic literature is an interesting one. If one accepts the census figures produced at Raffles' behest, then it appears that the population of the island in 1815 stood at approximately 4.5 million. In 1900 it was close to 30 million. This apparent explosion in population, in the absence of any substantial net immigration, has been the focus of a good deal of comment for decades, drawing attention from other, potentially more significant, aspects of Java's demographic history. Now that recent studies have begun to cast doubt upon the accuracy of the early nineteenth century population estimates, suggesting that the population of rural areas was, for a number of reasons, grossly under-reported, it appears that Java's population growth may not have been quite as astonishing as it once seemed. Such studies do, however, highlight an important aspect of the past distribution of the population on the island, particularly in the Javanese-speaking areas of central and east Java: despite its heavy population, Java has not until recently been significantly urbanized. The 1815 figures indicate that at that time there were only five towns on the island with more than 20,000 inhabitants; at the end of the nineteenth century, towns of that size or larger still contained less than 3 percent of the population, and 90 percent of the population lived in communities of fewer than 5,000 inhabitants,[1] despite the administrative and eco-

I wish to thank the British Academy for providing the funds that supported part of the research discussed below. I would also like to express my gratitude to the members of the Pusat Penelitian Arkeologi Nasional for the aid and facilities provided. My sincere gratitude goes to Drs. Boechari for sharing with me some of the epigraphic research in which he is currently engaged, and to Drs. Mundarjito for discussing with me some of the survey material which he is currently assembling.

[1] Peter Boomgaard, *Children of the Colonial State: Population Control and Economic Development in Java, 1795–1880* (Amsterdam: Free University Press, 1989), p. 111; discussion of the early nineteenth-century figures can be found on p. 166. Some of the recent debates are summarized in G. J. Hugo, T. H. Hull, V. J. Hull, and G. W. Jones, *The Demographic Dimension in Indonesian Development* (Singapore: Oxford University Press, 1987).

nomic restructuring and rapid growth of rail links brought about by the Dutch colonial government.

This dispersal of population, particularly in central and east Java, did draw the attention of colonial commentators, who tended to explain the demographic situation by reference to the structure of the Javanese colonial economy, which acted as a feeder of unprocessed and semi-processed agricultural produce to European industries and markets. Most assumed that the colonial economy damped the native tendency towards urban growth. Anthony Reid has taken this argument a step further by suggesting that European interference in Southeast Asia actually reversed trends towards urbanization, and that in the sixteenth and seventeenth centuries Southeast Asia had been one of the most urbanized areas of the globe.[2]

Although Reid's suggestion may be a valid one in the case of coastal trading states whose port cities suffered under colonial rule, there is no evidence that Java was significantly urbanized before the arrival of the Dutch. The port towns of the north coast of Java described by Tomé Pires early in the sixteenth century, based upon actual observation rather than hearsay, were surprisingly small, most having fewer than 2,000 inhabitants.[3] The situation seems not to have changed significantly before the middle of the eighteenth century, the size of towns fluctuating wildly over periods of months or years depending upon the fortunes of war and the movements of rural populations,[4] but showing no overall tendency towards long-term growth. In the period of peace following the signing of the treaty of Giyanti in 1755, the rise in population in rural districts far out-stripped that of the towns.[5] Dutch colonial policies of the following century, far from impeding urban growth, seem actually to have encouraged it.

The underlying pattern of growth of population in central and east Java seems to have been, during the pre-colonial perod, that of short-term fluctuation in very mobile urban populations balanced against long-term (though not necessarily steady) growth in density of rural population in core regions of states. Not only did villages apparently grow at the expense of larger enclaves, but the data suggest that as villages grew they tended frequently to break down into two or more nucleated hamlets rather than acquire the characteristics of

---

[2] A.J.S. Reid, "The Structure of Cities in Southeast Asia, Fifteenth to Seventeenth Centuries," *Journal of Southeast Asian Studies*, 11, 2 (1980): 235–50.

[3] A. Cortesão (ed. and trans.), *The Suma Oriental of Tomé Pires and the Book of Francisco Rodrigues* (London: The Hakluyt Society, 1944), vol. 1, pp. 175–200. Figures for the population of settlements presented by Tomé Pires fall into two classes: those based upon hearsay (for Dĕmak and the state in the interior) and those based upon direct Portuguese observation (most of the Pasisir states). The figures based upon hearsay tend to be large. According to the head of Tuban, the lord of the interior state had some 200,000 fighting men at his disposal, and the state was "thickly populated, with many cities, and very large ones"; Pires, however, felt that this was clearly an exaggeration (pp. 175–76). Dĕmak, "according to what they say," was reported to be a town of some 8,000 to 10,000 dwellings and its lord had some 30,000 fighting men at his disposal from the country as a whole (p. 185); yet direct observation appears to have indicated a lower population for the town (p. 186). The figures based upon direct observation reveal that the ports of the other Pasisir states of the time were quite small. Tuban, for instance, had only some 1,000 inhabitants within its walls (p. 190), yet its lord could apparently raise 6,000 to 7,000 fighting men from the town and its limited hinterland (p. 192). The port of Gresik, "the great trading port, the best in all Java," which had a seasonally large foreign and archipelago trading population, appears to have had relatively few permanent residents. The population of the smaller states resided mainly in villages which were themselves apparently rather small.

[4] M. C. Ricklefs, "Some Statistical Evidence on Javanese Social, Economic and Demographic History in the Later Seventeenth and Eighteenth Centuries," *Modern Asian Studies* 20, 1 (1986): 1–32.

[5] Peter Carey, "Waiting for the 'Just King': The Agrarian World of South-Central Java from Giyanti (1755) to the Java War (1825–30)," *Modern Asian Studies* 20, 1 (1986): 59–137.

small towns.[6] Most of the towns and cities of modern Java owe their size, and many their very existence, to Dutch intervention. It will be argued below that this underlying pattern of relatively small-scale residential clustering within a densely populated rural landscape is a very old one, and that the economic and administrative structures of early Javanese states were not only adapted to this settlement pattern, but may in fact have helped to perpetuate it.

Background and Sources

The very limited archaeological data available at present suggest that rudimentary states of some sort may have begun to appear on the north coast of Java as early as the last three centuries B.C.E. The initial stages of political development seem to have occurred, at least in part, in response to an intensification of regional trade. This trade brought tin, copper, and iron into metal-poor Java; it also brought valuables in the form of large bronze drums from northern Vietnam. The distribution of these drums along the coasts of the Java and Banda Seas suggests that the Javanese may have dominated the spice trade of the eastern islands as early as the second or third century B.C.E., which may in turn explain the unusually large concentration of these drums in Java itself. With the connection of this regional trade network into the Old World trade system in the first century C.E., Javanese states were exposed to ideas from the Indian subcontinent, and the long process of "indianization," a phenomenon related to the growth of these states, had begun. Thus, by the time that legal documents were first recorded on permanent materials on the island, early in the ninth century, Javanese states could draw upon perhaps a millennium of accumulated political tradition and economic development.

Despite a century of archaeological investigation on the island, these legal documents, preserved on copper plate or on stone, remain the best source of data relating to demographic and economic development in the heartlands of central and east Java. Most of the recovered structural remains, which are largely religious and frequently monumental, are located in the two regions known to have formed the foci of the major states of pre-colonial Java: the uplands skirting Mount Merapi and the Perahu chain in central Java, and the Brantas river valley and adjacent Malang uplands of east Java. Unfortunately, dense modern settlement and heavy dependence upon wet-rice farming, along with certain geological factors,[7] have made the location of non-religious sites nearly impossible. Only the politically marginal region of Rembang, Pati, and Blora, near the north coast, has provided any useful data on early settlement patterns.[8]

Written sources do to some extent compensate for the gaps in the archaeological record. The most important records in this respect are the indigenous inscriptions in Old Javanese

---

[6] Boomgaard, *Children*, p. 115.

[7] In the immediate environs of the central Javanese temple of Borobudur, to the south of Magelang, some 207 sites of the eighth to early tenth centuries have been found to date, including the remains of 43 temples and small shrines: Sub-Konsorsium Sastra dan Filsafat, *Laporan Kerja Lapangan, Borobudur* (Jakarta: Departemen Pendidikan dan Kebudayaan, 1976). However, further to the east, in the region between Yogyakarta and Solo, sites of the late first millennium C.E. have been buried under layers of lahar ranging in depth from two to seven meters in some areas, and almost no surface finds of material from the period are found in this area. Similar problems are caused in the east Javanese heartland by volcanic activity in the Malang uplands and adjacent areas, and by flood-borne alluvium in the Brantas delta.

[8] E. W. van Orsoy de Flines, "Onderzoek naar en van keramische scherven in de bodem in Noordelijk Midden-Java, 1940–42," *Oudheidkundig Verslag* (1941–47), Bijlage A; Jan Wisseman, "Archaeological Research in Rembang District, north central Java, 1975," *Indonesia Circle* (1977): 8–14.

language. The surviving corpus includes over 300 *sima* (tax transfer) documents and a much smaller number of *jayapattra* (lawcourt decision) records, most of which deal with financial matters. The majority of these documents were issued between the beginning of the ninth century and the end of the fourteenth, the largest number of original charters being issued late in the ninth century, early in the tenth, and again during the first half of the eleventh century. The early decades of the fourteenth century saw a spate of reissues of earlier charters, many of which were updated in response to changing circumstances. From the middle of the fourteenth century a major literary work, the *Nagarakrtagama,* has survived which contains passages describing the landscape and settlements of the time in east Java. Added to these sources are the small collection of descriptions of Java recorded by a series of foreign observers, geographers, and trade officials over this period of several centuries. These last are far from reliable and can thus be used only when their contents appear to confirm information available from local sources.

Early Settlement Patterns and Demographic Trends

The impression one receives from Javanese written sources of the ninth to fourteenth centuries is that the vast bulk of the population lived in rural settlements of varying size, complexity, and antiquity, but all of which were primarily farming communities. These settlements were distributed somewhat unevenly across a landscape dominated by a series of volcanoes, many of which were at least partially active, and by two major and numerous minor river systems. Before 929 C.E. the dominant state on the island clung to the skirts of the volcanoes of central Java; after that date the center moved east to the Brantas river delta and the adjacent Malang uplands of east Java. This move appears to have occurred in response to at least two pressures: the long-term positive pull of the Brantas delta region and its trading opportunities during a period when Java was probably gaining trade at the expense of its more economically volatile rival Srivijaya[9]; and the short-term, catastrophic effects of volcanic activity in central Java during the later ninth and early tenth centuries.[10]

[9] Jan Wisseman Christie, "Patterns of Trade in Western Indonesia: Ninth through Thirteenth Centuries A.D." (University of London: PhD thesis, 1982), vol. 1, pp. 30–33.

[10] See the following: R. W. van Bemmelen, "The Influence of Geographical Events on Human History. (An example from Central Java)," *Verhandelingen van het Koninklijk Nederlandsch Geologisch-Mijnbouwkundig Genootschap,* geologische serie 16, (1956), pp. 19–36; H. Th. Verstappen, "Geomorphological Observations on Indonesian Volcanoes," in *Drie Geografische Studies over Java* (Leiden: Brill, 1963), pp. 237–51; M. Boechari, "Some Considerations on the Problem of the Shift of Mataram's Centre of Government from Central to East Java in the 10th Century," in *Early South East Asia,* ed., R. B. Smith and W. Watson (London: Oxford University Press, 1979), pp. 473–92. It appears, from more recent observations, that the layer of lahar which swamped the temple of Sambisari, near Yogyakarta, to a depth of seven meters, was not the result of one overwhelming flood of volcanic mud and sand, but probably of at least five separate episodes of deposition during a relatively brief period. There is no evidence at present that the surface of any of the major layers weathered sufficiently for vegetation to gain any widespread foothold before the next layer was deposited. The volcanic activity which produced this outflow of lahar may have built up over some decades. Deposits of volcanic sand relating to this period of volcanic activitiy are shallower to the west, in the region of Borobudur, but those at the site of Borobudur itself indicate that the settlement suffered a series of minor volcanic episodes before it was abandoned to the meter of sand dumped on it. Occupation of the site just below the monument appears to have begun late in the eighth century. At least two, and possibly three, narrow bands of sand interrupt the occupation layer accumulated before the early tenth century, indicating that there was a series of minor eruptions towards the end of the period of occupation. As in the seventeenth century, these may have been accompanied by a series of earth tremors. In the seventeenth century the tremors and eruptions caused widespread alarm and fostered the belief that the ancestors and spirits were unhappy with the incumbent political order. A parallel period of political instability occurred between 884 and 898 C.E., when, according to the recently discovered Wanua Tengah charter of 908 C.E., two rulers were driven out of the palace within a year of taking the throne, a third "fled the palace" after eight years in power, and a fourth survived only four years on the throne. Political instability during that four-

Since no inscription dating to the period after 928 C.E. has been found in central Java, it is assumed that a large proportion of the population followed the political center east to the Brantas delta. As, however, there is some evidence for continuity of place names in central Java between the ninth and later centuries, it seems likely that central Java was never actually depopulated, although it certainly became a political backwater.

After 929 C.E. the political center remained for some centuries in east Java, although during the later eleventh century the east Javanese state appears to have split into two smaller states, one on the coast and one in the interior, centered at Kadiri on the upper Brantas. These states were reunited once more in the early thirteenth century. The unified east Javanese state reached its peak in the fourteenth century, at which point it appears to have exercized some degree of power over much of the island of Java, as well as those of Madura and Bali, and to have included within a wider sphere of political clients many of the coastal states of eastern Indonesia, Borneo, and the Malacca Straits. By the fifteenth century, however, this state began to disintegrate, as a number of port enclaves along the north coast of Java began to pull away, financed by a major trade boom in the region, to form the Pasisir trading states. Shortly after 1500 C.E. the interior state was overrun from the north.

Against this background of shifting political fortunes, certain demographic trends appear to have been cumulative and largely unidirectional, reflecting several underlying developments: growth in population, growth in wealth both from agriculture and trade, and administrative attempts to cope—with varying degrees of success—with these long-term trends.

Several factors, including location of political centers and trade routes, as well as distribution of soil types, available surface water, and the steepness of incline, influenced the size and location of settlements. Judging from the distribution of *sima* charters and the number and size of settlements mentioned in them, it appears that settlement in central Java, during the ninth and early tenth centuries, formed a series of enclaves in the more fertile upland regions of Kedu, Magelang, Wonosobo, and the area to the north and east of Yogyakarta. Archaeological data seem to indicate that most villages were located along the banks of rivers draining the Merapi and Perahu massifs, between 100 and 400 meters above sea level.[11] This, at least, is where almost all monumental remains and inscriptions have been found, along with the large number of scattered *yoni* and *lingga* stones which may indicate the location of early village shrines.[12] While pollen samples from the site of Borobudur, south of Magelang, indicate that by the time of the construction of the monument late in the eighth century the site was located in a large tract of agricultural land and palm groves,[13] the inscriptions indicate that most villages had direct access to forest resources.

Although this general pattern of uneven, perhaps even discontinuous, distribution of population within states was maintained over a number of centuries, certain important differences between patterns in the core regions of central and east Java were apparent by the

---

teen-year period may well have been fed by natural disaster. The Wanua Tengah charter has been transliterated by Drs. M. Boechari, but has yet to be published.

11 Mundarjito, personal communication.

12 Jan W. Christie, "Raja and Rama: the Classical State in Early Java," in *Centers, Symbols and Hierarchies: Essays on the Classical States of Southeast Asia*, ed., L. Gesick (New Haven: Yale University Southeast Asia Studies Monograph 26, 1983), p. 16.

13 J. Nossin and C. Voute, "Notes on the Geomorphology of the Borobudur Plain (Central Java, Indonesia) in an Archaeological and Historical Context." Paper delivered at the Symposium on Remote Sensing for Resources Development and Environmental Management, Enschede, The Netherlands, 1986. Proceedings, p. 858.

tenth century and tended to become more marked over time. The center of the independent state which existed in east Java during the eighth and early ninth centuries appears, like that of its sister polity in central Java, to have been located on the upland skirts of active volcanoes, in this case the Malang valley. After this state was annexed by that of central Java, later in the ninth century, population appears to have begun to build up in and around the Brantas delta in the lowlands. Following the shift in political center to the east, the rate of population growth in the delta region appears to have accelerated considerably, and the distribution of monumental and epigraphic remains indicates that location of settlement from this period onwards was as much influenced by a network of roads and overland tracks as by the drainage system. The description, published in about 916 C.E. by the Arab writer Abu Zaid, of what can only have been the Brantas region of east Java,[14] provides a vivid, if perhaps somewhat exaggerated image of what the region's settlement looked like:

> The authority of the Maharaja [of Zabag] is exercized over these various islands and the island in which he resides is extremely fertile, and patches of settlement succeed each other without interruption. A very trustworthy man affirms that when the cocks crow at daybreak, as in our country, they call out to each other throughout the whole extent of a hundred *parasangs* [@500 kilometers] or more, showing the uninterrupted and regular succession of villages. In effect, there are no uninhabited places in this country and no ruins. He who comes into the country when he is on a journey, if he is mounted he may go wherever he pleases; if he is tired or if his mount has difficulty in carrying on, then he may stop wherever he wishes.

By the early eleventh century the landscape in the delta region was already a crowded one. The settlements of Cane, Patakan, and Baru, lying just to the south of Surabaya,[15] each

---

[14] G. R. Tibbetts, A Study of the Arabic Texts containing Material on South-East Asia (Leiden: Brill, 1979), p. 33. Tibbetts is inclined to believe that the term Zabaj was originally applied by the Arab writers to the island of Java, and that it only later became confused with references to Srivijaya, during a period when there was little direct Arab contact with the region and changes were occurring in the regional balance of economic power. The fact that successive authors plundered earlier manuscripts for information led to a great deal of confusion. At the time that Abu Zaid wrote, however, there seems to be no doubt that Zabaj was Java (p. 100–16). Chinese records and inscriptions from mainland Southeast Asia, as well as archaeological data, tend to support the impression that from the late eighth to the early or mid tenth century, Java was the most important trading power in the maritime region of Southeast Asia (Christie, "Patterns," pp. 30–33ff.).

[15] The charters are: Cane (1021 C.E.), Patakan (eleventh century), and Baru (1030 C.E.). Sources for the charters referred to in this article are as follows: In J.L.A. Brandes, *Oud-Javaansche Oorkonden*, ed., N.J. Krom (The Hague: Bataviaasch Genootschap, 1913): Baru (1030 C.E.) lx, Cane (1021 C.E.) lviii, Hantang (1135 C.E.) lxviii, Jaring (1181 C.E.) lxxi, Kamalagyan (1037 C.E.) lxi (and also in Christie, "Patterns," vol. 2, pp. 492–503), Kambang Putih (eleventh century) cxviii (and also in Christie, "Patterns," vol. 2, pp. 528–29), Kemulan (1194 C.E.) lxxiii, Padlĕgan (1117 C.E.) lxvii, Panumbangan (1120 C.E.) lxix, Patakan (eleventh century) lix, Pĕrtapan (1198 C.E.) lxxv, Petungamba (1269 C.E.) lxxx, Sangguran (928 C.E.) xxxi, Tuhañaru and Kusambyan (1323 C.E.) lxxxiii. In A.B. Cohen Stuart, *Kawi Oorkonden in Facsimilie met Inleiding en Transscriptie* (Leiden: Brill, 1875): Lintakan (919 C.E.) i, Waharu (931 C.E.) vii. In Th. G. Th. Pigeaud, *Java in the 14th Century*, 4 vols. (The Hague: Nijhoff, 1960–63): Ferry Charter (1358 C.E.) vol. 3, pp. 156–62. In H.B. Sarkar, *Corpus of the Inscriptions of Java* (Calcutta: Firma K.L. Mukhopadhyay, 1971–72): Mantyasih (907 C.E.) lxx. In W.F. Stutterheim, "Transscriptie van een Defecte Oorkonde op Bronzen Platen uit het Malangsche," *Oudheidkundig Verslag* (1928), pp. 105–8: Manañjung (eleventh century) and also in Christie, "Patterns," pp. 504–12. In W. F. Stutterheim, "Oorkonde van Balitung uit 905 A.D. (Randoesari I)," *Inscripties van Nederlandsche-Indie* 1 (1940): 3–28: Randusari 1 (905 C.E.). In F.H. van Naerssen, *Oudjavaansche Oorkonden in Duitsche en Deensche Verzamelingen* (Leiden: University of Leiden Proefschrift, 1941): Watukura (ninth century) viii, ix, x, and also in Christie, "Patterns," p. 527. Wanua Tengah (908 C.E.) has been transcribed by Drs. M. Boechari, who has also transcribed and translated the charter of Garamān (1053 C.E.); both of these have yet to be published. The charter of Dhimaṇāśrama (eleventh century) has plates scattered through three collections: plates 8, 9, and 10 appear in Brandes, *Oudjavaansche* as charter number cxii; plates 1(?), 7, and 10 appear in P.V. van Stein Callenfels, "Stukken betrekking hebbend op oud-Javaansche opschriften in de

appear to have supported populations exceeding a thousand persons, belonging to over three hundred households; their markets were large and frequented by foreign traders. The charter of Kamalagyan (1037 C.E.) lists seven settlements lying along the twenty-five kilometer stretch of river between Kamalagyan and the port of Hujung Galuh on the coast, along with an unspecified number of holy places of nine different classes.[16] This rise in density of population continued up the length of the Brantas, particularly around Kadiri and the area to the east of Blitar, where overland routes between the mountains descended to the river,[17] and along the overland routes themselves.[18] In the middle of the fourteenth century the Brantas and Solo rivers were crossed by a network of roads served by a lengthy list of villages with official ferry charters. The incomplete set of copper plates of the Ferry Charter (1358 C.E.) lists thirty-four such ferry-operating villages in the lower Brantas region alone and over twenty on the lower stretch of the Solo, downstream from Bojonegoro. Since an entire plate bearing the beginning of the list is missing, the total number of ferry settlements along the two rivers may have exceeded 150.[19]

MacDonald's guess[20] that the population of Java could have reached five million by the fourteenth century may not be wildly inaccurate. Yet from none of the sources, either historical or archaeological, does there emerge a single clear description of a settlement which can confidently be called a city. In fact, despite the greater tendency of settlement in east Java's lowlands to conform to a man-made pattern of distribution, and despite the clear increase in both the size of the population and the number of settlements in the broad lowland plains area, there appears to have been no pressure for a classic central place hierarchy of economic centers to evolve. The only concentrated accumulations of population to appear before the fourteenth century seem to have developed around one or two ports, and even these concentrations seem to have fallen short of the size and stability that characterize true urban centers. The capital of Majapahit itself seems to have been little more than a series of large royal and elite compounds with attached religious monuments, surrounded by a cluster of large villages.

The continuing diffuseness of settlement was probably, in fact, due partly to the nature of the political centers in Javanese states, and to the considerations that governed their locations and their movements. Literary sources suggest that the residence of the ruler (*kadatwan* in Old Javanese, *kraton* in Modern Javanese) was, by the eleventh century at least, broadly similar in function, structure, and residential population to the *kratons* of the Later Mataram

---

Bibliotheque Nationale te Paris," *Oudheidkundig Verslag* (1924), pp. 23–27; and half of plate 12 was transcribed by F.H. van Naerssen, "Inscripties van het Rijksmuseum voor Volkenkunde te Leiden," *Bijdragen* 97 (1937): 507–8. See also Christie, "Patterns," pp. 513–21.

16 The holy places mentioned included *sima, kalang, kalagyan, thāni jumput, wihara, śala, kamulan, parhyangan,* and *parapatāpan*. Of this list, the first four were, in fact, special-status communities with religious connections of some sort in this context. The *wihara* was a monastery, *sala* a type of temple, *kamulan* apparently an ancestor shrine, *parhyangan* a place associated with the spirits, and *parapatapan* meant "the several hermitages of ascetics."

17 See the charters of Padlĕgan (1117 C.E.), Hantang (1135 C.E.), Panumbangan (1120 C.E.), Jaring (1181 C.E.), Pĕrtapan (1198 C.E.), Kemulan (1194 C.E.), Petung-amba (1269 C.E.), Tuhañaru and Kusambyan (1323 C.E.), and others from the upper Brantas region.

18 See especially Kemulan (1194 C.E.), Panumbangan (1120 C.E.), and Petung-amba (1269 C.E.), as well as Hantang (1135 C.E.).

19 See Pigeaud, *Java*, vol. 3, pp. 156–62, and commentary, as well as J. Noorduyn, "Further Topographical Notes on the Ferry Charter of 1358," *Bijdragen* 124, 4 (1968): 460–81, for a summary of other discussions of the topographic information in the charter.

20 P. MacDonald, "An Historical Perspective to Population Growth in Indonesia," in *Indonesia: Dualism, Growth and Poverty*, ed., R. G. Garnaut and P. McCawley (Canberra: Australian National University Press, 1980).

period. While there are indications in the legal literature of a growing social and ceremonial distance between the ruler and the populace after the tenth century, as numbers of officials multiplied and the chain of intermediaries between royal patron and village client lengthened and each official enlarged his own retinue of clients, there is no real evidence that palace settlements became truly urban either in size or in function.

In fact, one characteristic shared by states both in central and east Java was the relative mobility of the political center. The royal center appears to have moved at least twice in the eighth and ninth centuries in central Java, each time shifting further to the south and east and apparently locating itself in a region already heavily populated. One of the moves probably carried it at least sixty kilometers. Then in 929 C.E. the *kadatwan* was shifted some six hundred kilometers to the east. Although this was the most striking of the moves of the palace, it was far from the last. The royal center moved between the Malang uplands and the Brantas valley a number of times over the centuries before coming to rest at Trawulan in the Brantas delta during the late thirteenth or fourteenth century. The period between the mid tenth and early thirteenth centuries appears to have been marked by at least three civil wars, each necessitating at least one move of the political center. This degree of mobility of the royal settlement appears to reflect a relatively low level of investment in the physical premises and the surrounding physical infrastructure. The fact that abandoned royal centers appear to have left little but rural villages in their wake, as in the case of that mentioned in the thirteenth century *Sumanasantaka*,[21] seems to indicate that whatever population build-up occurred outside the palace gates was not translated into formal or enduring urban structures. Nor were royal centers apparently located in settlements which already had major economic functions. Rulers in both central and east Java avoided, for strategic or symbolic reasons, placing their palaces in port enclaves before the fifteenth century, and the heads of the various *watek* tax groupings appear to have maintained their own residences away from the palace settlement; consequently, administration, patronage, and trade wealth did not converge on the same settlement, as was the case in the contemporary states of the Malacca Straits. Nor did they apparently remain attached to fixed settlements for any great length of time.

The patterns of distribution of settlement and the direction of the flows of wealth and power across the Javanese landscape appear to have been for centuries in a constant, if not always rapid, state of flux. Until the fifteenth century, when the three centuries of disintegration and warfare began on the island, these fluctuations occurred against the background of, and perhaps partly in response to, a substantial rise in population and a marked proliferation and growth of rural settlements. Two clear trends emerge from the archaeological and epigraphic records. The first, which is most clearly attested to archaeologically, is of the expansion of states through pioneering in peripheral areas. The sudden growth of population and proliferation of settlements in the marginal Rembang-Pati-Blora region after the turn of the millennium appears to have occurred as a result of this process.[22] The *sima* charters of certain strategic peripheral areas indicate that rulers actively promoted this pioneering through the granting of tax concessions. Grants stipulating that swidden land or forest be converted to *sawah* (irrigated rice land) in order to settle and stabilize territory bordering major road and river connections with the coast were made both in central and east Java. In central Java between 872 and 882 C.E. a series of at least ten *sima* grants was made to several temples in the mountains to the north of Magelang, along the route to the north coast. In many cases these grants involved *tgal* (dry field, swidden land) or *sukat* (brush

[21] 154.7: see P. J. Zoetmulder, *Old Javanese-English Dictionary* (The Hague: Hijhoff, 1982), p. 1932.

[22] Wisseman, "Archaeological Research," p. 13.

land, fallowed swidden), which was to be converted to *sawah*.[23] A few years later similar grants were made in east Java along the route between the Malang uplands and the coast, the stated reason being the danger presented to travelers by the *tgal* fields along the road.[24] At the beginning of the tenth century, during a period of expansion and consolidation in central Java, another grant was made in connection with forest and *sawah* land on the slopes of mounts Sumbing and Sundoro to the north of Magelang for the stated purposes of protecting the high road.[25] At the same time in east Java a grant was made concerning forest to be cleared for *sawah* because the forest was said to present a danger to traders and people traveling to the coast.[26]

The second trend, most apparent at the level of the village community, was the coupling of growth with fission.

Settlement and Community

The diffuseness and mobility of political and economic foci within early Javanese states was echoed at the village level. Unlike ancient villages on the mainland of Southeast Asia, which often remained in one place long enough to build up substantial mounds reflecting centuries or even millennia of occupation, Javanese villages seem not to have occupied the same precise location for more than a few generations. This does not, however, mean that there was no long-term continuity in villages or that the communities broke up and reformed in other places. Villages remained fixed within a defined region and they had boundaries that apparently remained stable over a period of centuries. Village names appearing in charters of the tenth century can still frequently be found on maps of the twentieth century, particularly in the Brantas valley. In some cases the boundaries of old *sima* territories can still be traced on modern maps. Land, once cleared, bunded, and irrigated for rice cultivation, was not abandoned casually, even if a proportion of the population moved or died during periods of warfare. However, within the fixed village territorial borders, the community's population appears to have shifted the location of their dwellings frequently enough to prevent the build-up of any tell-tale mounds.

The relative impermanence of dwelling units was apparently one of the factors underlying what was perhaps the most interesting development in the Javanese interior before the fifteenth century. This process, which might be termed the "disintegration" of the village, seems to have been provoked by population growth. It appears to have contributed, in turn, to certain administrative changes. This process of the restructuring of the rural communities and their relations to the court is reflected in the changing terminology applied in the legal literature to these settlements. Between the early–ninth century and the mid–fourteenth century several clear shifts occurred in the terms by which communities were defined for administrative purposes. The terms are, in order of appearance, *wanua, thāni/karaman, duwan/duhan i dalem thāni, paraduwan/paraduhan*, and *desa* or *dapur* .[27]

---

[23] See M. Boechari, *Prasasti Koleksi Museum Nasional I* (Jakarta: Museum Nasional, 1986), inscriptions E5, E6, E7, E9, E10, E15, and E18; in Machi Suhadi and M.M. Sukarto, *Laporan Penelitian Epigrafi Jawa Tengah* (Berita Penelitian Arkeologi 37, Jakarta: Departemen Pendidikan dan Kebudayaan, 1986), inscriptions 2.7.1, 2.7.3, 2.7.4, and 2.7.6.

[24] Sarkar, *Corpus*, lvi and lvii.

[25] Ibid., lxx.

[26] A. M. Barrett Jones, *Early Tenth Century Java from the Inscriptions* (Dordrecht: Foris Publications, 1984), p. 181.

[27] J. Wisseman Christie, "*Wanua, thāni, paraduwan:* The 'Disintegrating' Villages of Early Java?" in *Texts: Oral and Written Traditions*, ed. W. Marshall (Bern: University of Bern, 1991).

The oldest term to be applied to Javanese settlements in the legal literature is *wanua*. It appears in the earliest surviving *sima* document, dated 804 C.E., and with a single known exception was the only term used in charters until 991 C.E.. The term is a very old one. Given the wide distribution of the word and its variants in maritime Southeast Asia, the Pacific, and Madagascar, it was certainly present in the basic proto-Austronesian vocabulary by the time the Austronesians moved south through the Philippines, about five thousand years ago, with a meaning that must have been something like "settled territory" or "dwelling place." In the Old Javanese legal literature the term had several related meanings. It meant both "group" and "settled territory." The "group" was in all cases human and the word appears to carry overtones of internal structure or stratification. The closest English language equivalent is "community." When the term was placed in the landscape, it referred to settled land belonging to a structured community whose rights derived from deified ancestors rather than from the state. The *wanua* in this sense was acknowledged by the court to have had clearly identified boundaries and to have included all of the land within those borders, cultivated or not. This territory appears to have been large, based perhaps upon the territorial requirements of mixed agricultural systems including swidden. The formulas in the charters relating to *wanua* land include such phrases as, "the forests, swidden fields, and rivers, in the valleys and on the hills," "their valleys and mountains . . . their *sawah* and orchards," "their *sawah*, dry rice fields, marshes and orchards," and others in the same vein. The *wanua* was administered by a council of heads of land-owning households—the *karaman*—a number of whom held named community offices. However, no single figure can be identified as headman in the legal literature before the fourteenth century, and it is doubtful that such a figure appeared uniformly until much later, when state authorities (frequently Dutch) imposed headmen on villages for administrative convenience.[28]

The legal charters of the ninth and tenth centuries refer to only three classes of settlement: the *wanua*, the religious community (*kahyangan*), and the palace enclave (*kadatwan*), as in the Mantyasih charter of 907 C.E.:

> "O ye Holy Spirits of past [kings],who once were lords of the *wanua*, masters of the *kahyangan*, builders of *kadatwan*. . . ."[29]

All communities subject to *sima* grants before 991 C.E. were called *wanua*, and so were the surrounding communities who sent witnesses to the ceremonies and all of the communities from which the middle and lower-ranking state officials were drawn. The use of this single term in these charters did not reflect poverty of vocabulary. Judging from the Indian literary works available by that time in Old Javanese—notably the *Ramayana*, and the *Adiparwa* and other parts of the *Mahabharata*—the full range of Sanskrit terms for settlement and city was available to the court clerks who inscribed the charters. There appears to have been very little resistance at the time to borrowing Sanskrit terminology where it proved to be useful, and a wide range of legal, political, and administrative terms were already part of the working vocabulary of courtier and villager alike. The more obvious Sanskrit terms which could be used to describe a city—*pura* and *nagara*—didn't filter into the Javanese vocabulary until the thirteenth century, and even then, in Javanese legal contexts (rather than "Indian" literary contexts) the terms appear to have referred only to the palace enclave and its dependent settlement complex, replacing and amplifying the older term *kadatwan*. Use of the terms in the thirteenth and fourteenth centuries does not appear to reflect the addition of

---

[28] J.C. Breman, "The Village on Java and the Early-colonial State," *Journal of Peasant Studies* 9, 4 (1982): 189–240.

[29] Sarkar, *Corpus*, lxx.

a new category of settlement to those recognized, although it may indicate some growth in the size of the population living just outside the palace walls.

The names of over four hundred *wanua* appear in the surviving records from central Java, most of which date to the brief period between 850 and 928 C.E. It remains unclear what proportion of the total number of settlements belonging to the central Javanese state and located in that region this represents. The fact that few overlaps occur from one charter to the next in the names of *wanua* from which witnesses to the various *sima* ceremonies were invited (in nearly a hundred charters) probably means that those listed represent less than half of the total extant in the regions where grants were made. Since both religious foundations and *sima* territories that supported them formed a series of clusters, rather than being uniformly distributed across the settled landscape, there must have been a substantial number of areas whose *wanua* were not mentioned at all in the *sima* charters.

Most *wanua* subject to tax transfers appear to have had a number of close neighbors. Some of these *wanua tpi siring* ("adjacent bordering settlements") who sent witnesses to *sima* ceremonies clearly shared boundaries with the *sima* villages. Since, however, the number of *wanua tpi siring* mentioned in any one charter ranged from one or two to over sixty, as in the case of Randusari I, issued in 905 C.E., the term appears to have been applied somewhat loosely to villages within a recognized catchment region that cross-cut the 120 or so *watek* tax-groupings (the precursors to later appanage holdings) mentioned in texts of this short period.

The ninth- and tenth-century *wanua* were by no means uniform blocks of population. They varied considerably in size, in wealth, and possibly in internal structure and economics. These differences seem to have become more marked over time. By the end of the ninth century the *sima* charters mention large and small (*magöng, madmit*) *wanua*, whose representatives were ranked accordingly in the ceremonial gift lists. Lists of heads of households in ninth-century settlements affected by *sima* transactions range in length from a handful to nearly a hundred, and these households appear to have represented only one class in the community hierarchy, so it is conceivable that some settlements could have harbored close to a thousand individuals. In the large *wanuas* of the ninth and tenth centuries, two, three, or even four or more individuals shared the same community office. By the early tenth century, sub-communities within the *wanua* were often distinguished. These appear to have comprised groups of residents whose primary occupation was not farming, as in the case of the merchant group (*kabanyagan*) of Galuh, mentioned in the Lintakan charter of 919 C.E. At the same time there appear to have been named territorial subunits of at least some *wanuas*.

It may have been in response to this growth in diversity of rural communities that, late in the tenth century, the ancient term *wanua* was replaced in the legal literature by the terms *thani* and *karaman*, the word *karaman* referring to the body of heads of household who formed the community council, and the word *thani*, which referred to the place itself, emphasizing its rural character. This new terminology proved less enduring than the older word. By the middle of the eleventh century the word *thani* was beginning to give way to the term *duwan* (later also *duhan*), meaning "hamlet," found in the phrase *duwan i dalem thani* ("hamlet inside the *thani*"). One *thani* could consist of several *duwan*, as in the case of Baru (Baru, 1030 C.E.), whose four *duwan*, named Punasa (? "purified"), Gunung ("mountain"), Dèpur ("cluster"), and Pkan ("marketplace"), comprising about 100, 40, 70, and 90 households respectively, provide some indication of the manner in which the community was distributed. At much the same time the term *babad* ("forest clearing, pioneer settlement") begins to make a regular appearance as a description of a settlement sub-unit belonging to the community, and from the way in which it is mentioned it appears that the *babad* settlement may in many cases have lain outside of the old community boundaries. If so, then at least some of the pioneering settlement in east Java appears to have been carried out under the auspices and administration of existing communities, through the creation of daughter settlements and the annexation of territory. By the beginning of the twelfth century, the term *thani* appears to have been largely replaced by the word *paraduwan* ("the several *duwans*") or phrases indicating the number of *duwan*. Most communities whose *duwan* were enumerated at this time comprised about four or five hamlets, but others incorporated up to a dozen, particularly in the upper Brantas valley where there appears to have been more room for territorial expansion. In these large, sprawling settlements the old term *wanua* occasionally appeared in the phrase *wanua tengah* ("core/original settlement"), but not in its old general usage. Late in the twelfth century a new term, *desa*, borrowed from the Sanskrit, began slowly to replace other terms for the community as a whole, while in the fourteenth century, the term *dapur* ("cluster") appears to have taken over some of the meanings of *duwan*. Usage appears to have remained in flux until the Dutch standardized the use of the word *desa* five centuries later.

This rapid series of shifts in terminology, after what may have been several thousand years of use of the term *wanua*, could reflect changes in administrative relations between court and populace, or changes in the demographic structure of Javanese states. In fact, it probably reflects both. Only two of the terms—*desa* and possibly *thani*—were borrowed from Sanskrit. The word *desa* meant "area, region" in Sanskrit, and it was originally used in Old Javanese with that meaning, only very gradually taking over the meaning of settlement territory. The term *thani* probably derives from the Sanskrit term *sthanin* ("abiding, permanent") or *sthaniya* ("large village, town"). The original Sanskrit term never appears in the legal literature in connection with settlements, and the Javanized version, *thani*, is so stable in orthography both in the charters and in metric literature that it seems likely that the term had been thoroughly adapted to the local context, acquiring a new set of indigenous meanings, well before it began to replace the term *wanua*. Both of the borrowed terms have one common feature, however, which may have influenced their adoption: they both implied relative largeness in scale. The replacement of *wanua* by *thani* may reflect a perceived growth in the average size of communities, although the constant coupling of the term with that of *karaman*, distinguishing the place from its population may also indicate some adjustment in administrative relations between state and village, foreshadowing the growth in direct patron-client links between official and individual household, bypassing the village. This shift may also represent an attempt on the part of the tax-collecting authorities to redefine the status of communities by abandoning a term that carried too many overtones of political autonomy.

Subsequent changes, which followed one another in such rapid succession from the eleventh century onwards that they overlapped even in the same charters, tell us a good deal about the changing demographic structure at the village level and administrative attempts to deal with them. The population of east Javanese states appears to have risen fairly consistently from the early tenth century through the fourteenth, despite at least three periods of internal strife: during the second two decades of the eleventh century, and again in the second half of that century, followed by another, possibly briefer struggle early in the thirteenth century. Not all of the excess population was syphoned off into pioneering communities on the states' peripheries. Established communities grew, but instead of forming ever larger clusters of dwellings and taking on the characteristics of small towns, they apparently began to break up into smaller residential units. This process was almost certainly under way as early as the ninth century, in central Java, where larger communities developed multiple sets of officials, probably representing different hamlets within the communities' territories. Named subunits of *wanuas* appear in *sima* charters by the early tenth century, not all of them located within the boundaries of the original *wanua* territory. This trend may reflect a growing confidence in the state's power to maintain order, as well, perhaps, as a beating back of the surrounding forest and its dangers, since convenience and pressures to reduce social tensions appear to have over-ridden considerations of defense in the location of housing. It is at about this time that domestic architecture in Java appears to have begun to change, bringing houses, once set high on pilings, much closer to the ground. This in turn allowed for the expansion of roofed domestic space, but characteristically, the process of enlargement appears to have led to the development of clusters of small structures rather than to an expansion of space under one roof, judging from the structures illustrated in temple reliefs. The processes of growth and sub-division appear to have been linked at every level in Javanese society.

After the move of the main political center to east Java, this trend towards the subdivision of larger communities accelerated. By the early eleventh century many of these communities were expanding into the remaining forest areas and claiming as part of their establishment newly–cleared land apparently beyond the borders of the communities' territories. The daughter communities set up in these forest clearings remained attached to the original community—a fact that may explain some later law suits between communities over conflicting administrative rights.[30] That the communities continued to exercise rights over clearly bounded territories at this time is indicated by the boundary pillars mentioned in descriptions of the borders of tax-transferred territories, and the assumption made by all charters that these borders would never be breached. It appears that communities could expand, but were not expected to shrink. Expansion, however, brought the subdivisions of the community more and more into the fore in legal documents. Hamlets within the village were listed as a matter of course by the mid-eleventh century, although the community continued to be recognized as a unit with administrative rights. The hamlets do, however, appear to have developed stable identities under the umbrella of the larger community. For instance, the edict of Panumbangan (1120 C.E.) refers to a community at a crossroads to the east of Blitar as *lima duwan i panumbangan i dalem thani* ("the five hamlets of Panumbangan inside the *thani*"), listing the five hamlets as Palampitan ("rattan-mat place"), Kamburan (?), Padagangan ("trading place"), Byetan (?), and Kidul-ning-Pasar ("south of the covered market"). A century and a half later, the charter of Petung-amba (1269 C.E.), referring to the same community as the *paraduhan panumbangan* ("the several hamlets of Panumbangan") lists at least three of the original hamlets: Kamburan, Padagangan, and Kidul-ing-Pasar, as well, possibly, as two new units: Banak ("goose") and (?) Tiwir. The inscription is too fragmentary for it to be clear whether the other two original hamlets survived intact, disappeared entirely, or developed new identities, but three of the hamlets clearly retained enough of their identity to keep the same names, and probably roughly the same locations, even if some degree of shift and expansion had occurred.[31]

---

30 One such dispute is recorded in the Majapahit period Walandit inscription from the Malang uplands, where the dispute hinged upon the claims of autonomy by Walandit and the counter claims of authority by Himad; while these were both holy places, the dispute appears to have concerned financial dispositions and Himad's claim that Walandit was a daughter community of some sort. See J. G. de Casparis, "Oorkonde uit het Singosarische (Midden 14e Eeuw A.D.)," *Inscripties van Nederlandsch-Indie* i (1940), pp. 50–60.

31 Brandes, *Oud-Javaansche*, lxix and lxxx.

The increase in prominence of hamlets within a village in tax transfer charters occurred as state authorities began to shift their tax concessions, in at least some cases, away from entire—and by then often large—community corporations, to the smaller subunits under community control. This shift in focus of tax-gathering interests was consolidated in the twelfth century, when the term *paraduwan* or *paraduhan* ("the several hamlets") replaced older terms for the community as a whole. The term *thani*, like the word *wanua*, was relegated to use in a few limited contexts, as it lost its former range of meanings. The community had become a sum of its parts, many of which were more or less self-contained farming communities. Other sub-communities, of a non-farming nature, emerged as regular features of these expanded settlement complexes: the incorporated groups of artisans (*kalang*), small religious establishments (*kalagyan*), and merchant enclaves (*kabanyagan*) were the three classes of non-farming community most frequently mentioned.

Late in the twelfth century, this expansion of the community and the rural sprawl it created resulted in the adoption of yet another term for community: the word *desa*, and in the following century the term *dapur*, which seems to refer to a cluster of housing, joined the word *duwan/duhan* in references to the smallish residential subunits of the community. During a period when old charters were being reissued and updated, in the fourteenth century, several terms occasionally appeared in the same inscription, apparently in an attempt to avoid some of the confusion that the accumulated changes in legal terminology must have created.

What seems clear from this record of administrative attempts to accommodate changes in the demographic structure of increasingly populous states is that the changes to which the authorities were reacting were not those leading to increased concentration of population, but rather to the proliferation of smallish residential clusters within an increasingly hierarchical administrative structure. The hierarchy was expanding at the bottom as well as at the top, and it was not a hierarchy that depended upon size of coresidential population. The only centers that appear to have seen any long-term growth of nucleated settlement were the port areas, whose populations appear, in any case, to have continued to fluctuate seasonally. It was precisely those enclaves that precipitated the breakup of the state of Majapahit.

The Economics of Decentralization

There is a tendency in academic literature for rural communities to be equated with isolation, ignorance, and poverty, and for economic systems not served by an orderly placement of greater and lesser urban centers to be equated with inefficiency and inelasticity. Neither of these truisms seems to be supported by the early Javanese data. States of early Java were demographically dispersed, but by no means inefficient in their handling of flows of goods and information. Java's lucrative trade with the Spice Islands was financed by exports of rice, beans, and other staple crops (Mananjung charter, eleventh century), and, by the twelfth century, Java had become a major producer and exporter of black pepper, feeding the Chinese market. The list of taxable goods traded in Javanese rural markets of the time included tin from Malaya, copper from China and mainland Southeast Asia, iron from sources perhaps as distant as the East African coast, silver perhaps from Burma, and gold from many sources. With these metals came dyestuffs from the forests of Borneo and Sumatra and from the dry islands of the Lesser Sundas, skeins of silk from China and of cotton from Bali and the east Javanese lowlands, salt and salt fish from the coast, and other regional products from Java itself. Local pottery was widely traded and Chinese ceramics are so widely dispersed in non-elite sites after the tenth century[32] that they must have circulated through the market system. Chinese reports of the twelfth and thirteenth centuries speak of exports to Java not only of such finished goods as silk cloth, lacquer-ware, ceramics, and cast iron implements, but also of a wide range of industrial chemicals used in dyeing and metal working.[33] Gold and silver coins were minted in both central and east Java,[34] and they were used by all strata within the society to pay taxes and debts, and to purchase everything from cloth and buffaloes to land and buildings. At the same time Java imported Chinese copper cash, and the boundless Javanese appetite for copper coinage seriously worried Chinese treasury authorities after the turn of the millennium. So much of this versatile small-denomination coinage appears to have been in circulation in Java by the fourteenth century that it was adopted as the standard currency. By the standards of the time, Java's economy—both domestic and import-export—was efficient and its market sophisticated.

Several factors appear to have contributed to this efficiency in the flow of goods through an obstinately rural landscape. Administrative involvement appears to have been largely passive in nature, even in the import-export trade. In this sector Javanese rulers of successive states seem to have resorted, like their later counterparts, to tax farming as a means of acquiring income without reforming the very decentralized tax-collecting system.[35] These tax farmers apparently included in their ranks both local and foreign merchants,[36] and port areas seem to have become the foci of collection of taxes in kind, and of administered sales at fixed prices, largely in connection with rice, black pepper, beans, salt, and *wungkudu* dye, from the coastal regions in their immediate vicinity, under authorities other than the court and political hierarchy. This development of an alternative administration of major classes of taxation in the vicinity of ports may have been a key factor in the eventual breakdown of the Majapahit state during the trade boom of the fifteenth century. The Javanese court seems not to have been equipped to deal with the increasingly autonomous, powerful, and wealthy enclaves it had inadvertantly created by trying to derive maximum benefit from the export of agricultural produce without reforming its own administrative structure and practices. Since ports appear also to have become centers of industries dependent upon imported raw materials (the main iron-working centers of east Java were, for instance, located in the Surabaya-Sidoarjo coastal region[37]), and they harbored large fishing industries,[38] it is not surprising that these areas began to develop characteristics reminiscent of the Malay states of neighboring islands, whose economic and administrative arrangements were broadly similar.[39]

Port areas aside, the economy of Javanese states remained largely decentralized. Although the ports played an essential role in providing a number of critically important

32 Orsoy de Flines, "Onderzoek" and Wisseman, "Archaeological Research."

33 F. Hirth and W. W. Rockhill (trans. and ed.), Chau Ju-kua: His Work on the Chinese and Arab Trade in the Twelfth and Thirteenth Centuries, entitled Chu-fan-chi (New York: Paragon Reprints, 1966), p. 78.

34 R. S. Wicks, "Monetary Developments in Java between the Ninth and Sixteenth Centuries: a Numismatic Perspective," *Indonesia* 42 (1986): 42–77.

35 See, for instance, the charters of Watukura (tenth century), Manañjung (eleventh century), and Garamān (eleventh century).

36 Christie, "Patterns," pp. 252–68.

37 See the charters of Sangguran (928 C.E.) and Manañjung (eleventh century).

38 See Dhimaṇāśrama (eleventh century).

39 Christie, "Patterns," pp. 332ff.

goods and raw materials for circulation, and in renewing supplies of copper currency and bullion to feed the domestic economy, they appear not to have become central places in the classic sense. Some of the more valuable and prestigious finished goods, such as Indian cottons and swords, Chinese silks and ceramics, and so forth, may have gone to the court in the first instance as payment for tax farms, and from there trickled down to other members of the state. Most of the more mundane items—and many of the more valuable items as well—seem to have entered the interlocking networks of circulating markets of the interior fairly directly, without passing through any identifiable intermediate level of centers of distribution of goods.

Markets and the trade associated with them are mentioned frequently and prominently in the *sima* charters, particularly of the tenth and eleventh centuries. These markets (*pkan*) circulated amongst groups of neighboring communities, at the village rather than hamlet level, on a five day schedule (this Javanese five–day week also bearing the name of *pkan*). By the tenth century, if not before, the market held on the day Kliwon in the five-day market week appears to have been the dominant market of the circuit,[40] feeding goods into those held on other days in the same catchment area. These markets drew varying ranges and volumes of trade, those in the densely populated and apparently well-off Brantas delta region providing a particularly impressive range of goods and services. The professional traders who frequented them were expected to cover large territories in their circuits, as they still are today.[41] No single trader's circuit could, however, have carried goods from the coast to the far interior. Such a distance could only have been covered by overlapping and interlocking circuits in patterns still present in the market systems of central and east Java for some goods.[42] While metal-workers may have developed their own network based upon port industries and relations to certain exclusive holy places, most of the trade in perishables seems, as early as the tenth century, to have been handled through a system very similar in broad terms to that still present in rural Javanese market networks.

The key to this system is the *bakul* trader, a market-based trader who buys from farmers and peddlars and sells both locally (on a retail basis) and to carriers moving on to other markets (on a wholesale basis). The modern *bakul* is, in turn, wholesaler, retailer and provider of credit, bulking goods for more distant markets and breaking down lots that arrive from outside. Without the *bakul*, modern Java's market system, which *can* operate in the absence of large urban supply-markets, would collapse. This entrepreneur appears, under the name of *adagang bakulan* ("*bakul* trader") or *abakul*, as early as the beginning of the tenth century, operating in the larger markets of the Brantas delta communities,[43] though not, apparently, in markets at the ports themselves. They seem to have been then, as now, the essential middlemen who kept trade moving:

> . . . those *bakul* traders who trade in areca and betel . . . sesame and oil . . . all the produce of the marshes . . . tamarind . . . cotton . . . may receive goods from other, distant

[40] See the charter of Waharu (931 C.E.).

[41] The most common formula to be found in passages relating to the removal or transfer of state taxes on certain classes of trader is similar to that found in the charter of Patakan (eleventh century), which states that thise traders "are not to be subject to the *sang mangilala drawya haji* tax collectors, no matter what region they go to..." The Kambang Putih charter (eleventh century) is more explicit, stating that these traders are not to be subject to state tax "should they trade to the limits of the kingdom of His Majesty."

[42] See A. Dewey, *Peasant Marketing in Java* (New York: Free Press, 1962); G. Chandler, *Market Trade in Rural Java* (Clayton: Monash University Centre of Southeast Asian Studies, Papers on Southeast Asia, No. 11, 1984); J. Alexander, *Trade, Traders and Trading in Rural Java* (Singapore: Oxford University Press, 1987).

[43] Christie, "Patterns," p. 224.

regions and sell them in the neighborhood without being subject to the merchant tax farmers of the five regions. . . . (Garaman charter, 1053 C.E.)[44]

. . . those who act as *bakul* traders, handling all the contents of the dry rice fields, all the contents of the *sawah* fields, all the contents of the marshes, all the contents of the sea, all the contents of the mountain slopes—two of each only [shall be freed from tax]. . . . (Tuhanaru and Kusambyan charter, 1323C.E.)[45]

The *bakul*-centered market network sustained flows of goods of at least certain classes through the heartlands of the east Javanese states. Whether they performed the same functions in the earlier markets of central Java is less clear, since passages in *sima* charters of the ninth century are less specific in relation to trade. The periodic market system does, however, appear to have been a major agency through which horizontal cohesion was maintained at the village level in all of the early states documented by inscriptions. By the ninth century, administrative groupings of villages under *watek* heads were already too dispersed to perform this function. The fact that the states of early central Java were even less "urbanized" than their east Javanese successors may indicate that a trader similar to the *bakul* was already beginning to appear in markets of the central Javanese interior.

This *bakul* system does not seem to have led to the formation of markets above a certain size—nor does it seem to have generated permanent, daily markets specializing in wholesale trade. It may be that this manner of articulating wholesale and retail trade was self-limiting in its scale. If so, then the *sima* system of state finance for religious foundations, with its commercial tax concessions, must have reinforced this tendency to limitation in scale of operations. The tax provisions of the charters of the ninth century were fairly vague and sweeping. By the tenth century, however, when market trade began to receive greater administrative attention, limits were imposed upon the volume of trade that could be carried on by individual professionals resident in *sima* villages without being subject to state taxes. Since limitations were also placed upon the number of professionals who could operate free of these taxes within a given community, this may have reduced competition; it certainly ensured dispersal of such professional trading activity. The *sima* tax concessions must have encouraged the build-up of trade in the affected community until it reached the tax ceiling (assuming, of course, that the religious community to which the tax rights were transferred was not overly greedy in exercising those rights). But the same concessions must have discouraged growth in professional trading activity beyond that ceiling.

New finds of charters continue to be made, and the exact provenance of some of those found in the past is uncertain, but from the record as it now stands, it seems that the pattern of creation of *sima* territories was correlated more closely with periods and areas of population growth than with those of temple building, particularly in east Java. Thus, the creation of *sima* trading enclaves must, to some extent, have kept pace with the growth of consumption demand and of the market network as a whole. This may have acted as a brake on the growth of commercial centers in the interior. At least thirty such *sima* trading enclaves appear to have been established in the Brantas delta and on its fringes between 900 and 1060 C.E., all in areas with the population, wealth, and transport infrastructure to produce commercial towns or even cities but which, in fact, did not.

In sum, then, a number of factors may have contributed to the failure of clearly urban centers to develop in the populous heartlands of the early states of Java. The major ones—

---

44 Transcribed and translated by Drs. M. Boechari, but not yet published.

45 Brandes, *Oud-Javaansche*, lxxxiii.

the nature of Javanese communities and their persistent tendency to subdivide into smallish residential clusters within traditional village territories that were large enough to accommodate a good deal of rural sprawl, and the decentralized, periodic, *bakul*-centered market network that supplied those communities—were reinforced, and even amplified, by certain of the states' administrative procedures and peculiarities. These included the *sima* tax-transfer system and tax-farming arrangements that obviated the need for administrative centralization of state finances, as well as the relative mobility of the political center. Political ties and tax rights in Java tended, over time, to devolve into somewhat unstable and territorially unfocused chains of patron-client ties, as tax-collecting authority, like everything else, tended to subdivide rather than accumulate.

Urbanization is not a process which can be automatically coupled with that of state-formation and development: in central and east Java, population growth and the increase of wealth and trade appear to have encouraged growth of communities of the interior only until they reached a threshold beyond which fission began to occur. Those coastal enclaves which managed to pass that threshold eventually detached themselves from the main body of the state, becoming the foci of smaller states of a somewhat different nature.

The Merchant and the King Political Myths of Southeast Asian Coastal Polities

Pierre-Yves Manguin

"Maka kapal pun dapat dan dapati real lima puluh laksa lain dagangan. Maka baginda pun menjadi raja di Siantan."

Hikayat Raja Akil[1]

The relationship between the rise of maritime trade and the formation and subsequent development of coastal polities in Southeast Asia has become the focus in recent years of many a study by archaeologists, historians, and anthropologists.[2] The nature of this rela-

---

The final form of this essay owes much to the critical comments and suggestions of Oliver W. Wolters, William H. Scott, Jean-François Guermonprez, Bernard Sellato, and Jacques Leclerc. I wish to express my gratitude for all their help. It goes without saying that I assume full responsibility for its conclusions.

[1] From the unpublished Roolvink manuscript of the "Siak Chronicle" (*Hikayat Raja Akil*), as quoted by A. C. Milner, *Kerajaan: Malay Political Culture on the Eve of Colonial Rule* (Tucson: University of Arizona Press, 1982), p. 26. It translates as "A ship was captured and 500,000 dollars and other goods were taken from it; then the prince [who had been responsible for obtaining the booty] became raja in Siantan."

[2] Among other such studies dealing with Insular Southeast Asia, see J. Wisseman Christie, "Markets and Trade in Pre-Majapahit Java," in *Economic Exchange and Social Interaction in Southeast Asia: Perspectives from Prehistory, History and Ethnography*, ed. K. L. Hutterer (Ann Arbor: Center for South and Southeast Asian Studies, 1977), pp. 197–212; J. Wisseman Christie, "Raja and Rama: The Classical State in Early Java," in *Centers, Symbols, and Hierarchies: Essays on the Classical States of Southeast Asia*, ed. L. Gesick (New Haven: Yale University Southeast Asian Studies Monograph 26, 1983), pp. 9–44; J. Wisseman Christie, "Trade and State Formation in the Malay Peninsula and Sumatra, 300 BC–AD 700," in *The Southeast Asian Port and Polity: Rise and Demise*, ed. J. Kathyrithamby-Wells and J. Villiers (Singapore: Singapore University Press, 1990), pp. 39–60; P. Wheatley, "Satyanrta in Suvarnadvipa: from Reciprocity to Redistribution in Ancient Southeast Asia," in *Ancient Civilization and Trade*, ed. J. A. Sabloff and G. C. Lamberg-Karlovsky (Albuquerque: University of New Mexico Press, 1975), pp. 227–83; P. Wheatley, *Nagara and Commandery: Origins of Southeast Asian Urban Traditions* (Chicago: University of Chicago Department of Geography Research Paper 207–208, 1983); O. W. Wolters, *Early Indonesian Commerce: A Study of the Origins of Sri Vijaya* (Ithaca: Cornell University Press, 1967); O. W. Wolters, *History, Culture, and Region in Southeast Asian Perspectives* (Singapore: Institute of Southeast Asian Studies, 1982); A. Reid and L. Castles eds., *Pre-Colonial State Systems in Southeast Asia* (Kuala Lumpur: Malaysian Branch of the Royal Asiatic Society, 1975).

tionship is essential to the understanding of both the early formative stages of Southeast Asian statehood (sometime between the last few centuries of the first millennium B.C.E. and the beginnings of the first millennium C.E.) and subsequent state development. In very simplified terms the question posed boils down to the following: to what extent were local coastal polities a product of indigenous developments, and was overseas trade—interregional and later international—a major factor in this process?

Because of its subject matter, the present paper places itself at the center of this debate; indeed, it deals with the place of trade in the early phases of the development of coastal polities of Insular Southeast Asia, as perceived by themselves. Due to the category of sources used, the problem cannot be directly addressed in chronological terms: it threads through the relatively unexplored land that lies between history and myth as an attempt to explore and better understand, in the societies under consideration, what appears to be the very special relationship they maintained and encouraged between overseas trade and political power. What we will be dealing with is a historical process or mechanism, not actual, tangible events.

* * *

I shall start by summarizing a few tales. They all originate from coastal—*pesisir*—societies, and most of them were told or recorded in the harbor-cities on the Javanese, Balinese, Sumatran, or Kalimantan coasts.

We will first go to Buleleng, on the north coast of Bali.[3] The tale, according to the *Babad Buleleng*, runs as follows. A **ship from overseas** (*banawa sunantara*) got **stranded** (*kandas*) on the beach. The owner, Ki **Mpu Awang**, made an agreement: he would offer the whole cargo of the ship to whoever could put her back to sail. She was **fully laden** (*sarat*) with the finest products, cloth, [ceramic] dishes, plates, and bowls. After attempts by other people, Ki Gusti Pañji, with the help of his sacred kris and of the Gods, passed the **test** and put her back afloat. Ki Mpu Awang kept his word. Henceforth Ki Gusti Pañji possessed considerable **wealth** and, after some time, was **consecrated** as King Ki Gusti Ngurah Pañji.[4]

If we travel slightly west to Sumenep, in Madura, we find another story. On his way from Majapahit to Sumenep, Jokotole lived through various adventures. He met his father at his meditation place and learned that he would have to **fight** against an admiral from China named **Dempo Abang** (alias Sampo Tua Lang), who was said to show off his strength to all the kings of Java, Madura, and surrounding places. Jokotole fought Dempo Abang who had a **ship** that could sail on the sea as well as above mountains between clouds and sky. Jokotole himself rode a flying horse and managed to destroy the enemy's ship. He is said to have become the **first historical ruler** of Sumenep, under the name of Pangeran Setjoadiningrat.[5]

A Central Javanese *lakon* tells us about a prince of Java, from a country rich in rice, who entered into a **competition** with a shipmaster (*juragan*) from Banjarmasin named **Dampu**

---

[3] Relevant passages or motifs in the following stories are emphasized. It should also be noted at this point that the tales, as told in this paper, are selected episodes of much longer texts, the global meaning of which is clearly more complex than the one offered here for these particular episodes. For a broader analysis of the *Babad Buleleng*, see P. J. Worsley's introduction to his translation of the text, *Babad Buleleng: A Balinese Dynastic Genealogy* (The Hague: Bibliotheca Indonesia 8, 1972); also J.-F. Guermonprez, "Rois divins et chefs de guerre, variations et complexites des images de la royaute a Bali," *L'Homme* 95 (1985):39–70.

[4] Worsley, *Babad Buleleng*, pp. 145–47; for this and other versions of the Dampu Awang story, see also I Gusti Ngurah Bagus, *Tokoh Dempu Awang dalam Dongeng Bali* (Singaraja: Lembaga Bahasa dan Kesusastraan, 1966).

[5] Abdurachman, *Sedjarah Madura Selajang Pandang* (Sumenep: np, 1971), pp. 10–11.

Awang (alias Sampukong), who was asking for rice against his **shipload** of gold, jewels, and spices. The prince, of course, won the fight against the overseas trader and got the **riches.**[6]

We also learn from various legends that Ratu Kali Nyamat, the famous mid-sixteenth century queen of Japara, was **established as the ruler** after receiving help from a **Chinese merchant** whose **ship** had become **stranded** there.[7]

We now come to Cirebon, some time during the fifteenth century. The hero is Jeng Maulana. While traveling to China, he met the daughter of the Emperor, **Putri Cina** ("the Chinese Princess"). The Chinese ruler put him to a **test.** Jeng Maulana won and was subsequently expelled. However, the lady had fallen in love with the hero and she asked the emperor to be sent over to Cirebon to marry him; her father accepted and she went off together with a **fleet of ships loaded with men, ceramics (*guci, panjang*), and all sorts of riches.** All were duly accepted by Jeng Maulana: he married the princess and they had many children. Jeng Maulana eventually **established the kingdom** of Cirebon, which he ruled as the famous Sunan Gunung Jati (alias Sunan Cirebon). So, at least, goes the tale.[8]

Sumatra's west coast can also provide some examples of similar tales. One such example explains the origin of the name Minangkabau by the usual "victorious buffalo" motif. But it is associated with a theme by now familiar: the founding brothers of the kingdom, Dato' Katumanggungan and Dato' Parpatih see a **ship** coming ashore. It carries a gigantic buffalo. The **captain** (*Nakhoda Besar*) offers his ship and all her **cargo** to whoever can beat his buffalo in a fight. Using a young buffalo and a stratagem, the local people **win the bet** and are therefore given the ship and the shipload. After this, they rename their abode as Minangkabau and **reorganize the polity.**[9]

In Barus, the story runs with a twist, as follows: Guru Marsakot, one of the sons of the founding father of the polity, separates from his brother and moves to Lobu Tua, a site he

[6] S. Cohen, "Wajang Dampoe Awang," *Tijdschrift voor Indische Taal-, Land- en Volkenkunde uitgegeven door het Koninklijk Bataviaasch Genootschap* [hereafter *TBG*] 45 (1902):144–67; also, see references in note 13. The proposed exchange of the cargo for rice—a staple production of the Javanese hinterland—appears again in Sundanese episodes in connection with the myth of Sri, a goddess always associated with fertility and rice growing. Dampo Awang, however, appears right in the middle of the myth of origin for rice. He was a merchant who came from a country suffering from famine and tried to buy rice from Prabu Siliwangi; when the latter refused—rice should not be sold—Dampo Awang became angry and spread all sorts of plagues to destroy rice and other plants. Only divine intervention could defeat Dampo Awang and his allies and save cultivated plants. K. A. H. Hidding, *Nji Pohatji Sangjang Sri* (Proefschrift, Rijksuniversiteit te Leiden, 1929), pp. 34, 61 n. 1, 86 n. 1; V. Sukanda, *Le triomphe de Sri en pays soundanais* (Paris: École Française d'Extrême-Orient Publication No. 101, 1977), pp. 80ff; I wish to thank Viviane Sukanda for data on the Sundanese appearances of Dang Puhawang. This diversion of the rather profane shipmaster into the sacred world of origins appears to be unusual in Insular Southeast Asia. However, this branching into motives relevant for inland, agricultural polities should also be explored. The present paper cannot address this problem.

[7] Liem Thian Joe, *Riwajat Semarang (dari djamannja Sam Poo sampe terhapoesnja Kongkoan)* (Semarang: Ho Kim Yoe,, 1934), p. 7; Th. G. Th. Pigeaud, *Literature of Java. Catalogue Raisonné of Javanese Manuscripts in the Library of the University of Leiden and Other Public Collections in the Netherlands*, 4 vols. (The Hague: Koninklijk Instituut, 1967–80), 2: 363; Th. G. Th. Pigeaud and H. J. de Graaf, *De eerste moslimse vorstendommen op Java* (The Hague: *Verhandelingen van het Koninklijk Instituut voor Taal-, Land- en Volkenkunde* [hereafter *VKI*] 69, 1974): 104–6, 271 n. 112.

[8] P. S. Sulendraningrat, *Babad Tanah Sunda/Babad Cirebon* (Cirebon: np, 1984), pp. 31–37. For historical background on Cirebon, see P. Abdurachman, ed., *Cerbon* (Jakarta: Yayasan Mitra Budaya/SH, 1982). Paramita Abdurachman (p.c.) heard a similar story from Buton, involving the local ruler, a Tartar (i.e., Chinese) princess and a shipwreck with a valuable cargo (said to be found in Selayar).

[9] E. Netscher, "Een verzameling van overleveringen van het rijk van Minangkabau uit het oorspronkelijk Maleisch vertaald," *Indisch Archief* 2, 3 (1850): 53–54. The tales published by Netscher carry a few more such motifs with variants; see, for instance, pp. 64–65.

owns. He discovers Indian merchants (*Ceti* and *Hindu*) are already established there after their ship got **stranded**. They had attracted many foreigners (*orang dari lain tempat dan segala bangsa*) and the settlement had therefore become a **prosperous** settlement (*negeri*). Guru Marsakot decides to stay and rule over the land named Pansur. After he **becomes the *raja*,** the land grows even more **prosperous** and attracts trade from many overseas places.[10]

The same motifs are found again in Kutei. After the setting is prepared and the founding hero Aji Batara Agung Dewa **Sakti** and other characters are introduced, a Chinese prince sails into the harbor. He lures Aji Batara Agung into **betting** on a cockfight, which he loses. He thus has to surrender **his ship, together with her cargo and crew**. Aji Batara Agung **builds a new settlement** (*pindah bernegeri*), following which he sails to various places in Kalimantan and keeps **acquiring riches** (*harta agung*).[11]

Up in the Philippines, on the Island of Palawan, a tale recalls that there was once a conflict between the King of Brunei and a local hero as to who would rule over the island. After **winning a bet** against his Brunei rival, the Palawan contender gained five **ships with their cargoes** and consequently **ruled** over Palawan.[12]

One could go on narrating such tales, for there is quite a repertoire originating from the multitude of harbor-cities that have sprung up, at one time or another, along the coasts of the Java Sea, from Palembang to Buleleng, through Lampung, Banjarmasin, and the Javanese *pesisir*, as well as, seemingly, in other areas of Maritime Southeast Asia.[13]

At times, the stories appear only vaguely related and, as is often the case in a predominantly oral context, the characters or events undergo permutations that may obscure the contents of the tale, at least at first sight. However, a careful breakdown of their formative elements can bring to light the underlying and recurrent motifs: in other words, the structure of the tales. The tales above may easily be trimmed to the parts that interest us, i.e. into the seven following motifs (not all of these necessarily being always present in a single tale):

1. a local character has exceptional powers/*sakti*;
2. then comes an overseas ship fully laden/*sarat* with rich merchandise,

[10] J. Drakard, ed., *Sejarah Raja-raja Barus: dua naskah dari Barus* (Jakarta: École Français d'Extrême-Orient, Collection de texts et documents nousantariens, no. 7, 1988), pp. 81, 133.

[11] C. A. Mees, ed., *De Kroniek van Koetai* (Santpoort: np, 1935), pp. 72–73, 140–53.

[12] R. B. Fox, *Religion and Society among the Tagbanua of Palawan Island, Philippines* (Manila: National Museum Monograph No. 9, 1982), p. 18.

[13] Th. G. Th. Pigeaud, *Javaanse volksvertoningen, bijdrage tot de beschrijving van land en volk* (Jakarta, 1938), pp. 81, 91, 192–95; and Pigeaud, *Literature of Java*, 2: 61, 495, 516, 850, 853, gives brief summaries of Javanese *lakon* and local legends of Dampu Awang. R.T.A.A. Probenegoro, "Djoeragan Dampoehawang," *Djawa* 21, 1 (1941): 1–11, also has various references to this theme, including some from the *ketoprak* repertoire. I have myself heard such stories told by fishermen in the Tuban area in 1983. On a different tales for Dampu Awang's occurrence: in Palembang, see L. C. Westenenk, "Boekit Segoentang en Goenoeng Mahameroe uit de Sedjarah Melajoe," *TBG* 68, 1 (1923): 222 (but he also is associated there with the Putri Cina and Chinese customs in local lore); in Lampung, see J. A. Du Bois, "De Lampongsche districten op het eiland Sumatra," *Tijdschrift voor Nederlandsch-Indie* 14 (1852): 245–75, 309–33; in Banjarmasin, J. J. Ras, ed., *Hikayat Banjar, A Study in Malay Historiography* (The Hague: Bibliotheca Indonesica 1, 1968), where Dampu Awang is the name of a sea-going merchant who is associated with a story different from that in our tales. H. O. Beyer, "The Philippines before Magellan," *Asia Magazine* (Oct.-Nov., 1921), states that "the most reliable of the pre-Mahommedan traditional histories of Sulu states that the first civilized foreigners to establish a settlement in that island were the Orang Dampuan"; this appears to be some corrupt quotation from a comparable tale. In association with most of these tales, one finds explanations for local toponyms that carry names of boats (*banka*, *jong*, etc., or even the name Dampu Awang itself, as in Lampung) resulting from the events described in the tales.

(3. usually under the captainship of shipmaster Dampu Awang, alias Sampo);
(4. the ship may get stranded/*kandas*[14] and)
5. a competition takes place, either a fight or a bet, the prize of which is the ship cargo;
6. the local character, thanks to his *sakti*, wins over the riches in the ship and thus acquires considerable wealth, after which
7. he rules over his now prosperous country.

Before we start trying to understand the underlying meaning of such tales, some further motifs which appear to have been blended into the rich symbolism of Indonesian textile decoration and are clearly associated with the above tales should be investigated. These textiles have been found within the area where the tales were collected. These are not narrative motifs, but the statements they make can be read as "texts" in the very same way.

The first motif is the so-called *jong sarat*. The meaning of the phrase itself poses no problem: what we have here is a "fully laden ship," the same motif we encountered in the above tales. It always seems to be mentioned in relation with various rites of passage and—this is essential—with high-ranking or royal-blooded heroes. In Perak (Malaysia) we find mentions of a mat embroidered with the *jong sarat* motif, in an East Javanese *Babad Blambangan* it is a *songket jong sarat*, in the Malay *Hikayat Dewa Mandu* we get a *kafan jong sarat* and in Lampung there is a *tampan jong sarat*.[15] Despite the fact that, in Lampung, depictions of sailing vessels are a common feature of textiles, the name *jong sarat* has no connection with such graphically obvious textiles: it is actually associated with a cloth that does not carry a ship design and is worn by the bride at marriage ceremonies. It is, however, richly decorated with gold thread and has valuable silver coins hanging from its lower side.[16] What we have here, therefore, are "fully laden" pieces of cloth that were associated, in rituals, with wealth deriving from maritime trade.

The other textile motif I shall mention is still a popular pattern among *pesisir* people (mostly Cirebon and Indramayu): this is the *pola kapal kandas*, which translates as "stranded ship pattern." The story associated with it relates that this ship, which was not set afloat again, was that of the Putri Cina—therefore, as we have seen, it was a "fully laden" one. No wonder, then, batiks bearing the *kapal kandas* motif are still worn in special circumstances, where wealth and prosperity are asked for. The design of the motif is purely abstract (no *kapal* is represented) and were it not for the tale of the Putri Cina quoted above, it would be difficult to figure out its actual meaning.[17]

---

[14] The acquisition by a ruler of the cargo of a stranded ship reminds one of the shipwreck laws current in Southeast Asian seas: the rulers automatically inherited the contents of the lost ship. But such laws are also common in the Indian Ocean, not to say universally, and I therefore do not believe that this coincidence is relevant. In any case, the stranding of the ship is not an essential motif in our tales.

[15] On the *jong sarat* expression and an analysis of the broader meaning of ship motifs in textiles from Lampung and elsewhere, see P.-Y. Manguin, "Shipshape Societies: Boat Symbolism and Political Systems in Insular Southeast Asia," in *Southeast Asia in the 9th to 14th Centuries*, ed. D. G. Marr and A. C. Milner (Singapore: Institute of Southeast Asian Studies, 1986), pp. 187–213, and the references quoted therein.

[16] I owe many thanks to the late Paramita Abdurachman for having taken the trouble to carry out her own personal inquiry on these textiles.

[17] On the *pola kapal kandas* in Cirebon and Indramayu, see Abdurachman, *Cerbon*, p. 153. W. Warming and M. Gaworski, *The World of Indonesian Textiles* (Tokyo/New York: Kodansha International, 1981), p. 178, are mistaken when they say this motif is only found in Lasem; when they explain it by stating that "it was customary for villagers who helped push a beached ship back to sea to share in some of the wealth on board," they seem to have noted down and possibly misunderstood a local interpretation of the motif akin to the stranded ship theme. The

An odd occurrence of the "fully laden boat" motif appears in the Javanese *Kidung Angling Darma*, as well as in other texts. These carry references to *banawa sarat*, the literal meaning of which is the same as *jong sarat*. Drewes discusses the use of the phrase but does not understand its appearance in the *kidung* to designate a house in a forest which is full of riches, a wealth that will be acquired by the hero of the tale.[18] It is only in the comparison with other appearances of the *sarat*/"fully laden" motif that sense can be made of the *banawa sarat* phrase in this particular context. Except for the fact that the riches are referred to as a "ship (*banawa*) cargo," there is no reference here to sea-going trade. This raises questions about both Javanese perceptions of the forest and remanent maritime motifs in an essentially inland and agrarian context. Answers to such questions are beyond the scope of this essay.

One other aspect of these tales should be investigated. This is the name of the character who most often appears in them, though he is not the actual hero (a role reserved for the founder of the polity), i.e. Dampu Awang (and his aliases Sampo, Sampo Kong, Sampo Tua Lang, etc.). It is used in the examples above as a proper name, but its origin is in the Javanese title *dang mpu hawang* (or possibly in cognate forms in other related languages). *Dang* is an honorific prefix denoting persons of distinction, or high rank; *(m)pu* has a similar usage; the title *(h)awang* conveyed among various Malay World people (Minang, Malays, etc.) the idea of a non-noble official of high rank, at times associated with shipmasters (*nakhoda*). This last meaning is precisely that of the title *puhawang* when it first appears in the Old Malay Sriwijayan inscription of Telaga Batu, dated from the last quarter of the seventh century C.E. It is often found again with the same meaning in late first millennium Malay and Javanese epigraphs, as well as in Old Javanese literature (in twelfth-century texts such as the *Bharatayudha*, the *Smaradahana*, or the *Hariwangsa*). So what we have in our tales is a character clearly bearing the title *Dang Puhawang* (turned into the proper name Dampu Awang by folk tradition) who has from early times been associated with shipping and trading at the highest level. He is not a petty trader: in the tales, he owns the ship and the rich cargo with which she is laden. Inscriptions make it clear the *puhawang* were part of the ruler's chosen retinue. In Central Java, they make offerings to royal sanctuaries (Dang Puhawang Gelis inscription of 827 C.E.). In East Java, enough revenue was derived from transactions with *puhawang* and merchants (*banyaga*) from other islands (*dwipantara*) to prompt the ruler into launching hydraulic works, so as to facilitate their mooring in Ujung Galuh (Kamalagyan inscription of 1037 C.E.).[19]

The other names Dang Puhawang is given in some of the tales, and never as obviously as in the Semarang tradition, are Sampo Kong or Sampo Tua Lang, etc.[20] These are the

---

National Museum in Jakarta holds in its collections a *dodot* with the *kapal kandas* pattern said to come from Yogyakarta.

[18] G. W. J. Drewes, ed., *The Romance of King Angling Darma in Javanese Literature* (The Hague: Bibliotheca Indonesica 11, 1975), pp. 87 & n 9, 329. I am grateful to Henri Chambert-Loir for having attracted my attention to this unusual example of the motif.

[19] The best philological analysis of the term so far will be found in L.-Ch. Damais, "Quelques titres javanais de l'époque des Song," *Bulletin de l'École Française d'Extrême-Orient* 50, 1 (1960):25–29. See also Manguin, "Shipshape Societies," pp. 197–99, to which one may refer for more references to existing literature on the subject.

[20] On the Dampu Awang/Sampo tradition in Semarang, there is an abundant literature. One may refer to I. W. Young, "Sam Po Tong, La grotte de Sam Po," *T'oung Pao* 9 (1899):93–102; D. E. Willmott, *The Chinese of Semarang: A Changing Minority Community in Indonesia* (Ithaca: Cornell University Press, 1960); Oen Boeng Ing, "Het een en ander over Sam Poo Toa Lang of Kjiahi Dampoe Awang," in *Supplement op Het Triwindoe-Gedenboek Mangkoe Nagoro VII* (Soerakarta, 1940), pp. 221–23; Liem Thian Joe, *Riwajat Semarang*, pp. 1–10; Th. G. Th. Pigeaud and H. J. de Graaf, *Chinese Muslims in Java in the 15th and 16th Centuries: The Malay Annals of Semarang and Cerbon*

clearly recognizable aliases of the famous Chinese historical character Admiral Zheng He, a Muslim who conducted seven great Ming fleets across Southeast Asia and the Indian Ocean between 1405 and 1433.[21] Why this other great historical Chinese "shipmaster" became associated with our legendary Dang Puhawang (who carries an Austronesian name) can only be answered later in this paper, after the riddle of the tales is solved.

* * *

We therefore are presented with a set of folk-tales that were commonly popular among coastal societies of the western part of Insular Southeast Asia. These societies are relatively well known to historians, at least during the post-fifteenth century stages of their development.[22] The social context of such tales may therefore be examined to investigate the "king and merchant" relationship, which appears so prominently in them.

A first step in this process will be to check what we presently know about trade—particularly with overseas merchants—and acquisition of wealth in Malay World political systems. We are fortunate to be able to refer to recent historians who have conducted their research by studying Malay texts, thus providing us with a referential relationship with the folk-tales under consideration.

What first comes to mind is that political power and wealth cannot be dissociated in a Malay World context. The symbolic value of the ruler's "treasure" is essential in this regard. Wealth is an attribute of the ruler, one of the requisite sources of his power (wealth, however, is not an accumulative process: it should flow towards the ruler as well as from him[23]). Now, in coastal polities or harbor-cities, where trade was the foremost economic activity, in societies where not only luxuries but above all the basic daily necessities were obtained through overseas trade, it would be normal to find among the requisite attributes and duties of a good ruler an ability to convene a sufficient number of traders into his harbor. In doing so, he would reinforce his sovereignty over potentially rival neighboring harbor-cities. Through this initiative, in proportion to the success of the trade, he would also generate income for his followers, and he would therefore accumulate prestige as the dispenser of material wealth. Milner, in fact, writes about the "excessive partiality for trade" among Malay rulers whose "kingdom was, in the final analysis, a commercial venture." Thomaz, basing himself on early sixteenth century Portuguese sources, portrays pre-Portuguese

(Monash: Monash University Papers on Southeast Asia No. 12, 1984); P. Pelliot, "Les grands voyages maritimes chinois au debut du XVe siècle," *T'oung Pao* 30 (1933): 257–58; P. Pelliot, "Notes additionnelles sur Tcheng Houo et sur ses voyages," *T'oung Pao* 31 (1935):280, 311; C. Salmon, "A propos de quelques cultes chinois particuliers à Java," *Arts Asiatiques* 26 (1973): 243–64; Amen Budiman, *Semarang Riwayatmu Dulu*, vol. 1 (Semarang, 1978): 8–35.

[21] J.J.L. Duyvendak, "Ma Huan re-examined," *Verhandelingen der Koninklijke Academie van Wetenschappen, afd. Letterkunde* 32, 2 (1933); Pelliot, "Les grands voyages" and "Notes additionnelles."

[22] As mentioned in note 2, many studies have been devoted to trade, state formation, and statecraft. The following paragraphs were mostly inspired by A. C. Milner's study of Malay perceptions of their *kerajaan* in nineteenth-century Deli and Pahang; Milner, *Kerajaan*, particularly chapter 2, which deals with economic aspects. See also A. Reid, "Trade and State Power in 16th and 17th Century Southeast Asia," in *Proceedings, Seventh IAHA Conference, Bangkok, August 1977* (Bangkok, 1979), 1: 391–419. Wolters, *History, Culture, and Region*, pp. 34ff discusses the importance of the notion of "treasure" for Southeast Asian rulers.

[23] It is always when the flow of wealth is unidirectional, when there seems to be accumulation without redistribution, that the rich merchants of Java are accused of being helped by the malevolent genii named *tuyul*.

Melaka in very similar terms: "everything in Malacca points to a market economy. . . . The State existed there because of trade, not trade because of the State."[24]

The various conditions a potentially successful ruler would need to perfect the foundation of a coastal state could therefore be summarized as follows (this is done with a considerable measure of simplification: because of the theme of this essay, the economic aspects of kingship are artificially over-emphasized, leaving aside other crucial attributes such as ritual, kinship, etc.):

—being imparted with some measure of legitimacy and/or endowed with enough charisma (derived from "prowess," "divine radiance," "soul-stuff," or *sakti*) to build up local networks of alliance and exchange;[25]

—assuming authority over a potential harbor-centered polity;

—luring in, retaining, and regulating overseas exchange at this site to provide external income (a variety of technical possibilities are offered: tap the economic resources of the hinterland, conduct entrepôt trade, etc.);

—mobilizing, manipulating, and redistributing the subsequent wealth as a political weapon, to extend his secular authority and attract a larger clientèle, thus achieving the desired state of *ramai*.[26]

A comparison of the list of structural motifs extracted from the Dang Puhawang tales with that of conditions set up in Malay literature for a ruler to be able to proceed with the foundation of a viable coastal polity will at once reveal striking similarities. The statement in the tales uses the language of a society, that of the *pesisir* harbor-cities of Southeast Asia or rather of two of their literary genres—"histories" and folk-tales—which this society uses to express and explain concepts that are critical to her. In this particular case, the statement is made to explain in symbolic or metaphoric terms the economic mechanism leading to the foundation of a state: the message carried by this particular episode, encountered in a wide variety of (more complex) texts, is that overseas merchants and trade are a prerequisite for the kind of prosperity (*keramaian*) considered befitting a successful polity. In the *Hikayat Hang Tuah*, it is said that the founder of the Melaka dynasty, shortly after descending from Heaven to Bukit Seguntang, became widely known as a king bestowed with many qualities, among which loomed large the fact that "he was very fond of all merchants"; Bukit Seguntang/Palembang is later said to have become a large country, "many merchants came and went to trade there. And all the people from countries without a *raja* congregated there."[27] Curiously, Marco Polo's description of Java in the late thirteenth century rings a bell by now familiar: "This island is full of great wealth. . . . And unto this land come very great numbers

---

[24] Milner, *Kerajaan*, p. 16; L.F.F.R. Thomaz, "Malaca's Society on the Eve of the Portuguese Conquest: A Tentative Interpretation based on the Extant Portuguese Documents," Paper presented at the *Persidangan Antarabangsa mengenai Tamadun Melayu*, Kuala Lumpur (1986), p. 5.

[25] For a discussion of these various attributes of power in Southeast Asia, see Wolters, *History, Culture, and Region*, particularly pp. 101–4.

[26] The term *ramai* (or the form *keramaian* describing the state of being *ramai*) is the most common attribute of a successful kingdom. A Bengkulu folk-tale expresses this in a nutshell: *Lama-kelamaan kampung menjadi ramai, dan hampir menjadi sebuah kerajaan* ("As time passed the settlement became *ramai* and came short of becoming a kingdom."); Anonymous, *Cerita Rakyat Daerah Bengkulu* (Jakarta: Proyek Penerbitan Buku Sastra Indonesia dan Daerah, 1981), p. 113.

[27] *Hikayat Hang Tuah* (Kuala Lumpur: Dewan Bahasa dan Pustaka, 1961), pp. 6, 9. The expression this text uses in many similar examples is *dagang santeri*, in a context where sea-going or "foreign" merchants are called for (as in *kasantrian*, the name of foreign quarters in harbor-cities such as Banten). See also note 38 below.

of ships and of merchants who come there to trade and buy many goods there and make very great profit there and very great gain. There is so great treasure in this island that there is not a man in the world who could believe or tell or say it."[28] It is admitted by now that Polo never actually sailed to Java and he may well have heard this description from the mouth of Southeast Asian merchants in North Sumatra, where he spent some time. This would explain the striking similitude with local statements. The same could be said about Tomé Pires' hearsay remark on Demak in the mid-1510s: "because . . . [Demak's ruler] has not done any trade for three or four years he is greatly exhausted . . . and the people are already leaving his land for other places because there is no trade in merchandise."[29]

One element of the tales still needs elaboration: why has Dang Puhawang, a character with an Austronesian name (or title), been given the name of, or been assimilated with a well-known Chinese historical character? Dang Puhawang is, by trade, a ship-master who arrives from "overseas," literally from across a sea. Depending on the context of the tale, this notion of "overseas" may be left with its vague definition (as in *sunantara*), or it may be given a more precise connotation: the overseas merchant may come from other harbor-cities within the Malay World (Banjarmasin, Aceh, etc.) or from countries across the China Sea or the Indian Ocean (generally China or Keling). In a word, he is a *sabrangan*, somebody who has crossed over the seas (though I have not found in the above tales this particular term, common in Javanese *lakon* for overseas characters). The emphasis in the tales is therefore on "overseas," not on a determined place of origin: the shipmaster in the tales may stand for inter-regional (i.e. essentially Malay World) as well as "international" traders (including Chinese), both of which would be part of a suitable trade network. Early epigraphy—particularly that of East Java—appears not to distinguish among merchants from "international" and inter-regional backgrounds: the classification of traders is functional, not based on place of origin. In later Malay literature the presence of numerous foreign merchants is conventionally seen as a desirable feature in a polity.[30] Maritime trade is the main source of income of harbor-centered polities and, by nature, this can only be "overseas" trade.

The answer to the Sampo riddle therefore lies in the economic role played by China and the Chinese market in Southeast Asian history. No factor in the international environment of harbor polities in the region would have been more significant than overseas trade with China, whether it was conducted by Southeast Asians themselves or by Chinese.[31] Yet another tale relates that the ruler of Kan-to-li, a trading kingdom somewhere on the shores of the Malay Peninsula or South Sumatra, had a dream in 502 C.E.: if he would send tribute (i.e. trading) missions to China, his land "would become rich and happy and merchants and travelers would multiply a hundredfold." Though recorded by a Chinese chronicler, this dream of a southern king bears a striking resemblance to the statements we have come across in local tales and provides a vivid illustration of the osmosis between the two markets at the northern and southern ends of the South China Sea. In the eleventh century, in a

---

[28] A. C. Moule and P. Pelliot, eds., *Marco Polo. The Description of the World*, 2 vols. (London, 1938), 1: 368.

[29] A. Cortesão, ed., *The Suma Oriental of Tomé Pires*, 2 vols. (London: Hakluyt Society, 1944), 1: 186.

[30] Christie, "Markets and Trade," pp. 204–9; Milner, *Kerajaan*, p. 23 and n. 82.

[31] The ups and downs of *pesisir* states (including such prominent polities as Sriwijaya and Melaka), and their close relationship with the fluctuations of the Chinese overseas trade have been studied in detail by Wolters in his two books on the rise and fall of Sriwijaya: *Early Indonesian Commerce*, already cited, and *The Fall of Srivijaya in Malay History* (Kuala Lumpur: Oxford University Press, 1970); also Wang Gungwu, "Early Ming Relations with Southeast Asia: A Background Essay," in *The Chinese World Order*, ed. J. K. Fairbank (Cambridge: Harvard University Press, 1968), pp. 34–62.

pragmatic but nonetheless evocative statement about Sriwijaya, a Chinese chronicler writes: "Merchants from distant places congregate there. This country is therefore considered to be very prosperous." Closer to us, we know that Chinese overseas activity and patronage—at the precise time of the great naval expeditions of the Ming under Zheng He—were crucial in the launching of the early kingdoms of Pasai and Melaka.[32]

It is no wonder, then, that a character such as Zheng He (alias Sampo, i.e. *Sam bao*, the "Three Jewels" eunuch) would be remembered in local lore by those who stood to gain from the increased economic activity as an expeditor of trade, hence a promoter of wealth and political power, hence a replication of Dang Puhawang. The fact that the Ming expeditions were carried out with such considerable pomp, with fleets of dozens of enormous ships loaded with merchandise, could only have further stamped the imagination of *pesisir* populations in Southeast Asia. By coincidence (?), the Ming Chinese called their huge junks "treasure-ships" (*bao-chuan*), a striking rejoinder to the ships "fully laden" with riches of the Dang Puhawang tales. Moreover, these memories were further cultivated among an economically active and well integrated Chinese merchant community: in Melaka, in Semarang, in Jakarta, they kept the Sampo cult alive, blending local and Chinese statements into one single story. The appropriation by the Chinese community of the local Dang Puhawang theme parallels that of the recuperation in the temples they dedicated to Sampo of indigenous cults rendered to local *kramat*.[33] In a sense, therefore, this very appropriation confirms the interpretation of the Dang Puhawang tales.

In a second step, one may find another transformation of the above motifs in some texts, at times in combination with the "real" Dang Puhawang motif. In the *Hikayat Raja-raja Pasai*, for instance, ships loaded with regalia coming from Mecca are found among the various elements that consolidate Malik al-Saleh's power over the harbor-state. During this Islamic moment of the Archipelago, when a new "age of commerce" and the expanding Islamic consciousness were indiscernible, it would appear that the political statements made in "historical" literature had their emphasis shifted towards religion: legitimization had now to come from the Caliph. Transformation of the myth to accommodate Islam was facilitated by the fact that the trader and the preacher of the Islamic faith were, by then, more often than not one single person. But the "treasure-bearing merchant" motif—in a debased form—still appears in the *Hikayat Raja-raja Pasai* immediately after lip-service has been paid to the new "mentalité": a trading ship from the land of Kalinga carries a man who has the power to detect reefs of gold and, sure enough, gold is then found in great quantities, and Malik al-Saleh's polity is accordingly bolstered.[34] A similar variation on the theme—with a humorous twist—can be found in a folk-tale from Kalimantan Selatan: Datu Baduk is a learned *jin* who sails from Mecca on board the ship of Haji Muhhammad Arsyad, returning from studying Islam in the Holy Land to spread the new religion and to become an adviser at the Banjar court. The ship gets stranded (*kandas*); it turns out that the *jin ulama* is responsible for holding the ship immobile. He only releases her after it is agreed that he shall be

---

[32] Wolters, *Early Indonesian Commerce*, p. 165; O. W. Wolters, "A Few and Miscellaneous *pi-chi* Jottings on Early Indonesia," *Indonesia* 36 (1983): 55; Wolters, *Fall of Srivijaya*, especially chapter 11 and appendix C.

[33] Salmon, "Quelques cultes"; C. Salmon and D. Lombard, *Les Chinois de Jakarta: temples et vie collective* (Paris: Etudes insulindiennes-Archipel No. 1, 1980), pp. 86ff.; C. Salmon and D. Lombard, "Islam et sinité," *Archipel* 30 (1985): 73–94.

[34] A. H. Hill, ed., "Hikajat Raja-raja Pasai," *Journal of the Malaysian Branch, Royal Asiatic Society* 33, 2 (1960): 123.

authorized to settle in Banjar, where he will be revered and will teach the Religion to non-Islamic *jin*.[35]

One should also elaborate on a recurrent motif of these tales, that of the competition between king and merchant. Its outcome is positive (the founding of the polity), but it is clearly a conflictive rapport. Does the historical context in which these tales were produced provide elements that would allow us to decipher this motif? As discussed earlier, the title associated with our merchant, *hawang*, is that of a non-noble but high-ranking class in Malay World societies often associated with ship-masters (*nakhoda/puhawang/juragan*), trade and wealth. One social class in such societies—as known from post-fifteenth century sources—that immediately comes to mind is that of the ubiquitous and often all-powerful *orangkaya*. A lot has been written on their role and position, and this is not the place to elaborate again on the subject. Suffice it to say that, in the sixteenth to eighteenth centuries, the *orangkaya* merchant class was the mainstay of many societies of Insular Southeast Asia. But it has also been a constant threat to the power of the ruler. Exactly like the folk hero Dampu Hawang, the *orangkaya* could both do and undo a king. Too much wealth on their part was usually felt as a threat to the ruler's own power, challenged as it was by the rise and parallel development of commercial elites. Beaulieu, who visited Aceh in the early seventeenth century, puts this in concise but appropriate terms: the *orangkaya* usually lost their life when the king became suspicious of two circumstances, "their good reputation among the people and their wealth."[36] Earlier in time, in fact in the first ever written mention of a *puhawang* in a late seventh century C.E. Sriwijayan inscription, the ship-master class appears among those who threaten the "treasure" of the ruler (and, interestingly enough, they are among the few that bear an Austronesian, non-imported, title). No doubt, if merchants stopped patronizing a harbor-city, the ruler's "treasure" would rapidly fade away. Similarly, in an inscription from Champa dated 797 C.E., merchants are mentioned, together with warriors, brahmins, and ministers, among those prone to steal the riches of the polity.[37] This ambivalence of merchants is possibly what prompted the author of a ninth century Javanese inscription to classify them among migratory birds: they were unattached, liable to transfer their trade activities to a rival harbor-city, hence dangerous.[38] Again, a similar notion could have been conveyed by the 1079 C.E. Sriwijayan inscription at Canton which describes merchants as "flying."[39]

It therefore appears that the competition motif can itself be explained when the context of the tales is examined and reference made to the dialectical relationship between ruler and

[35] Anonymous, *Cerita Rakyat Kalimantan Selatan* (Jakarta: Proyek Penerbitan Buku Sastra Indonesia dan Daerah, 1981), pp. 92–95.

[36] A. Reid, "Trade and the Problem of Royal Power in Aceh, c. 1500–1700," in *Pre-Colonial State Systems in Southeast Asia*, ed. A. Reid and L. Castles (Kuala Lumpur: Malaysian Branch of the Royal Asiatic Society, 1975), pp. 45–55; Reid, "Trade and State Power"; J. Kathirithamby-Wells, "Royal Authority and the Orang Kaya in the Western Archipelago, circa 1500–1800," *Journal of Southeast Asian Studies* 17, 2 (1986): 256–67; Beaulieu's quotation is from his *Mémoires*, as published in M. Thevenot's *Relations de divers voyages* . . . (Paris 1696) 1: 109ff.

[37] L. Finot, "Notes d'épigraphie VII: Inscriptions du Quang Nam (i: Première stèle de Dong-duong)," *Bulletin de l'École Française d'Extrême-Orient* 4 (1904): 91, 95.

[38] J. G. de Casparis, *Prasasti Indonesia II* (Bandung: Masa Baru, 1956), pp. 2 n. 12, 326. One should note here that Casparis' clarification on the obscure verse that regroups birds (of the migratory sort) and merchants is only tentative. Could the term *santeri* used in classical Malay literature with a possible connotation of "wandering" be a reminiscence of this "migratory" trait of sea-going merchants (see above note 27)?

[39] Tan Yeok Song, "The Sri Vijayan inscription of Canton (AD 1079)," *Journal of Southeast Asian History* 5, 2 (1964): 17–24.

merchants in harbor-centered polities. This in turn further confirms the analysis offered here.

* * *

The exact nature of these stories that I have, for convenience sake, called the Dang Puhawang tales should at this stage be examined in more detail. As told in available literature (oral as well as written), they appear to belong to two genres: chronicles of the *babad, sejarah,* or *hikayat* type (therefore a local "historical" genre) and plain folk-tales (the latter closer to an oral, more popular tradition, but having nevertheless been transformed while passing into a written form). In whichever literary genre they have been transmitted to us, the underlying motifs always relate to that event of momentous importance for the narrator, i.e. the foundation of the polity he is telling us about. This is an event which can only happen once in his story, which is a "history" of that particular polity. I therefore believe that such tales should be interpreted as desacralized, transformed political myths of trade-oriented *pesisir* states. Their function would have been to elicit the legitimacy of the ruler's power and, as far as the Dang Puhawang motif is concerned, to clarify the position of a specific social group, that of the merchants, within the society.[40] The episode of the *Babad Buleleng,* possibly the most elaborate and eloquent of those we found, no doubt points in that direction.[41] The court rituals that may have been associated with such myths appear to have long disappeared in the societies under consideration. But the association of the "fully laden" or "stranded ship" motifs with textiles that remained until recently very much part of state or rank-related rituals is another indication of the origins of such tales.

Ceramics are often mentioned among the goods obtained after the competition described in the tales (where they usually appear as *piring* or *piring panjang*). The use of imported ceramic dishes in a variety of court rituals, as well as in the decoration of buildings found in harbors along the Javanese *pesisir,* has been routinely but loosely associated with past overseas trade. However, when attention is paid to the constant reference to such ceramics in *jong sarat* cargoes, a close correlation with the popular tales quoted above is inescapable. Gifts of ceramics loom large in foreign relations of Southeast Asian polities with overseas powers, mainly China. To quote just one example, the *Hikayat Banjar* lists among other gifts brought back by an embassy to China, "a thousand large bowls, a thousand small bowls, a thousand plates of various colours." It is remarkable in this context that ceramics still used in rituals at various courts in Central or *pesisir* Java, as well as in other islands (Sulawesi, Kalimantan, Maluku, Mindanao, etc.) are consistently said to be ancient

---

[40] On the historical origins of tales and the transformation of myths into profane tales or "histories," see C. Lévi-Strauss, *Anthropologie structurale deux* (Paris: Plon, 1973), particularly chapters 8 (an analysis of Propp's *Morphologie du conte*) and 14 ("Comment meurent les mythes?"); V.J.A. Propp, *Les racines historiques du conte merveilleux* (Paris: Gallimard, 1983); G. Condominas, "Le souverain époux de son peuple: variations madécasses sur un thème malais," in *Variant Views: Five Lectures from the Perspective of the "Leiden Tradition" in Cultural Anthropology,* ed. H.J.M. Claessen (Leiden: ICA Publicatie No. 84, 1989), pp. 39ff ("La triade mythe, ethnologie, histoire"); P. E. Josselin De Jong, *Ruler and Realm: Political Myths in Western Indonesia* (Amsterdam and Oxford: Mededelingen der Koninklijke Nerderlandse Akademie van Wetenschapen, afd. Letterkunde, Deel 43/1, 1980); P. E. Josselin De Jong, "Myth and non-Myth," in *Man, Meaning and History,* ed. R. Schefold, J. W. Scholl, and J. Tennekes (The Hague: *VKI* 89, 1980), pp. 109–28.

[41] Worsley, when editing the text, understood it as such (*Babad Buleleng,* p. 25); Guermonprez ("Rois divins," pp. 44–45, 50–51) concurs in his study of Balinese perceptions of kingship: he writes about a "prosperity contract" between the ruler and his people.

imported pieces, and, in places (Imogiri), more precisely gifts from foreign rulers.[42] Having some of these ceramics inlaid into the walls of important buildings must have been tantamount to making a statement akin to that conveyed by the Dang Puhawang tales, or better to "illustrate" such a statement.[43] Foreign textiles also appear prominently in lists of goods traded or received from overseas and we also know how important they were in rank-related and other rituals. Goods acquired in shipments from overseas were thus naturally incorporated into the sign system of the society that produced the "fully laden junk" tales.

The existence of such trade-biased political myths underscores the fact that commerce played a prominent role in the early formative stages of coastal, harbor-centered political systems. Since what myths describe is a process—not an event—we are left with the problem of chronology. Is it possible, from the evidence at hand, to provide these myths with some sort of chronological depth, i.e. with a measure of referentiality to historical events? Is the process explained by the myth a recent one, that would for instance have taken place only during the fifteenth–seventeenth century economic boom of Southeast Asia? If so, this would substantiate the emergence of a new mercantile ethos in association with—as often claimed—this modern "age of commerce."[44] Or has this process been central to local societies from much earlier times?

The fact that practically no referential readings are available for pre-modern times may be only a reflection of the extreme scarcity—both quantitative and qualitative—of pre-fifteenth century sources that may be of use in textual interpretations. In no way does this paucity of sources allow us to conclude that the emergence of the Dang Puhawang motif is contemporary with the first texts that include the above tales. Indeed, I have quoted earlier in this paper a few first and early second millennium C.E. references that fit in closely with the motifs in the tales. That of the Kan-to-li ruler's "dream" about trade and associated wealth is particularly relevant in this context. This in turn points to the earliness of the process explained in such myths. I also identified two specific clusters of transformations undergone by the motifs that can be traced down to the fifteenth–sixteenth century period (which corresponds to trade expansion and to the rise of Islamic consciousness): the Sam Po/Zheng He variation and the shift of the legitimization process towards Mecca and Islamic values. Such transformations can only have been initiated when the producing societies further elaborated on their myths, generating a new set of referents within a pre-coded narrative. The myth must therefore have antedated this elaboration and cannot merely be a by-product of this recent "age of commerce."[45]

However, for such a conclusion to be given a firmer recognition, one would need to investigate the relationship of the above motifs with seemingly comparable ones that appear

[42] S. Adhyatman, *Antique ceramics found in Indonesia, various uses and origins* (Jakarta: The Ceramic Society of Indonesia, 1981), pp. 142ff., describes in detail the traditional use of ceramics in a variety of rituals as well as in decoration. For the *Hikayat Banjar* passage, see Ras, *Hikayat Banjar*, pp. 258–59.

[43] Surviving buildings that bear testimony to this practice are mainly religious—the burial complex of Sunan Bonang at Tuban, that of Sunan Gunung Jati at Cirebon, etc.—but texts point to a much broader usage of this type of decor in court buildings: in the *Serat Arok*, Vietnamese ceramics (*piring Koci*) are said to have decorated the palace of the *adipati* of Surabaya; S. Robson, "The Serat Arok," *Archipel* 20 (1980): 293.

[44] D. Lombard, "Le sultanat malais comme modèle socio-économique," in *Marchands et hommes d'affaires asiatiques dans l'Océan Indien et la Mer de Chine, 13e–20e siècles*, ed. J. Aubin and D. Lombard (Paris: Editions de l'EHESS, 1987), pp. 117–28; A. Reid, *Southeast Asia in the Age of Commerce, 1450–1680, Volume One: The Lands below the Winds* (New Haven and London: Yale University Press, 1988); A. Reid, "An 'Age of Commerce' in Southeast Asian History," *Modern Asian Studies* 24, 1 (1990): 1–30.

to be found in other, mainly Eastern Indonesian perceptions of similar or less elaborate exchange systems.[46] I would submit as a working hypothesis that these myths could possibly be generated when the economy of a society crosses over the border between simple forms of exchange—restricted to kin-ordered, alliance, or tributary modes—and wider ranging networks in closer connection with market forces and, ultimately, with world economies. Jan Wisseman Christie convincingly argued that an active participation in inter-regional and later international trade networks would have been at the origin of state formation process in the Melaka Straits and Northern Javanese *pesisir* as early as the turn of the first millennium C.E.[47] The dramatic broadening of the *espace social* brought about by such a direct involvement in far-ranging trade networks would then naturally have given birth to myths that established an explicit relationship between sea-going merchants, trade, and the founding of a viable polity.

---

45 These variations on the older Dang Puhawang theme may well have been conscious manipulations for political use by social participants; on such manipulations, see Josselin de Jong, "Myth and non-Myth," p. 115.

46 Comments on an earlier version of this paper suggested a relationship between the "cargo" in the *jong sarat* motif and cargo cults of Melanesia. I believe this is only a superficial resemblance. Nowhere in the Puhawang myth is there a messianic connotation (despite the fact that messianic or millenarian movements are common in Indonesia). The acquisition of the "cargo" is only one among many other prerequisites for state formation and development in Southeast Asia. This acquisition is not thought of as a means to obtain "wealth" comparable to that of a dominant force (the intruding "whites" in the Melanesian cargo cult). Finally, the Puhawang myth is in no way central to the formation of a full-fledged cult. A reverse proposition may, however, be conceivable: the modern cargo cult may actually have evolved on a favorable terrain where myths comparable to those of Southeast Asia would have been present.

47 Christie, "Trade and State Formation."

Competing Hierarchies: Javanese Merchants and the *Priyayi* Elite in Solo, Central Java

Suzanne A. Brenner

> "Everyone wants to be priyayi. The ones who are already priyayi want to become even more priyayi. The rich ones want to be richer. The ones with rank want higher rank. All of them are priyayi. Rank, wealth, title, that's what being priyayi is about. Any one of those alone, that's priyayi. Not to mention all three of them at once. Prepare yourself, my daughter. The time has come."
>
> —Arswendo Atmowiloto, *Canting* (1986)

The eighth month of the Islamic-Javanese lunar calendar is called Sadran, Sya'ban, or, more commonly, Ruwah. During this month, which directly precedes the Muslim fasting month (Ramadhan), Javanese villagers and city folk alike make individual and group visits to the grave sites of ancestors and other relatives, venerated Islamic teachers, mystics, legendary figures, the first settlers of their villages, and any others from whom they wish to request blessings (*nyuwun pangèstu, nyuwun berkah*), or for whose souls they wish to offer prayers. The ritual of visiting graves during this month is known as *sadranan* or *ruwahan*. Ruwah is the time when people return to their natal or ancestral villages to make offerings at the graves of their forebears, and make pilgrimages to grave sites too distant for a casual weekly visit on a Thursday night or Friday morning, the usual time to "send" (*ngirim*) flowers, prayers, and incense to the spirits of the dead.

It was toward the end of the month of Ruwah that I was invited to accompany several neighbors on a day-trip to Kotagede, in the Special Region of Yogyakarta. Early on a Monday morning five of us piled into a chauffeur-driven passenger van belonging to the

Research for this article was conducted as part of my dissertation research from 1986 to 1988 in Solo, Central Java, under the auspices of the Indonesian Institute of Sciences and the Center for Cultural Studies of Gadjah Mada University. Research and writing were funded by a Fulbright-Hays Dissertation Research Fellowship, a Social Science Research Council Dissertation Research Grant, and a Woodrow Wilson Research Grant in Women's Studies. I am grateful to James Siegel, Benedict Anderson, Nancy Florida, P. Steven Sangren, and Kathryn March for their comments on earlier drafts of this essay.

wealthy merchant couple that had organized the trip, the Sapardis[1], who were in their late sixties. About two hours later, we arrived at the royal cemetery of Kotagede, established in the late sixteenth century. This is the burial place of the founders of the kingdom of Mataram, ancestors to the present-day royal houses of Solo and Yogyakarta.[2]

Upon entering the high-walled complex, which had only a few other visitors, we removed our shoes as a sign of respect, and changed our clothes in a room designated for that purpose. The one man in our group, Pak Sapardi, changed his Western-style clothing for full formal Javanese attire, donning a high-collared white jacket, a Solonese batik sarong, and a *blangkon,* the stiff batik headdress worn by men. The women, who were already wearing batik sarongs, replaced their usual long-sleeved blouses (*kebaya*) with *kemben,* a simple breast cloth that leaves the shoulders bare, in the style worn at court by female servants and noblewomen of all but the highest ranks. Before entering the inner courtyard, a gatekeeper wearing the regalia of a court retainer (*abdi dalem*) asked us politely to remove our jewelry and watches. The reason, I was told by a member of my party, was so that we would not appear to be "trying to put ourselves on the same level" with the royalty buried there: in the presence of royal graves one dressed the same way that one would dress for a formal audience if their inhabitants were still alive. So, barefoot and dressed in the unadorned style of courtiers, we proceeded to *sowan*—to pay a visit to someone of superior status—to the tombs of the royal personages interred in the inner sanctum of the cemetery.

Walking past the more minor graves, which were outdoors, we stopped at the doorway of a large mausoleum. Each member of the party sat cross-legged outside the door for a few minutes, without speaking, once again in the respectful manner of a courtier. Before going inside, everyone performed a *sembah,* an obeisant gesture made by holding the hands before the face, palms pressed together and thumbs approaching the nose.

The inside of the mausoleum was dimly lit, illuminated only by occasional thin rays of sunlight that streamed through a few glass roof tiles and bevelled glass windows emblazoned with the insignia of Sunan Pakubuwana X of Solo (r. 1893-1939). The damp air was heavy with incense and the smell of fresh and decaying rose petals strewn liberally over all the tombstones. Members of the group greeted several male caretakers in formal Javanese clothing, who wore the yellow sash around their necks that indicated their status as *abdi dalem.* The Sapardis knew these men from their regular biannual visits to the cemetery during the months of Sura (Muharram, Arabic; the first month of the Islamic-Javanese year) and Ruwah.

---

[1] The name Sapardi is a pseudonym.

[2] Kotagede was established by Kyai Ageng Mataram, also known as Pamanahan (died 1575). The kingdom of Mataram was founded at Kotagede in 1587 by Panembahan Senapati Ingalaga, Kyai Ageng Mataram's son, after he destroyed the kingdom of Pajang. Senapati died in 1601 and was buried in the graveyard of the town mosque, next to the grave of his father. Other members of the royal family and high officials of the kingdom were buried there as well. This graveyard was subsequently made into a special compound and designated a royal cemetery. Even after the seat of Mataram was moved from Kotagede to Kerta by Sultan Agung, who built a new royal cemetery at Imogiri, the cemetery at Kotagede continued to be treated as a venerated site housing the graves of the ancestors of Later Mataram. Following the division of Later Mataram into the Sunanate of Surakarta (Solo) and the Sultanate of Yogyakarta in 1755, it was agreed that the royal cemeteries at Kotagede and Imogiri would be maintained jointly by the two courts as "ancestral lands" (*tanah pusaka*). For more on Kotagede and its royal cemetery, see H. J. van Mook, "Kuta Gede," in *The Indonesian Town: Studies in Urban Sociology* (The Hague and Bandung: van Hoeve, 1958) and Mitsuo Nakamura, *The Crescent Arises over the Banyan Tree: A Study of the Muhammadiyah Movement in a Central Javanese Town* (Yogyakarta: Gadjah Mada University Press, 1983).

As we approached the tombs of the most senior figures, which were on a dais raised above the level of the other graves, each person dropped to his or her knees and moved forward in a humble, half-crouching posture (*laku dhodhok*) used in the palaces for approaching someone of high rank. We sat cross-legged in front of the most important tombs. Two of the women burned incense in a small brazier and scattered flower petals over the tombstones. Pak Sapardi made a short introductory speech in very high Javanese, mentioning the names of the members of the party (excluding the anthropologist) who had come to pay respects to the dead buried there, and to pray that the souls of the deceased would be accepted by God and given a place in Heaven. He asked forgiveness from the spirits of the dead for any mistakes or offenses the members of the group might commit in their presence.

After he stopped speaking, the three *abdi dalem* whose services he had enlisted sat down before the tombs on the raised platform and chanted Arabic prayers for the souls of the dead. When these prayers were finished, Pak Sapardi, followed by the other members of the party in turn, inched forward in the same crouching walk until he was directly in front of one of the tombstones, uttered a prayer under his breath, then wiped his face afterwards with both hands in the gesture that follows an Islamic prayer. After this he moved even closer to the tombstone. With one hand touching the base of the tombstone, he knelt deeply in front of it, almost prostrate, his forehead and nose also touching the base. He moved his lips in a whisper for several minutes while remaining in that position. Upon completing this part of the ritual, he made a *sembah* before the tomb, then moved on to the next grave, where he repeated the whole routine. This went on at about ten tombs, which were arranged in tiers according to rank and seniority. The progression of the ritual was from the tombs of the most senior figures to those of lower rank.

Having gone around to each of the major tombs, the members of the group left the chamber, turned around, knelt, and performed a final *sembah* before departing the graveyard. After a brief chat with a few of the *abdi dalem*, a stroll around the rest of the grounds, and a picture-taking session just inside the main gates, we changed back into our street clothes and exited the complex. On the way out, Pak Sapardi distributed small coins from a plastic bag to women and children beggars who sat at the outer gates.

As we left the cemetery, I asked one of the women what she had whispered at each grave. The first part, she told me, was a prayer to God that the sins of the dead would be forgiven and their souls (*arwah*) accepted in Heaven; this was the Arabic prayer that ended in the face-wiping gesture. The second part, when she "kissed" the base of the tombstone, was a prayer offered up directly in high Javanese to the spirit of the person buried there, and consisted of requests for various blessings. The other members of the group had followed the same routine, it turned out. I asked her husband what favors he had requested from the spirits of the dead. "Health, lots of good fortune, and great profits," he answered without hesitation.

This was only one of many cemeteries that were visited by the Sapardis during the month of Ruwah; during that day alone we went to three other grave sites in the Kotagede area, and Bu Sapardi let me know that during a typical Ruwah she might visit well over fifty cemeteries. "It's better than just sitting around at home, isn't it?" she asked rhetorically. What was striking about this particular *sadranan* ritual at the Kotagede cemetery, however, was that it involved an open, completely unabashed display of obeisance and supplication to royalty—or at least, to the spirits of royalty—by people who on other occasions adamantly declared their absolute independence from, and disdain for, the hierarchies and values of the palaces.

The Sapardis were the consummate representatives of the prosperous Javanese *sudagar* (merchant) couple: both had been born into well-established families that had enjoyed uninterrupted prestige in Solo's merchant community for several generations, not a small accomplishment considering the wild swings in fortune that many other merchants had experienced.[3] The Sapardis' own textile business, founded in the 1930s, had continued to thrive in the 1980s, a period when many similar businesses were foundering or had gone bankrupt. Their opulent home and gardens, situated behind a high wall crowned with barbed wire and impeccably maintained by a large house staff, were extraordinary by any standards. Their wealth, acumen in business, and family heritage gave them a degree of status in the Javanese merchant community that few others could match. Their female servants were expected to kneel while serving them and to avert their eyes submissively while speaking to them. Residents of Laweyan, a stronghold of ethnic Javanese merchants on the outskirts of the city who specialized in the manufacture and trade of batik cloth, the Sapardis had the self-assured air of people who had reached the pinnacle of success, at least by local standards.[4] When they walked down the street, those of lesser status would move aside respectfully to let them pass.

Only a few days after arriving in Laweyan, a neighborhood that was known throughout Solo and beyond for its well-to-do, independent-minded Javanese *sudagar* families, I had been escorted to the Sapardis' home by a senior member of the household in which I was living. It soon became clear to me that this was a couple that commanded great respect, and not a little envy, serving as exemplars for the rest of the community. During the course of our conversation, Pak Sapardi stated proudly and in no uncertain terms, "The people of Laweyan have always had the spirit of entrepreneurs. Since the time of our ancestors, we haven't liked people telling us what to do. We don't like serving people. Our souls are the souls of entrepreneurs—we work for ourselves." He made no effort to hide his scorn for those whose livelihood depended upon catering to the will of others, especially those who served the palaces and the government bureaucracy. His wife indicated her full agreement, and I was to hear this sentiment expressed by many other residents of the neighborhood in the months to come.

Given their own almost "royal" stature in the Laweyan community, and their vehement declaration of independence from the true Solonese royalty and the values that they espoused, it was, then, most remarkable to see the Sapardis on their knees in Kotagede, nearly prostrate before the tombs of the ancestors of that same royalty. Their willingness to

---

[3] The term *sudagar* (*saudagar*, Indonesian) means a medium- to large-scale merchant. It can refer to people who are involved in trade alone or in manufacturing as well as trade.

[4] Laweyan is one of a relatively small number of indigenous merchant enclaves found in Java. Other such communities include the devout Muslim community of West Kudus, long known for trade and for the manufacture of *kretek* (clove cigarettes), and the merchant community of Kotagede, which included batik and silver manufacturers as well as pawnbrokers and diamond dealers. Although trade in Java tends to be associated with other ethnic groups, especially Chinese and Arab, each of these enclaves was famous for its successful *Javanese* entrepreneurs and merchants, particularly in the period from the mid- to late nineteenth century through the 1930s (and continuing into the 1960s, for instance, in the case of Laweyan). It is the indigenous merchant group on which I focus here. For a lengthier discussion of Laweyan, the batik industry, and the Solonese merchant community more generally, see Suzanne A. Brenner, "Domesticating the Market: History, Culture, and Economy in a Javanese Merchant Community" (PhD dissertation, Cornell University, 1991). On the entrepreneurs of Kudus, see Lance Castles, *Religion, Politics, and Economic Behavior in Java: The Kudus Cigarette Industry* (New Haven: Cultural Report Series no. 15, Southeast Asia Studies, Yale University, 1967) and Gretchen G. Weix, "Following the Family/Firm: Patronage and Piecework in a Kudus Cigarette Factory" (PhD dissertation, Cornell University, 1990). On Kotagede, see Nakamura, *The Crescent Arises*.

humble themselves in this way was directly related, no doubt, to their expectation that they would receive the blessings of the dead in return. Implicitly, however, it was also an acknowledgment of their acceptance, if only partial, of the ideologies of the Javanese *priyayi* (aristocratic and bureaucratic) elite—the very ideologies that they claimed to disdain. Even when they made offerings at the graves of their own ancestors to ask for blessings of health and prosperity, they never performed the *sembah,* a sign of deference to those of high rank, since their forebears were, after all, only commoners.

Understanding the historical relationship between the Solonese *priyayi* and the *sudagar* class, two small but at one time very influential groups in the city, is important for what it reveals about the complexities of status and the cultural and ideological bases for the construction of hierarchy in Javanese society. Systemic conflicts between merchants and political elites are hardly unusual, especially in agrarian-based societies, where access to power and material wealth typically depends on control over land and labor rather than on control over commerce. In Java, where large-scale trade has been predominantly in the hands of people of foreign descent since the later seventeenth century—Dutchmen, Chinese, and Arabs, among others—one is not surprised to find the qualities generally linked with foreign trading minorities—avarice, a lack of social concern, a calculating rationalism and selfishness in place of a spirit of cooperation—attributed to the indigenous merchant class as well. During the colonial period, the indigenous merchants were unquestionably marginal to the mainstream of Javanese society, perhaps even more marginal than the nonindigenous merchants with whom they competed; for no clear niche was allotted to them in the colonial order, as was allotted, for example, to the ethnic Chinese, who had a well-defined position as middlemen. This marginality has continued into the postcolonial period, despite sporadic efforts of both the Old Order and New Order regimes to strengthen the position of indigenous entrepreneurs and merchants relative to nonindigenous groups.

The mistake of some scholars of Javanese society, however, has been to take this social marginalization as a sign of a basic difference in cultural outlook, a radical disjuncture between the values of the indigenous merchant class and those of the the wider population. In *Peddlers and Princes,* for instance, Clifford Geertz notes that "the *pasar* [marketplace] has tended to form a fairly self-contained cultural universe for its participants, while at the same time the status of the trader in the wider society has been ambiguous at best, pariah-like at worst." He writes in the same paragraph of the "historically persistent tension between the value system of the general society and that of the interstitial bazaar culture, and between peasant and gentleman on the one hand and trader on the other."[5] What I shall suggest in this essay is that the alleged cultural division between the Javanese merchant and "everyone else" is in important ways a fiction. In its internal social relations, linguistic formations, and cultural representations, the merchant community of Solo has recreated its own version of the hierarchies that underlie all other sectors of Central Javanese society. And hierarchy, as James Siegel has shown, is a fundamental value that permeates every sphere of Javanese society.[6]

But it is not quite accurate to assert that the values of the merchants are "the same" as those of other Javanese, for that, too, would be an oversimplification. Although the merchant community, like the peasantry or the aristocracy, has created its own patently

---

[5] Clifford Geertz, *Peddlers and Princes: Social Development and Economic Change in Two Indonesian Towns* (Chicago: University of Chicago Press, 1963), p. 44.

[6] James T. Siegel, *Solo in the New Order: Language and Hierarchy in an Indonesian City* (Princeton: Princeton University Press, 1986).

Javanese hierarchies, it has done so primarily on the basis of something that is, from the perspective of *priyayi* ideology, outside the sphere of culture: money. Only among merchants, "the social representatives of unfettered equivalence," as Arjun Appadurai puts it, can one find a former household servant, who managed through luck and skill to build up a lucrative textile business, being treated as the social equal of the most established elites of the community.[7] Yet the merchants of Laweyan, far from considering themselves to be "outside" Javanese culture, have done their utmost to uphold what they see as the most basic pillars of Javanese cultural life and tradition, particularly in their tireless attention to linguistic and behavioral etiquette and ritual detail—including some rituals that have been left behind by other sectors of the population.

The *sudagar*, then, have taken something that is, according to the dominant ideologies of the society, un-Javanese, and transformed it into something Javanese. This transvaluation of values[8] reproduces at a collective level a symbolic transformation that takes place daily at the level of the household: the conversion of money into a cultural object.[9] Just as Javanese ideology tends to deny women, who are closely associated with money in the household as well as in trade, the status of fully enculturated beings, merchants as a class, male as well as female, are often considered to be less than fully Javanese. But from the viewpoint of the merchants themselves, as well as from the perspectives of women (the two categories overlap significantly, in fact, but for the time being I shall speak of them separately), transacting money does not preclude participating in the broader cultural order; on the contrary, it makes such participation possible. Money provides the means for the reproduction of the family and its social status. In the merchant community, money begets deference. The assimilation of money to hierarchy, in short, is what gives it its cultural value.

I shall return to this later. At this point, I turn again to the division between merchant and *priyayi*, in order to illuminate the tensions inherent in a social system in which there is a basic disjunction between political power, wealth, and status, at the same time that the dominant ideologies of that society insist on their unity. I focus here on the major royal house of Solo, the Kraton Solo (Solo Palace) or Kasunanan (Sunanate), and on the merchant community of Laweyan.

A Legend of Defiance: Pakubuwana's Misadventures in Laweyan

In the context of modern Indonesia under the New Order regime, both the Kraton and Laweyan stand as vestiges of a bygone era. Behind the imposing whitewashed walls surrounding the Kraton compound one expects to find the inherited riches of an almost 250-year-old history. Instead, one finds timeworn buildings, sparsely furnished and inhabited, filled with little more than the lassitude of a dissolute and largely impoverished aristocracy. To speak of any real political power on the part of the Kraton would be absurd, since this descendant house of the once preeminent kingdom of Mataram had come completely under the control of the Dutch colonial regime by the end of the Diponegoro War (1825-1830). Moreover, the Sunanate of Solo, unlike the Sultanate of Yogyakarta, lost its claim to special political status after independence. While the Sultan of Yogyakarta and the Prince of the Pakualaman court (Yogyakarta's minor palace) maintained the right to participate in

[7] Arjun Appadurai, "Introduction: Commodities and the Politics of Value," in *The Social Life of Things: Commodities in Cultural Perspective*, ed. Arjun Appadurai (Cambridge: Cambridge University Press, 1986), p. 33

[8] I owe this phrase to James Siegel.

[9] Cf. Janet Carsten, "Cooking Money: Gender and the Symbolic Transformation of Means of Exchange in a Malay Fishing Community," in *Money and the Morality of Exchange*, ed. Jonathan Parry and Maurice Bloch (Cambridge: Cambridge University Press, 1989), pp. 117-42.

governing what became known as the Special Region of Yogyakarta, Solo was deprived of "Special Region" status and neither the sunan nor the ruler of the Mangkunagaran house have had any official role in the republican government since that time.[10]

Although the Kraton had lost a great deal of its effective power, then, by the mid-nineteenth century, it nevertheless continued to envision itself—and was in turn envisioned by much of the population—as the pinnacle of the Solonese social and cultural hierarchy for the duration of the colonial period and beyond. The symbiotic relationship between Dutch overlord and local nobility that characterized colonial rule in Java enabled the Kraton (like the Sultanate of Yogyakarta and the two minor royal houses of the Vorstenlanden, or Principalities) to maintain considerable symbolic power in Javanese society while its actual power to govern the populace became increasingly limited. Even as the functionaries of an alien regime, the royalty continued to dominate Solo's social landscape. However, the lack of education, gradual impoverishment, and self-absorption of the royal family after independence, along with its failure to gain permanent political concessions from the government of the republic, led to a marked decline in the respect that the Kraton was able to command from the population. While it is still prestigious in Solonese society today to hold a title from the Kraton, an indication that the nobility continues to carry some symbolic weight, there is at the same time widespread cynicism toward the royalty, and a general belief in the community that a noble title can be purchased from the Kraton by anyone who has the money and inclination to do so.

The neighborhood of Laweyan, too, has an eerily anachronistic and debilitated air about it. Many of its batik workshops and immense homes are empty and decaying, their cracked and peeling walls, cobweb-covered dye vats, and broken stained-glass windows a reminder of an earlier, more prosperous time in the *kampung*'s history, when the batik industry seemed an almost limitless source of wealth. There are exceptions to this general decline, such as the well-kept homes of the Sapardis and some of their neighbors, who continue to operate profitable businesses of one sort or another. But in Solo, the name Laweyan itself has become associated with a rapidly fading mercantile ethos and an old-fashioned way of life. In this latter sense as well it may be compared to the Kraton, which is seen as the symbolic center of Javanese tradition in Solo and throughout much of Java, but which is also considered to be largely irrelevant to the workings of the modern political, social, and economic order.

To speak of the relationship between Laweyan and the Kraton is to speak of the past, then, for although sentiments of mutual suspicion and resentment continue to be voiced on both sides late in the twentieth century, the sources of conflict between them date back to an earlier period. According to local legend, in fact, the strained relations between the merchants of Laweyan and the Javanese royalty originated just prior to the establishment of the Karaton Surakarta Hadiningrat (otherwise known as the Kraton Solo or Kasunanan) in 1746 by Sunan Pakubuwana II (r. 1726-1749), who was placed on the throne there by the expanding Dutch East India Company (VOC) in exchange for his cession to the Company of the portion of Java's north coast under his control.

Pakubuwana II had initially come to the throne in 1726 at the court of Kartasura, located about seven miles west of Solo, which was first established as a seat of power in 1680. Following a lengthy period of political intrigue, power struggles, popular discontent, and ulti-

[10] For an analysis of the events that determined the political fates of the Solo and Yogyakarta royal houses after independence, See Benedict R. O'G. Anderson, *Java in a Time of Revolution: Occupation and Resistance 1944-1946* (Ithaca: Cornell University Press, 1972), esp. pp. 350-69.

mately, an armed rebellion that pitted local Javanese and Chinese against the allied forces of Pakubuwana II and the Dutch East India Company, rebel forces ravaged the palace at Kartasura, and Pakubuwana II fled eastward in June 1742. As M. C. Ricklefs puts it, Pakubuwana II "fled into the arms of the Company, who accepted this . . . friendship on several conditions, most notably that the whole of the [north] coast would be placed under the Company's jurisdiction."[11] The rebels were finally put down later that year by the troops of Prince Cakraningrat IV of Madura, who was an ally of the Company and the brother-in-law of Pakubuwana II, and Pakubuwana was restored to the throne in 1743, his power, however, much diminished. Instead of attempting to rebuild the palace at Kartasura, which appeared to be an ill-fated site for the Kraton, he decided to move the entire court a few miles east to the village of Solo, near the banks of the Solo River (Bengawan Solo). The building of the new Kraton at its present site was completed in 1745, and Pakubuwana and his courtiers had taken up residence there by 1746.[12]

A legend that is told today in Solo, most commonly in Kraton circles, dates the inception of the antagonism between Laweyan and the Kraton to the historical moment when Pakubuwana II was fleeing Kartasura, after his palace had been overtaken by the rebels. Although there are quite a few variations on the story, I offer here an abridged translation of one popular version, which was written down in modern Javanese by Samsudjin Probohardjono, a courtier of the Kraton, in 1981:

> Three hundred years ago, the village of Laweyan was already famous as the home of wealthy merchants who dealt in thread (*lawé*), woven cloth, and batik. Their large walled houses loomed up everywhere. Their vast yards were surrounded by brick walls that were as thick and high and strong as the walls of the palace.
>
> There are some who hold the opinion that the people of Laweyan were by nature strongly inclined toward trade, working only for themselves, and being entrepreneurs. This was a far cry from the honor and prestige of serving the King or the State. The greatness of their rank, the loftiness of their status, what was good and bad, were all determined by wealth and worldly riches.
>
> The story is told that on June 30, 1742 A. D., the Palace at Kartasura was ravaged by Chinese soldiers. His Royal Highness Pakubuwana the Second, together with his son the Crown Prince and his entourage, all of whom had just fled from the palace, were traveling east on horseback. Passing Pajang, they reached the eastern side of the Premulung River, where they rested for a spell to put all their things in order, as well as to rest their tired horses, which had not been tended to for several days due to the battle that raged, and because the Chinese soldiers were hot in pursuit.
>
> While they rested there, His Highness sent a retainer to the village of Laweyan to borrow fresh horses that could be used to ride and to carry their supplies for the remainder of the journey. But none of the people of Laweyan were willing to offer their horses, since all were being used to transport their wares, trade being very brisk at the time.

[11] M.C. Ricklefs, *Modern Javanese Historical Tradition: A Study of an Original Kartasura Chronicle and Related Materials* (London: School of Oriental and African Studies, University of London, 1978), p. 11.

[12] For a straightforward account of the events leading up to and following the move of the Kraton from Kartasura to Solo, see M. C. Ricklefs, *A History of Modern Indonesia c. 1300 to the Present* (London: Macmillan, 1981), chapters 8 and 9; see also Ricklefs, *Modern Javanese Historical Tradition*, esp. pp. 10-11. A more interpretive and thoroughly enlightening account of the "royal progress" from Kartasura to Solo is found in John Pemberton, "The Appearance of Order: A Politics of Culture in Colonial and Postcolonial Java" (PhD dissertation, Cornell University, 1989), chapter 2.

His Highness Pakubuwana the Second received this report with a heavy heart, thinking of how bad his luck was, facing the trials that the Almighty God was setting him. But then, calming himself, he said to himself clearly and firmly: "The people of Laweyan are not of the stature of *priyayi,* but are by nature traders who calculate profits and losses, who strive for wealth and treasures. May God the Almighty grant them these things."

The words of his Royal Highness Pakubuwana the Second, otherwise known as the Floating Sunan, have been true to this day. Many of the people of Laweyan have been successful in trade and in their firms. Many have become large-scale traders and entrepreneurs, very wealthy, their property and riches overflowing. But few have become *priyayi* or servants of Court and State with distinguished rank.[13]

This version of the story places the uppity people of Laweyan within the symbolic sphere of Kraton control by attributing their long-lasting success as merchants to the charity of Pakubuwana II and to the power and efficacy of his Word (*sabda*). In spite of their refusal to serve the sunan, he proves his own superiority and the superiority of the *priyayi* ethos by blessing them instead of cursing them.

In other versions of the story, though, Pakubuwana II is not quite so generous. Several people told me that when His Highness's request to borrow horses was turned down, he *cursed* the people of Laweyan, swearing that none of their descendants would ever be permitted to marry his descendants, and that henceforth, the people of Laweyan would be barred from attaining high rank in the Kraton, doomed forever to be low-status traders instead of honored *priyayi.*[14] In fact, there does seem to be an informal rule in the Kraton, still in effect today, which enjoins high-ranking members of the royalty from marrying residents of Laweyan. Those who told me of this prohibition invariably cited the unfortunate experiences of Pakubuwana II in Laweyan as the reason for the prohibition.[15]

This legend was understandably more popular in Kraton circles than in Laweyan; many people in Laweyan seemed not to know the story or, if they had heard it, gave it little credence. However, an older Laweyan woman and her daughter related a version of the story that was generally similar to others but differed in one significant respect. I had asked the woman whether any member of the royalty had ever married into a Laweyan family, to her knowledge. "No," she answered simply, "That wasn't allowed by the Kraton. It was the word (*sabda*) of the sinuhun [sunan]." Her daughter, who was in her fifties, explained further. "People say that a woman from Laweyan was going to be made a concubine of the sinuhun, but she refused. The sinuhun was mad, and swore (*nyebda,* from *sabda*) that from that time on, from generation to generation, the people of Laweyan would never be close to the king, but they would be blessed with abundance" (*Sa'turun-turuné wong Laweyan bakal adoh karo raja, nanging diparingi keluwihan*). The older woman added that the name "Laweyan" came from *luwih sembarang,* meaning "more of everything." "More riches (*luwih bandha-bandha*), for instance," she explained.

---

[13] Samsudjin Probohardjono, "Sejarah Laweyan" (unpublished ms.), pp. 5-7. The translation is my own.

[14] According to one man, also a Kraton retainer of high rank, the sunan said to the people of Laweyan, "In the future, you will never become one with me" (*sésuk, kowé ora isa manunggal karo aku*).

[15] A few people suggested that the sunan, wishing to travel by water instead of by land, asked to borrow a ship, not a horse. Since the word *kapal* can mean either "ship" or "horse" in Javanese, the source of the ambiguity is understandable. This is not an implausible twist on the legend, since Laweyan is said to have bordered on a sizable tributary of the Solo River at that time. I might also mention that according to a resident of the Kraton, it was not Pakubuwana's request for transportation that was turned down, but his request for opium. That is not implausible, either, as local tradition has it that opium was one of the commodities traded widely in the area.

This version of the story is especially telling, since it points to the unwillingness of the independent-minded women of Laweyan—for women clearly dominated trade in the neighborhood, as was typically true among Javanese merchants in the Solo-Yogyakarta region—to be placed under the control of aristocratic men. While many Javanese would have considered it an honor and a privilege to be made the wife or concubine of the sunan, Laweyan women were in general agreement that it was preferable to be a common but autonomous trader than to be kept as a royal consort, pampered but confined like a bird in a gilded cage, and forced to compete with other wives and mistresses for the attentions and favors of the men of the court. They found the idea of being dependent on men for everything (their stereotyped image of what it meant to be a woman of the nobility) to be especially unappealing, because most were accustomed to earning and saving their own money, with the freedom that provided. On several occasions people in Laweyan remarked disapprovingly that the ladies of the palace were little more than "vessels" (*si wadhah*) for bearing aristocratic children.[16] They also took a dim view of the fact that Kraton consorts of common origin were expected to address their own royal children in the deferential language of high Javanese, while their children spoke ordinary low Javanese to them in return—a linguistic configuration that would be unthinkable in Laweyan or elsewhere outside of aristocratic circles.

Underlying the last version of the legend is a central but often overlooked point of distinction between the nobility and the merchant class in Solo. I shall argue presently that the different positions of women—or at least, the imagined differences—and their relations with men in these two groups accentuated, and in critical ways even defined, the social and symbolic gaps between them. For now, however, I merely wish to observe that, while this variant of the story highlights an important factor in the rift between aristocrat and merchant which hinges on the contrasting symbolic, social, and economic roles of women in the two communities (with the contrasts sometimes exaggerated, as will become clear), it does not stray from the basic theme that runs through all of the other versions. Like the others, it points to the averseness of the merchants of Laweyan to acknowledge Kraton hegemony, as indicated by their refusal to acquiesce to the sunan's wishes. It should be noted, however, that even in the rendering of the story by two Laweyan merchants, it is ultimately the sunan who decides the fate of Laweyan. He forbids its residents to attempt any rapprochement with the Kraton through marriage alliances or through direct service to the Sunanate, yet provides them with perpetual abundance by means of the magical potency of his word.

This legend expresses a palpable rift between the Javanese merchant class and the *priyayi* in Solo. It is difficult to pinpoint the origins of this fissure. Clearly one cannot make generalizations in this regard for the whole of Java, for the situation in the agrarian interior of the island, where Solo is situated, differed significantly from that of the commercially oriented north coast. In the thriving trading ports of Java's north coast in the centuries prior to colonization, political power and access to revenue among the nobility depended upon their ability to control commerce.[17] While there may have been competition between aristocrats and merchants, there was little basis for a deep ideological conflict between them, because both depended in one way or another on trade for their livelihood and social status. Only when colonization permanently altered the face of socioeconomic relations in the region by

[16] Cf. Peter Carey and Vincent Houben, "Spirited Srikandhis and Sly Sumbadras: The Social, Political, and Economic Role of Women at the Central Javanese Courts in the 18th and Early 19th Centuries," in *Indonesian Women in Focus: Past and Present Notions* (Dordrecht: Foris Publications, 1987), p. 15, n. 5.

[17] See Pierre-Yves Manguin, "The Merchant and the King," above pp. 41–54, esp. pp. 47–48.

shifting trade into the hands of Europeans, Chinese, and other foreigners did commerce cease to be a major source of political and economic strength for local elites.

In the fertile inland of Java, on the other hand, where economic and political power were based to a greater extent on control over land and the labor with which to work it, it is possible that trade was seen as a subordinate occupation that was ill suited to men (though perhaps not women—I shall come back to this point later) of rank. But there is little evidence from the precolonial period to sustain or disprove this speculation, and it is equally possible that the marginalization of the Javanese merchant in the interior was entirely a colonial development. Without question, this process of marginalization was carried to an extreme during the colonial period. From the very start of colonial intervention in the Indies, the Dutch East India Company had determined that it was safest and most efficient to put economic power into the hands of those who (besides themselves) had no political power—most notably, Chinese and other trading minorities, whom they could manipulate to their own advantage. In addition, the Company, and the government of the Netherlands East Indies that followed on its heels, made sure that indigenous rulers had limited access to wealth save through their ever-growing dependence on the colonial regime.

The divide-and-rule policy of the regime, then, extended to the economic as well as the political sphere. The formula was simple and quite effective: to keep independent access to wealth out of the hands of those with power, and power out of the hands of those with independent access to wealth. While Solo's palaces commanded substantial economic resources, including control over extensive agricultural lands and eventually over profitable sugar factories, their gradual erosion of power during the nineteenth and twentieth centuries made it evident to just what extent they relied on the Dutch for their well-being. Beginning in the early to mid-eighteenth century, Dutch subsidies were what really sustained the courts of Central Java.[18] This was all the more apparent after the Indies government instituted the agrarian reorganization of the Vorstenlanden in the 1910s and 1920s, including the abolition of the long-standing appanage system, through which court functionaries had been assigned rights over fixed percentages of the produce of particular lands, as well as rights to a certain amount of corvée labor from the peasants. The abolition of this system, in conjunction with the spread of large European plantations, which cultivated crops like sugar, tobacco, and coffee for the international market, led to a serious reduction of power, prestige, and wealth on the part of the sunan and the Solonese *priyayi* as a whole.[19]

Whether or not the division between *priyayi* and *sudagar* actually originated with Dutch rule, the nature of colonial policy clearly served to exaggerate and rigidify that division. While supporting—and creating—*priyayi* ideologies that stressed service and self-sacrifice on behalf of the state as the noblest profession for a Javanese,[20] and identifying the *priyayi*,

---

[18] M. C. Ricklefs, *Jogjakarta under Sultan Mangkubumi 1749-1792: A History of the Division of Java* (London: Oxford University Press, 1974); Ann Kumar, "Javanese Court Society and Politics in the Late Eighteenth Century: The Record of a Lady Soldier," Part I: "The Religious, Social, and Economic Life of the Court," *Indonesia* 29:1-46 (April 1980).

[19] For more on the effects of the agrarian reorganization in the Vorstenlanden, see Anderson, *Java in a Time of Revolution*, pp. 348-351; Takashi Shiraishi, *An Age in Motion: Popular Radicalism in Java, 1912-1926* (Ithaca: Cornell University Press, 1990), chapter 1; George D. Larson, *Prelude to Revolution: Palaces and Politics in Surakarta, 1912-1942* (Dordrecht: Foris Publications, 1987), pp. 20-22; Nakamura, *The Crescent Arises*, pp. 40-44; and Van Mook, "Kuta Gede," pp. 320-31.

[20] Both Heather Sutherland and Ann Kumar point out that over the course of the nineteenth century, the period during which the Dutch consolidated their control over the whole of Java and over the Javanese ruling class, the ideal of being a warrior (*satria*) in service to a powerful Javanese ruler gave way to an ideal of being an aristocrat-cum-bureaucrat (*priyayi*) in service to the colonial state (through the courts). See Heather Sutherland, *The Making*

particularly those of the palaces of Central Java, as the standard-bearers of "high" Javanese culture,[21] the European colonizers also declared emphatically that the Javanese people were by their very nature unfit as traders. The colonial bureaucrat Van Deventer, for instance, commented in 1904 that

> Real thrift is foreign to the modern-day Javanese; money rolls through their fingers, or burns in their hands; the Chinese is thrifty, frugal, cautious at the same time. In the matter of free will, of the spirit of enterprise, the Native [Inlander] of Java has not come far either; his nature is rather docile. . . . Carefree also is the nature of the ordinary Javanese; they live from hand to mouth, and would rather think as little as possible about tomorrow; this source of a cheerful outlook on life, however, stands in sharp contrast with the inborn notion of the Chinese that people, as much as possible through material appearances, must uphold the sacred honor of their ancestors. Already in this one cardinal notion the Chinese possesses a mighty incentive to drive him to work, while the spirit of the Javanese knows nothing of this sort.[22]

Such assessments of "the Javanese character" appeared to justify the privileged position of nonindigenous sectors of the population with regard to trade, and the relegation of the Javanese themselves to the roles of happy peasant, carefree laborer, or docile government functionary. Although much small-scale trade remained in the hands of Javanese—mostly Javanese women[23]—intermediate trade was controlled largely by ethnic Chinese, who did not have access to the prestige of colonial service, and who were afforded important business privileges by the colonial regime.[24] The Dutch kept the very lucrative large-scale import-export trade for themselves. However, the increasing penetration of capital into the Vorstenlanden in the mid- to late nineteenth century was accompanied by the emergence of a small indigenous bourgeoisie, precisely at the time when the economic power and social prestige of the *priyayi* were waning as a result of colonial policies limiting their rights over land and the labor with which to work it.[25] This class of indigenous merchants remained marginal to the mainstream of Javanese society, however, never becoming large enough or influential enough to alter the basic shape of colonial society.

The effective marginalization of the Javanese merchant class guaranteed that it could not create a serious challenge to the colonial state. As long as the *priyayi,* thoroughly coopted by the colonial regime, maintained their place at the apex of Javanese society and continued to look down upon the activities of the merchant, the wealth held by members of the numerically insignificant *sudagar* class was certain to remain quite harmless.

---

of a Bureaucratic Elite: The Colonial Transformation of the Javanese Priyayi (Singapore, Heinemann, 1979) and Kumar, "Javanese Court Society and Politics," Part II: "Political Developments: The Courts and the Company 1784-1791," *Indonesia* 30: 67-112.

[21] Nancy K. Florida, "Writing the Past, Inscribing the Future: Exile and Prophecy in an Historical Text of Nineteenth-Century Java" (PhD dissertation, Cornell University, 1990); Shiraishi, *An Age in Motion*.

[22] C. Th. van Deventer, Overzicht van den Economischen toestand der Inlandsche Bevolking van Java en Madoera (The Hague: Nijhoff, 1904), pp. 100-101.

[23] See Thomas Stamford Raffles, *The History of Java,* Vol. I (Kuala Lumpur: Oxford University Press, 1965), p. 353, on the dominance of women in the marketplace in the early nineteenth century.

[24] On the collaboration of Chinese businessmen with the colonial regime, especially with regard to the opium revenue farms and the vast business networks that extended out from them, see James Rush, *Opium to Java: Revenue Farming and Chinese Enterprise in Colonial Indonesia, 1860-1910* (Ithaca: Cornell University Press, 1990).

[25] Shiraishi, *An Age in Motion,* chapter 1.

Benedict Anderson observes that the *priyayi* set themselves off from the rest of the Javanese population not only by rank and occupation, but also by lifestyle and the self-conscious adoption of a distinctive and highly elaborated system of ethical values. Within the *priyayi* ideology of spiritual potency, or Power, in Anderson's terminology, the active pursuit of material gain is seen as a sign of lack of refinement, which in turn indicates lack of status. As he writes:

> Personal acquisitiveness, like sexual indulgence and political ambition, is one of the most obvious types of personal indulgence or pamrih. Accordingly, the overt pursuit of wealth that is characteristic of the merchant or businessman shows a lack of Power and therefore lack of status. This judgment should not be taken to suggest that the typical high-status Javanese is not a man of wealth or that the Javanese tradition does not conceive of riches as an important attribute of the ruler and his closest associates. But money in itself should never be the object of active pursuit. Wealth should flow to the holder of Power, as a consequence of that Power, in the same way that pusaka [sacred objects or heirlooms], large populations, wives, neighboring kingdoms or states flow toward the ruler, as it were, magnetically attracted to the center. The vast wealth that the great rulers of the Javanese past are described as possessing is always an attribute of Power, not the means for acquiring it. Thus in the Javanese political tradition wealth necessarily follows Power, not Power wealth.[26]

Moreover, wealth should not only flow *to* the holder of Power, it should also flow *from* him, as the result of his beneficence: "[W]ealth (or property) is an *attribute* of power, not its provenance; and socioeconomic status is a quality which derives from the center and has no meaning except in relation to that center."[27] The legend of Pakubuwana II's encounter with the merchants of Laweyan affirms the ideology that wealth should emanate from the center of power. By attributing Laweyan's riches to the all-powerful word of the sunan, the story suggests that even these intractable merchants, who refused the great honor of serving the king because they were more concerned with making money, ultimately owed their wealth to the sunan's formidable concentration of power and his beneficent nature. In reality, the Javanese merchant owed little or nothing of his or her wealth to the "powerful center," whether that center be identified with the palaces or with the colonial state (the distinction is ultimately an artificial one, of course). The merchant's accumulation of wealth therefore challenged the notion that wealth should either flow to, or be bestowed by, persons of high status.

The "Suluk Mas Ngantèn": Rectifying Etiquette

Even if we cannot establish with any certainty that the schism between merchant and *priyayi* in Solo dates back to the establishment of the Kraton there in the mid-eighteenth century, as the legend of Pakubuwana II and his horses would have us believe, an extraordinary Javanese poem from early nineteenth-century Solo gives undeniable evidence that the social categories of *priyayi* and *sudagar* were already considered to be distinct, essentially immutable, and fundamentally at odds with each other by that time. Composed in 1818 by Radèn Mas Riya Jayadiningrat I, a *wayah dalem* (grandson of the sunan), the "Suluk Mas Ngantèn" (roughly, "The Song of Mas Ngantèn") has a didactic yet humorous, even farcical

[26] Benedict R. O'G. Anderson, "The Idea of Power in Javanese Culture," in *Culture and Politics in Indonesia*, ed. Claire Holt, Benedict R. O'G. Anderson, and James Siegel (Ithaca: Cornell University Press, 1972), p. 41.

[27] Ibid., p. 48.

tone.[28] The author states at the outset that his purpose in writing the poem is to advise young people never to fall short in following proper etiquette (*aywa kurang ing tatakrami*), so that they do not disgrace themselves. He then launches into a lengthy and very detailed description of some of the shameful shortcomings of people who aspire to be *priyayi,* but who do not know the *tatakrama,* etiquette or proper social conduct, of being *priyayi* (*Ana cacad ageng nistha malih/wong nora wruh tatrap tatakrama/pratingkahing kapriyayèn*).

The poem is divided into five sections, each describing a different scenario in which the failure to observe the etiquette proper to one's station in life leads to disastrous—and extremely comical—results.[29] The fourth section, which is most relevant to the present study, concerns a petty merchant of Butuh (a village located on the Solo River) who, despite his distinctly non-*priyayi* status, wants to marry his child off in a *priyayi*-style wedding (*kepengin cara priyayi*).[30] When the merchant, called simply "Mr. Merchant" (Ki Sudagar, Ki Juragan) confides his wish to "Mr. Adjutant" (Jajar Wajidan, Mas Wajidan[31]), a *priyayi* friend of his, Mr. Adjutant advises him that he would be better off not trying to imitate the *priyayi*. Mr. Merchant is determined, however, and Mr. Adjutant suggests that if Mr. Merchant is willing to entrust everything into his hands, he personally will see to all the preparations.

Ana maneh nisthane wong amemantu
ana ta sudagar cilik
sawatara sugihipun
kepengin cara priyayi
ana mitrane winanoh.

Kabeneran Jajar Wajidan ing ngayun
asugih mitra priyayi
rowang rembugan mantu
alah adhi kadipundi
gon kula arsa memanton.

Inggih kakang yen andhahar kula matur
tan kadi tata priyayi
kang raka alon amuwus
dereng dhenger kula adhi
tata pyayi kang sayektos.

Uwitipun kepengin celak priyantun
mas Wajidan anyaguhi
kakang sampun tumut-tumut

---

[28] Radèn Mas Riya Jayadiningrat I, "Suluk Mas Ngantèn" (orig. composed Surakarta, 1818) in *Serat Wulang* (Jakarta: Departemen Pendidikan dan Kebudayaan, 1981), pp. 131-201. This poem is composed in a Javanese verse form that was meant to be sung to prescribed melodies. I am grateful to Nancy Florida for information about the original date of this text and the identity of the author, as well as for her very helpful suggestions and important corrections on my translation. I am also thankful to John Pemberton for encouraging me to look at the poem and for making a copy of the text available to me.

[29] Each of the sections (*pupuh*) is written in a different meter with its standard corresponding melody and mood: Dhandhanggula, Sinom, Mijil, Megatruh, and Pucung.

[30] This fourth section is in the meter Megatruh, which Nancy Florida describes as a "melancholy metre." Florida, "Writing the Past," Vol. II, p. 668. Given the humorous nature of the scenes described here, the use of a melancholy sounding meter can only have added to the sharp satirical tone intended by the author.

[31] *Jajar* is the lowest rank of Kraton official. *Wajidan* is the same as *ajidan* or *ajudan*, meaning, not surprisingly, "adjutant" (in service to the palace). *Mas,* which is sometimes used in the text in place of the official title *Jajar,* means "older brother," but it is also a general term of address for a man. It can also indicate low noble status.

yen kakang sampun ngrojongi
sabarang dipun pitados.

Kang ngladosi miwah dandosan kang nyambut
ngamungna kula pribadi
ki sudagar teka nurut
mas Wajidan nuli pamit
wus mubeng dennya wewartos.

Ngajak-ajak pawong-mitra dennya nyambut
den ebang alungguh kursi
ana den ebang anayub
mitrane teka dalidir
wus pepak barang pirantos.[32]

Again there is the shame of one who held a wedding
There was a petty merchant
Middling was his wealth
He yearned to follow the style of the *priyayi*
He had a friend

A *jajar*, as it happened, an adjutant at court
Had a wealth of *priyayi* friends
He joined in the discussion of the wedding
"Alas, *adhi*,[33] how will it come to be
My desire to hold a wedding?"

"Well, *kakang*, if I may suggest to you
Don't try to do it *priyayi* style"
The elder one softly broke in
"I do not yet know, *adhi*
The true style of the *priyayi*

That is why I wish to be close to the *priyayi*"
Mr. Adjutant gave his promise
"*Kakang*, don't bother yourself
Kakang, if you agree
Just leave it all to me

For those who will serve, and the accessories, the procurer
Will be none but myself"
Mr. Merchant gave his assent

---

[32] Jayadiningrat I, "Suluk Mas Ngantèn," Pupuh Megatruh, verses 1-6, pp. 182-83. In keeping with the transliterated version from which I have taken the Javanese text, all diacritics are omitted. It should be noted that I have translated only selected passages from the text, and that some of the translations offered here are admittedly tentative.

[33] *Adhi* literally means "younger brother." Here, Mr. Merchant is addressing Mr. Adjutant, who is obviously younger than he is, in a friendly fashion. In return, Mr. Adjutant calls Mr. Merchant *kakang*, which literally means "older brother." Despite Mr. Adjutant's *priyayi* status, he speaks to Mr. Merchant in a somewhat higher level of Javanese (i.e., more respectfully) than Mr. Merchant speaks to him, although both speak to each other politely. For instance, Mr. Adjutant says that he wishes to *matur* (to speak to someone of higher status) to Mr. Merchant. The differences in language levels used by the two men fit with the junior and senior statuses indicated by their respective use of the terms of address "*adhi*" and "*kakang*." However, the language styles also show that Mr. Adjutant's *priyayi* status did not put him at a higher social level than Mr. Merchant. My thanks to Nancy Florida for pointing out the hierarchical nuances of the two men's speech styles.

Mr. Adjutant then took his leave
Going around to spread the news

He invited his close friends, and borrowed from them
Promising that they could sit in chairs
Some were offered the prospect of a *tayuban*[34]
His friends came in great number
The equipment was complete

Although the wedding is still twelve days off, Mr. Adjutant and a number of his companions arrive unannounced at the home of Mr. Merchant, bearing a complete set of *gamelan* instruments and more equipment than the house will hold. When Mr. Merchant worries about who will guard the gamelan for twelve nights, Mr. Adjutant informs him that he has already invited a few more of his friends to help out, and suggests that Mr. Merchant's wife should prepare some simple food, "nothing fancy" (*boten kedah opak-apik*), and a little liquor, to keep them from getting sleepy. Mr. Merchant readily agrees to this. However, much to his dismay, that evening a great many *priyayi* guests show up, expecting to be lavishly provided with food, liquor, and entertainment:

Lagi wayah mahrib dhayoh wus barubul
akathah tur pyayi-pyayi
ki Wisma susah arikuh
mas Wajidan ngacarani
lah suwawi sami lungguh.[35]

At sunset the guests poured in
Many were they, and all *priyayi*
The host was ill at ease
Mr. Adjutant welcomed the guests
"Please, have a seat."

As the nervous host to such a distinguished group of guests, Mr. Merchant follows whatever Mr. Adjutant tells him to do, acceding to an increasingly expensive list of demands. The Chinese liquor (*ciu*) and Dutch gin (*janéwer*) flow liberally, the card games begin—with gambling money supplied to the guests by Mr. Merchant—and professional female dancers and *gamelan* musicians are called in, the latter given opium at Mr. Adjutant's urging. Throughout all this, Mr. Merchant pointedly ignores his wife's repeated protests:

Nyai Wisma malengos asalang gumun
kapriye padone iki
durung jagongan wus nayub

---

[34] To be given a chair was a sign of honored status; people of lesser status would have sat on mats on the floor. *Tayuban* is a type of dance often performed in conjunction with weddings, annual village rites propitiating local tutelary spirits, and other ritual occasions. Male guests take turns dancing with one or two professional female dancers, known as *tlèdhèk* or *tandhak*, who signal that it is a man's turn by extending him a long scarf. On *tayuban*, see Robert F. Hefner, "The Politics of Popular Art: Tayuban Dance and Culture Change in East Java," *Indonesia* 43 (1987): 75–94; see also Claire Holt, *Art in Indonesia: Continuities and Change* (Ithaca: Cornell University Press, 1967), pp. 111-13 and John Pemberton, "Musical Politics in Central Java (or How Not to Listen to a Javanese Gamelan)" *Indonesia* 44 (1987): 17–30. In the latter article, Pemberton also discusses the ceremonial role of chairs and Kraton restrictions on their use dating from the eighteenth century.

[35] Jayadiningrat I, "Suluk Mas Ngantèn," Pupuh Megatruh, verse 17, p. 185.

ki Sudagar manthelengi
wruha heh sira wong wadon[36]

The lady of the house turned her head in astonishment
"What's going on here
The wedding celebration hasn't started yet but you're already putting on a *tayuban*"
Mr. Merchant glared at her [saying]
"What do *you* know, you're just a woman!"

Mr. Merchant, who after a few drinks has overcome his anxiety and is feeling quite pleased with himself, becomes happily drunk, as do his guests, and everyone dances the night away at the *tayuban*.

On the morning of the actual wedding ceremony, however, none of the *priyayi* appear to accompany the groom to the place across the Solo River where the ceremony will be held. Besides the inebriated Mr. Adjutant, only the *sudagar* guests come to serve as escort. Although the merchants are dressed in fine clothes and jewelry, the procession is nonetheless sloppy and disorderly:

. . .
duk panganten arsa kawin
pra priyayi tana rawuh
kapiran kang ngiring aring
kang saguh kabeh gedobrol.
Pra sudagar semune kemeren mutung
temah mangkat ting karenthil
mas Wajidan pijer wuru
sawiyah tungganganeki
wus mangkat nging reyah-reyoh.

. . .

Watak-wantu yen sudagaran memantu
sarwa emas sarwa keling
wus mangkat pangarakipun
sarwa mubyar busana sri
pangantene nunggang belo.

Meh kapiran turangga tan ana ngingu
punika napas barindhil
rada rengkik dhasar kuru
brang-wetan anambutneki
kyai Kapedhak ing Beton.[37]

. . .
When the wedding was nigh
None of the *priyayi* came
In disarray the escort
All of their promises had been empty

[36] Ibid., verse 39, p. 188.

[37] Ibid., verses 51-56, p. 190.

The merchants were all jealous and broken
And so their departure was not in unison
Mr. Adjutant was constantly drunk
Each of the vehicles
Had set off but was on the verge of collapse

. . .

Typical of a merchant wedding
All gold and silks
The procession was on its way
All shining in garments resplendent
The groom rode a young horse

Almost neglected was the horse, having received little care
It was a bald roan horse
Rather skinny and emaciated
At the eastern bank they were received
By Kyai Kapedhak of Beton.

When the members of the procession have been ferried across to the other side of the river, they discover that the *priyayi* guests have already arrived en masse. Feeling rather put out at this, many of the merchants decide to leave. The *priyayi* go off by themselves to sit in chairs, eat, and get drunk once again, paying no heed to the wedding ceremony that is taking place. While the nuptial rites proceed, the irrepressible men grab the hired female dancers to start up another *tayuban*:

. . .
tan dangu panganten prapti
ki tamu wus padha wuru
nora pati amarsudi
gendhing muni kebogiro.

Gendhing prapta ing kurmat penganten rawuh
anggepira para tami
kancane ingkang anjaluk
ringgit tinarik manginggil
samya jengklek pacak githok.

Pangantene kapiran duk apepangguh
mung para batur lan estri
kang upacara duk pangguh
datan kena den sayuti
panayube para dhayoh.[38]

. . .
Before long the groom arrived
The guests were already drunk
And didn't trouble themselves too much
The song that played was Kebogiro.

The song was played to hail the arrival of the groom
But the assumption of the guests
Was that one of their friends had requested it

[38] Ibid., verses 61-63, p. 191.

A dancer was pulled up
All of them turned their necks [i.e., all began to dance in the *tayuban]*

The bride and groom were ignored during the rites
Only the servants and women
Attended at the ceremony
It was impossible to restrain
The dancing of the guests

Those *sudagar* guests who did not leave from the start make a hasty exit when they realize that no chairs have been set out for them. Meanwhile, after dancing, eating, and imbibing to their hearts' content, the *priyayi* guests go home without bothering to congratulate the bridal couple and without offering the customary *sumbangan*, "contribution" or gift.

Night after night the *priyayi* continue to show up at the merchant's house to continue the festivities. At Mr. Adjutant's urging, they are provided with great quantities of food. Only when everything in the merchant's possession has been cleaned out are Mr. Adjutant and his *priyayi* friends finally satisfied:

. . .
wus entek kebo sepuluh
saben bengi akeh prapti
sumbangan tan ana katon.

Sinaosan bebeke anyar dha nyatus
kejaba kang kebo sapi
parandene nora cukup
kinurasan duwekneki
dalah darbeke wong wadon.

Mas Wajidan katutugan sedyanipun,
suka sagung mitraneki
sabubare ponang tamu
mitrane kang celak nglikik,
ki Juragan teka joto.[39]

. . .
Ten water buffalo were finished off
Every night many [people] came
Contributions were nowhere to be seen.

Even though a hundred new ducks [were slaughtered]
Not to mention the water buffalo and cows
Still it was not enough
His possessions were drained dry
Including the property of his wife.

Mr. Adjutant was fulfilled in every way
His friends were all happy
After the guests went home
His [Mr. Merchant's] close friends laughed at him
Mr. Merchant was left speechless with astonishment.

---

[39] Ibid., verses 66-68, p. 192.

Besides being dazed and disappointed, Mr. Merchant is also hungry, but he is ashamed to eat the food that has been set aside for others:[40]

Ana ingkang linorodaken ing ngayun
tinata bangku ing jawi
para sinoman kang nayub
ki Sudagar durung bukti
pijer ngladeni mring dhayoh.

Arsa milu pra sinoman bukti nayub
rumangsa tamu tur isin
jajan ora ana warung
sawisma pating kulikik
kang wadon gremeng memisoh.[41]

Some food had been left out front
Arranged on a table outside
The servers were dancing
Mr. Merchant hadn't yet eaten
Having been too busy attending to the guests.

Were he to join the servers eating and dancing
He would feel like a guest, and ashamed
Wanting to eat out, no foodstalls were open
The house was full of rumbling stomachs
His wife grumbled and cursed.

Realizing that he has been made a fool of, and that he has seen not a penny in gifts to compensate for his expenses, he comes to the conclusion that all of his efforts have been completely in vain.

The moral to be learned from this debacle, the author tells us in the final verses, is that one should do things in the manner appropriate to one's own station in life:

Iku uga cacade wong amemantu
dudu carane pribadi
yen ngindhung caraning ngindhung
priyayi cara priyayi
dadi tan nganggo geguron.

. . .

Aja kaya kawruhe si kaki Pengung
Sudagar cara Priyayi
yekti ngalor lawan ngidul
dudu carane pribadi
ngamungna kang wis kalakon.[42]

This is the fault of one who makes a wedding
Not in keeping with his own ways

---

[40] *Ingkang linorodaken* means "that which is set aside for those of lower status." Here, it refers to the food that has been put aside as a favor to the servers and other people of low status.

[41] Jayadiningrat I, "Suluk Mas Ngantèn," Pupuh Megatruh, verses 69-70, pp. 192-93.

[42] Ibid., verses 75-77, pp. 193-94.

If you're a peasant, then do things like a peasant[43]
A *priyayi*, then do things like a *priyayi*
Don't try to follow the ways of others.

. . .

Don't do what that old fool did
A merchant who tried to do things like a *priyayi*
He went south when he should have gone north
It was not his own way
Don't repeat what's already over and done with.

It is hard to say who is more the target of Jayadiningrat's biting sarcasm in this poem: the foolish merchant who ruins himself and his family for his visions of *priyayi* grandeur, or the greedy and decadent *priyayi* who care about nothing but satisfying their own sensual appetites and being treated with great deference. Although Jayadiningrat is more direct in his criticism of the merchant, whose downfall results from his attempt to be something that he cannot be, the poem is also an acerbic comment on the self-indulgent lifestyles and over-inflated egos of the members of the class to which Jayadiningrat himself belonged. These *priyayi* are not the noble, self-sacrificing pillars of morality, the brave and refined *satria* (knights), who would serve as aristocratic exemplars for the rest of the population. Rather, they are hedonistic, completely without shame, and totally unmindful of even the most basic etiquette (*tatakrama*).[44]

For all Mr. Merchant's troubles, he cannot cross the line between *sudagar* and *priyayi*; in the end, he is no more accepted by the *priyayi* than he was before. The only difference is that, whereas previously he was a merchant with a bit of money, now he is completely bankrupt. The author depicts merchant and *priyayi* as birds of a different feather, separate categories of people who have their own ways and travel in their own circles. It is significant, however, that, as a merchant, whom one would assume would place financial considerations above other concerns, Mr. Merchant is nonetheless willing to sacrifice all of his worldly possessions for the sake of the prestige that he would acquire should he succeed in being accepted into *priyayi* circles. His utter failure in this regard serves as a warning to anyone who would try to do the same. Still, this tells us something of the tremendous value placed on *priyayi* status. It also suggests that money and status were not equated—at least not in the eyes of the *priyayi*—and that even the most extravagant outlay of riches could not change the status of a merchant into that of a *priyayi*.

The poem points to the problem that wealth without power (power being a symbolic construct as much as a political one) creates in Javanese society. Wealth, of course, is what gives Mr. Merchant the illusion that he can break into *priyayi* circles, for the grandiose style

[43] "If you're a peasant" is a loose translation, for lack of a better English equivalent, of the Javanese *yèn ngindhung*, which means, roughly, "if you live in a house owned by another." Horne offers the following translation for *ngindhung*: "to occupy (without owning) a house one has erected—by permission—on someone's property." Elinor Clark Horne, *Javanese-English Dictionary* (New Haven: Yale University Press, 1974), p. 237. *Ngindhung*, then, suggests being propertyless and dependent.

[44] The "Suluk Mas Ngantèn" belongs to the genre of *piwulang* (poems of a didactic, often moralistic nature) literature. This was a common literary genre from the late eighteenth century through the nineteenth century. Soemarsaid Moertono writes that "*Piwulangs* were meant to fulfill specific contemporary needs, although of course they were based on traditional views and ideas. A careful reading of this genre of literature discloses the period's atmosphere of regret, of uncertainty and helplessness in the face of a reality too often unrelated to accepted standards of conduct." Soemarsaid Moertono, *State and Statecraft in Old Java: A Study of the Later Mataram Period, 16th to 19th Century* (Ithaca: Cornell University Modern Indonesia Project Monograph Series no. 43, 1981), pp. 46-47.

of *sudagar* weddings, "all gold and silks," was clearly modelled after the opulent displays of the aristocracy. In the *sudagar* community, it is the display of wealth that generates and reproduces status: where the wealth comes from is less important than the fact that it is *seen*. Among the *sudagar*, wealth itself is the source of authority and of the ability to command deference. It is the foundation upon which hierarchy is constructed. Without wealth, a merchant is nothing more than one of the *wong cilik*, the "little people."

In *priyayi* ideology, however, wealth signifies something else. It is a sign, but *not* the source, of authority, of power, of the right to expect deferential behavior and language. A show of wealth with power is magnificence; a show of wealth without power is mere garish display, particularly when the wealth originates with something as profoundly acultural as trade. The richest of traders is still a commoner. Mr. Merchant, then, is a nouveau riche (not even an especially well-heeled one, the poet tells us) among aristocrats, a source of entertainment for them. He and his fellow merchants can be ignored, and their wedding made a mockery of, because *sudagar* wealth does not stand for anything besides itself—power, rank, or authority, for instance. It is wealth without substance. Yet the *sudagar* must be ridiculed, it seems, precisely because of the threat that their money poses for *priyayi* ideology. The possibility that wealth can be translated to status challenges power, all the more so when that "power" itself is bestowed, and can be taken away just as easily, by the *real* power—the Dutch colonial authorities.

Firmly established by the early nineteenth century, if not earlier, the sharp conceptual division between *priyayi* and *sudagar* remained fixed throughout the remainder of the colonial era and beyond. I emphasize the word "conceptual" because, although this division did correspond in some cases to clearly demarcated social classes, the *perception* of difference often exceeded the social reality, as we shall see. "*Priyayi*" and "*sudagar*" were categories based on what sometimes amounted to little more than an illusion of difference.

Contested Hierarchies

The relationship between the merchant class and the *priyayi* in Solo was thus an ambivalent one. It was a relationship marked by mutual suspicion and condescension, but not infrequently tinged with jealousy. To the members of the nobility and colonial bureaucracy, the characteristics of the merchant class epitomized the qualities that they claimed to despise, Jayadiningrat's sarcastic portrayal of the *priyayi* notwithstanding: greediness, devotion to material rather than spiritual pursuits, and cultural boorishness. The *priyayi* saw themselves as the inheritors and protectors of a venerable cultural tradition that had been passed down from generation to generation, while the *sudagar*, in their eyes, were ostentatious bumpkins in fancy clothes and gaudy jewelry, with no taste, no culture, and no sense of proper etiquette. They were worse than peasants because they did not know their place, refusing to acknowledge the superior status of the *priyayi*. Moreover, as we have seen, their successes violated the ideological principle that wealth should emanate from the center of power. Coming to them through commercial activity rather than through power and service to the state, the wealth held by the merchants was illegitimate as far as the *priyayi* were concerned. It was, in short, wealth that refused to assimilate itself to the established hierarchies of the society.

The merchants were no less harsh in their judgments of the *priyayi* than the *priyayi* were of them. Criticisms that I heard in Laweyan about the nobility and civil servants (*pegawai negeri*), the modern-day *priyayi*, echoed complaints about the *priyayi* that had resounded for generations in the merchant community. The *priyayi* were accused of being lazy, decadent, corrupt, arrogant, and of being perpetually dependent on the good graces of their superiors in what was perceived as an endless chain of patronage and sychophancy. Members of the merchant class deliberately contrasted themselves with the *priyayi*, asserting their autonomy and taking pride in their willingness to work hard for a living, something that most *priyayi* were incapable of, they said. One entrepreneur I knew summed up this attitude rather bluntly: "People here [in Laweyan] aren't 'yes men' [she used the English term, even though she was speaking Indonesian]. We don't like to be told what to do. We have the spirit of traders, we work for ourselves. We don't like to receive wages from others. And we don't like to ass-kiss" (*ndak suka menjilat*, lit: "don't like to lick"; she stuck out her tongue to emphasize the point when she said this).

The contempt, mixed with envy, that the merchants held for the *priyayi* as a class was reflected in their responses to, and interactions with, local representatives of the Kraton and the colonial bureaucracy (and later, the postcolonial state). In the *sudagar* community wealth, not rank, was the key to status. Although the merchants were certain to act respectfully in personal encounters with the *priyayi*, they were privately scornful of those *priyayi* who had no wealth to show for their position. Writing in the 1920s about Kotagede, a town which, like Solo, had both a strong indigenous Javanese bourgeoisie and many *abdi dalem* (in this case, representatives of both the Yogyakarta Sultanate and the Sunanate of Solo), the colonial administrator H. J. van Mook remarked of the richer merchants and entrepreneurs that

> In them nothing is to be detected of the obsequiousness usual in the Principalities, for many of them are, on a lesser scale, what Rothschild was on a grand scale: the creditors of princes. They form a highly exclusive coterie which up to the present has held itself pretty much aloof from the activities of the recently created *kelurahans* [neighborhood or village administrative units].[45]

He also commented that

> The administrative officials [in Kotagede] have much less influence there than elsewhere, especially when they are not well-to-do. It is often difficult, and financially disastrous, for them to keep up with the wealthier inhabitants of Kuta Gede.[46]

Mitsuo Nakamura, confirming van Mook's findings, adds that "The majority of the wealthy merchants [in Kotagede] remained rather indifferent to the prestige deriving from the court."[47]

A number of Laweyan merchants whom I knew expressed sentiments that continued to reflect this attitude. Some were puzzled, even amused, at the notion that anyone would want to become an *abdi dalem* when the wages were so low. Of course, they recognized that people became *abdi dalem* because of the prestige associated with it, but obviously it was not a source of prestige or pride with which they could easily identify. Most saw service to the court as a rather foolish waste of time, time which could be better spent pursuing more remunerative activities. Serving the palace didn't pay, but it was work. And work, they believed strongly, should pay.

Examining the overt opinions and stereotypes of each group about the other brings into focus some of the ideological issues that divided them, but it does not reveal the discrepancies between ideology and practice, nor the underlying complexity of the relationship

---

[45] Van Mook, "Kuta Gede," p. 288.

[46] Ibid., p. 28

[47] Nakamura, *The Crescent Arises*, p. 53.

between the two groups. In order to better understand the nature of this relationship, it is helpful to look at the institution of marriage and how this served both to demarcate the differences and to obscure the commonalities between merchants and *priyayi* in Solo.

On the question of why there had been so few marriages between the *sudagar* families of Laweyan and Solo's nobility—for the wedding of wealth and noble status would seem to be a natural course of events—I received a number of opinions, each of which reflected a different source of tension between the two groups. Many merchants expressed doubt and even indignation when I suggested that it was the Kraton's decision not to allow marriages with Laweyan (cf. the reputed prohibition of marriage between the Kraton and Laweyan resulting from Pakubuwana II's experiences in the latter neighborhood) and not vice versa. Some insisted that, in fact, the opposite was the case: that the Laweyan *sudagar* wanted nothing less than to marry their children off to nobility. They pointed out that to marry into the royal family would likely mean bankruptcy for any merchant family, since the palace's demands for "contributions" would be unceasing (we need only refer to the "Suluk Mas Ngantèn" and Mr. Merchant's financial ruin to imagine this sort of scenario). Countering this, several *priyayi* argued that the *sudagar* would have been all too happy to have their children marry spouses with noble titles, but that the *priyayi* themselves found the merchants of Laweyan to be too concerned with matters of money to be acceptable as *bésan* (the parents-in-law of one's child).[48] They commented that many merchants would have counted themselves extremely lucky to have grandchildren with noble titles and a streak of "blue blood."

One batik merchant offered another opinion on why marriages between Laweyan men and women of the nobility had been so rare. She observed that in the past, almost all Laweyan women had earned a living as batik entrepreneurs and traders, but women of high nobility had rarely done anything productive besides cooking or making batik as a handicraft during their leisure time. "People in Laweyan probably thought that noblewomen wouldn't want to do the coarse (*kasar*) kinds of work that women here were used to doing," she suggested. Aristocratic ladies would not have been happy to do such work, she added, nor would their families have seen fit for them to do it.

The nobility looked askance at the involvement of women traders in the market, a place that they associated with things *kasar* and of low status: coarse language, lust for money, and too much unrestrained association between the sexes. As the appointed custodians of the *alus*, the refined, they declared it a place unsuited for their own women to work. A granddaughter of a former sunan remarked that in the old days, kings were forbidden to marry traders because of their reputation for being "loose." We can understand from this why, though it was not unusual for women of high rank to contribute substantially to the income of their families by crafting batik in their homes and selling it from hand to hand, it was unthinkable for them to trade their batik in the marketplace. Bu Kartika, whose father had been a Mangkunagaran regent (*bupati*) during the last decades of colonial rule, recalled how her aristocratic mother had quietly supplemented her father's income: "Even as a regent, my father didn't earn enough to support the family. He would turn his salary over to my mother, and say to her, 'Here—if this isn't enough, you'll just have to make do somehow.' So she made money by selling her batik. But she wouldn't sell it to just anyone, and

[48] *Bésan* is a convenient term for which English has no exact equivalent: it designates the relationship between two sets of parents whose children are married to each other. Thus, *bésanan* means "to be mutually related as parents-in-law." Since marriage in Java is seen as a union of families rather than of individuals, the relationship of *bésan* is an important one. The concept of *bésanan* puts the emphasis less on the relationship between husband and wife than on that between their two sets of families.

she *never* sold her batik in the market. There were prohibitions (*larangan*) on work for ladies of high status—the work they did had to be something that could be done at home, something that didn't stand out too much."

The different positions of women in these two classes of competing elites—the merchant class, in which women occupied pivotal economic and social roles outside the home, and the class of high-ranked nobility, in which women's productive activities were largely confined to the home—further symbolized the *alus/kasar* contrast and accentuated the social and ideological gaps between the two groups. If it was true that the nobility did not want their daughters engaging in "coarse" work, it was also the case that the merchant families of Laweyan had no use for women who would not work, because a work ethic for women was one of the most notable features of the community. As one woman merchant stated straightforwardly, "In Laweyan, the term *ndara* (a term of address used for someone of high rank) means someone who doesn't want to work."

Nor was the likelihood of Laweyan women marrying noblemen any greater: as I mentioned earlier in connection with the legend of Pakubuwana II's cool reception in Laweyan, *sudagar* women did not relish the thought of being dependent on aristocratic men. The most feared consequence of marrying a *priyayi* was being made a co-wife (*dimadu*), possibly one among several wives. Although polygyny was not unknown in the merchant community, it appears to have been less common than among the *priyayi*, perhaps because the typical *sudagar* man relied so heavily on his wife to manage the family business that he could not afford the possibility of incurring her wrath, or even the possibility of her demanding a divorce. Divorce was considered a preferable alternative by some women to being made a co-wife, but it was truly a dire prospect for a *sudagar* man of Solo, for it meant losing access to his wife's business skills and property.[49]

In the *sudagar* community, women's value was intimately linked to their economic productivity, which depended upon their ability and willingness to trade in the marketplace. Among the aristocracy, on the other hand, female value was tied much more to the domestic sphere, and to men's control over women's sexuality, fertility, and movement. Daughters were most valuable insofar as they could be used to forge politically expedient marriage alliances,[50] while wives were assigned the basic tasks of serving their husbands, reproducing their husbands' lines, and maintaining the household. The place of the noblewoman was in the home, her movement in public increasingly restricted the higher her father's or husband's rank.[51] The *pasar* (marketplace) represented the antithesis of the *dalem* (here in its double meaning of "home" and "an aristocratic residence"): it was a place where men could not control women.

---

[49] In her research on divorce practices in Java, Hisako Nakamura found that "sharing husband with another wife" (her translation of "*dimadu*"; this included the prospect of being made a co-wife as well as the fact of already having been made a co-wife) was recorded as the second most common cause of divorce in Kotagede from the years 1964-1971. The one reason given more commonly as the cause of divorce was "neglecting marital obligations" (on the part of either husband or wife). See Hisako Nakamura, *Divorce in Java: A Study of the Dissolution of Marriage among Javanese Muslims* (Yogyakarta: Gadjah Mada University Press, 1983).

[50] Cf. Carey and Houben, "Spirited Srikandhis."

[51] The best-known instance of female seclusion in Java is that of Radèn Ajeng Kartini (1879-1904), the daughter of a Jepara regent whose letters in Dutch were published under the title *Door Duisternis tot Licht* (Through darkness into light) seven years after her premature death at the age of twenty-five. Much has been made of the figure of Kartini, who attained the stature of a national heroine after Indonesian independence. An English translation of her letters was published under the title *Letters of a Javanese Princess*, translated by Agnes Louise Symmers, edited by Hildred Geertz (New York: Norton, 1964).

Between these two ends of the *priyayi-sudagar* spectrum, however, was a gray area in which the distinction was blurred. It was in fact quite common during the late colonial period for the wives of lower- and middle-ranked *priyayi* to support their families as batik entrepreneurs and merchants while their husbands worked in prestigious but low-paying jobs. This pattern was most pronounced in neighborhoods of Solo near the Kraton that had a sizable corps of court retainers: the Kauman, Kratonan, Pasar Kliwon, and Kemlayan; Keprabon was another such neighborhood, but associated with the Mankunagaran palace instead of the Sunanate. In the Kauman, for instance, which was the religious hub of the city and site of the Great Mosque (Mesjid Agung) of the Sunanate, many women supported their households through the batik trade while their husbands served as Islamic officials (*penghulu*) at the Kraton or as religious teachers in the community.[52] As Shiraishi comments, ". . . in central parts of the city such as Kauman there emerged no independent class of native bourgeoisie, even though there were numerous batik workshops and many batik entrepreneurs amassed wealth. In Marco Kartodikromo's words, batik entrepreneurs in this area were 'still in the family' with sunan's officials."[53]

From a practical standpoint, not many *priyayi* men could afford the luxury of keeping their wives at home.[54] In the case of those who were polygamous, small salaries had to be stretched even further to meet the needs of several wives and their children. Moreover, wealth contributed importantly to relative status: even for the *priyayi*, there was no honor to be gained in living on a pittance. A man of rank needed the material accoutrements of rank to support his claims to status. Thus, although *priyayi* ideology devalued trade, *priyayi* practice was not always in line with ideology. Because a family's status was defined much more by the social position of the husband than of the wife (which made it possible, for instance, for the sunan to marry a commoner woman and still sire royal children), the wife of a *priyayi* could engage in trade without her family being "demoted" from *priyayi* to *sudagar* status as a result. This was, of course, provided that neither her rank by birth nor her husband's rank was so high as to make trade out of the question.

Not all fields of trade were, however, equally acceptable. It would have been unseemly for the wife of a *priyayi* to peddle fruit, for example, or to open up a roadside foodstall at night. Since commodities, too, were evaluated hierarchically, it is no accident that the batik business was one of the few areas of trade open to *priyayi* women.[55] Batik cloth, especially that which is crafted by hand, is considered an *alus* object through its connections to court culture (though there are relative standards of *alus* and *kasar*, refined and coarse, by which

---

52 The practice of seclusion for women was strikingly absent even in the Kauman, among the most orthodox Javanese Muslims of the city (I stress *Javanese* Muslims because seclusion of women had not been uncommon in Solo's Arab community). Even relatively long-distance trading was not unusual for Kauman women, and trading textiles in the marketplace was considered quite respectable.

53 Shiraishi, *An Age in Motion*, p. 25; Mas Marco Kartodikromo, *Student Hidjo* (Semarang: N. V. Boekhandel en Drukkerij, Masman & Stroink, 1919), p. 6. A similar pattern existed in Yogyakarta, where batik families of the Kauman were often in service to the Sultanate as well. Mitsuo Nakamura, for instance, notes that Kyai Haji Ahmad Dahlan (1868-1923), the founder of the Islamic reformist organization Muhammadiyah, was both an Islamic official of the Yogyakarta Sultanate (for which he received a meager salary) and a batik merchant (*The Crescent Arises*, p. 46). Although Nakamura does not mention Ahmad Dahlan's wife's role in the business, women were as heavily involved in the batik trade in Yogyakarta as they were in Solo.

54 This was probably even more the case after the abolition of the appanage system in the first two decades of this century. The substitution of cash salaries for appanages meant that most officials had much less access to wealth than before.

55 Another object that was "respectable" for high-status women to trade was jewelry (especially gold and precious stones), which, like batik, had associations with court culture.

individual pieces of batik are judged). One might say that the commodity itself brings an aura of respectability to the field of trade that surrounds it. Women of the highest rank were expected to make batik at home; this was a sign of cultivation and a refined leisure-time activity.[56] The wife of a regent, as we have already seen, could unobtrusively sell the batik cloth she made to friends and acquaintances without being subject to criticism; for a "gift" of batik to be reciprocated with a "gift" of money was perfectly in keeping with standards of propriety. The shift, from making one's own batik and selling it to buying and selling other people's batik, was incremental; it did not require a great conceptual leap. Batik was still *alus*, even if trade was not. The batik business can therefore be seen as a nexus between *alus* and *kasar*, as culturally valued, *alus* objects are transacted in the *kasar* sphere of the market.

In another union of *alus* and *kasar*, many families of the Kauman and certain other neighborhoods of Solo were neither "purely" *priyayi* nor "purely" *sudagar*—they were hybrids. Here, *priyayi* and merchant lived under one roof as husband and wife. Some had ties of blood to the Kraton, as indicated by noble titles like Radèn Mas among the men or Radèn Ayu among the women. Batik workers and servants in such households addressed their employers deferentially as "Dèn" (from *radèn*) or "Ndara" (from *bendara*, master or mistress) instead of "Mbok Mas," the term of address commonly used in Laweyan for female employers without rank. This suggests that the boundary between priyayi and *sudagar* was not as impermeable as it seemed: it was an imagined boundary that could be crossed under numerous circumstances. Even inside the palaces of Central Java, there was a long history of women managing court finances and engaging in certain types of trade.[57] Peter Carey and Vincent Houben, for example, remark that in the early nineteenth century, members of the Sultan of Yogyakarta's elite corps of women soldiers (*prajurit èstri*) were involved in "frenetic trade in gold and precious stones between Yogya[karta], Kutagede, Surakarta and the north coast."[58] The Laweyan stereotype that women of the nobility "would not work," then, was not particularly accurate, for even those women who would have found selling batik in the marketplace unacceptable often earned money through other kinds of activities.

Being labelled as "*priyayi*" or "*sudagar*" was not solely a matter of occupation, since a woman could be a full-time merchant and still be identified as *priyayi* by association with her *priyayi* husband. It was *his* social standing that fixed the family's identity more or less irrevocably as *priyayi* or *sudagar*. Those who would posit a clear cultural division between merchant and *priyayi*, then, have not taken into account the actual overlap that existed between the two categories, made possible by the discordance between ideology and practice, and by the gendered division of symbolic labor in the household that enables men and women to produce status for their families in very different ways. In the courts, as in the wider society, women, unlike men, could handle money without loss of prestige. Hence, in the early nineteenth century it was usual for one of the high-ranked ladies of the Kraton to manage the household expenses and to look after all the contents of the inner court, including the sunan's gold and jewelry. "All this stood in marked contrast," write Carey and Houben, "to what was expected from the male members of the court, both relations of the ruler and senior officials, who were not supposed to soil their hands with business ven-

[56] See J. S. Furnivall, "The Weaving and Batik Industries in Java, with Notes on Hat Making and Soap Boiling," *The Asiatic Review*, 32 (110) (1936): 365-76.

[57] Nancy Florida, personal communication; Carey and Houben, "Spirited Srikandhis."

[58] Carey and Houben, "Spirited Srikandhis," p. 23; see Kumar, "Javanese Court Society," on the late eighteenth-century diary of a woman soldier in Solo.

tures."[59] The term "*sudagar*" did not only signify "merchant"—as a social and conceptual category, it also implied "those who are removed from the hierarchies of court and state." A peripheral neighborhood on the outskirts of town, Laweyan, unlike the Kauman, was the apotheosis of a *sudagar* community, for it identified itself precisely in opposition to the Kraton. Virtually none of its residents had any claims to *priyayi* status. Laweyan's merchants sought to create their own independent hierarchies based on wealth instead of title. A *bécak* (pedicab) driver, looking around at the imposing homes that dominated the neighborhood, put it most succinctly: "This is a place of royalty. But the rulers are all women. None of the men have any rank."

Even for Laweyan, however, the contrast between merchant and *priyayi* should not be overdrawn. Several of the most staunchly anti-Kraton merchants had grandfathers and great-grandfathers who had served the Kraton as *abdi dalem*. Furthermore, the wealthier and more established the *sudagar* became, the more they seemed to emulate the *priyayi* in certain aspects of their lifestyles, while continuing to voice their contempt for *priyayi* values. This was apparent, for instance, in their sharply asymmetrical relations with their employees; like the *abdi dalem* at court, the servants and batik workers of Laweyan employers were expected to speak to them in high Javanese and be answered in low Javanese, to come at their beck and call, and, in some cases, to kneel and avert their eyes when they served or spoke to them. Although most *sudagar* found the notion of serving others distasteful, this did not mean that they disliked having others serve them, or that they were any more egalitarian than the *priyayi* in their outlook.

The apparent "indifference" of the *sudagar* toward the *priyayi* frequently gave way to a more active rivalry, through displays of wealth reminiscent of those of the royalty, which few lower-ranked *priyayi* could match. *Sudagar* weddings and other ritual celebrations were extravagant exhibitions modelled after court ceremonial. No doubt the impressive diamond ornaments worn by women merchants and entrepreneurs and the bejewelled krisses sported by their husbands, visible indicators of success in business, were a constant, irritating reminder to the nobility that jewels did not necessarily go hand-in-hand with blue blood. This irritation, in fact, is still in evidence today. A woman from a high-born Mangkunagaran family whom I became acquainted with, herself involved in the batik business on a small scale, wrinkled her nose in distaste as she recalled the styles worn by Laweyan women in the past: "*We* never wore *selèndang* (a long scarf worn over one shoulder), because that was what all those traders in Laweyan wore. And then, they always went around showing off those big diamond earrings of theirs. . . ." Even the spirits of the dead could be annoyed by a display of jewelry, as I discovered at the Kotagede cemetery, where visitors not of royal rank were asked to remove their jewelry in the presence of the royal tombs.

What have often been construed as markedly different cultural values dividing merchant and *priyayi* must be understood instead as an inversion or transmutation of values. The central focus of life in Laweyan, like elsewhere in Solo, was the attainment of status within the hierarchical structures that underlie Javanese society. The crucial distinction was that in Laweyan, the foundation of hierarchy was money, and status was based almost entirely on the acquisition and conspicuous expenditure of wealth. Here, the "aristocracy" consisted of those who had the most wealth—and especially, those who could hold onto their wealth from generation to generation. If this basis for acquiring status was more flexible than one based on rank, it was also more tenuous, for even the richest of merchant families could not be assured of everlasting prosperity. Everyone in the neighborhood knew

59 Carey and Houben, "Spirited Srikandhis," p. 23.

families that had fallen from great wealth to near destitution from one generation to the next, sometimes even within the same generation. The higher the status a *sudagar* family attained, the more it became obsessed with maintaining and reproducing that status. When the Sapardis crawled on their knees in Kotagede to invoke blessings of good fortune and good profits from the ancestral spirits of Java's royalty, it was a sign of their willingness to enter into the dominant hierarchies of Javanese society, at least temporarily, in order to secure an exalted place in the hierarchies of their own, more marginal, sector of society.

Javanese Mysticism and Art: A Case of Iconography and Healing

Astri Wright

Some contemporary artists in Indonesia, specifically in Central Java, consider making and understanding art a part of their spiritual practices. Some strive to know the iconography of monuments of the past, not as archaeologists, but in order to understand the mystical messages embodied there. At the same time many of these artists are developing a personal, modern visual language of their own. Their spiritual orientation causes them to see mythology and monuments as living texts relevant to the choices contemporary Indonesians make in their daily lives. These spiritual views in turn influence the artists' perception of the creative process and the self in relation to this process. I will be discussing below an instance in which a mystically inclined Javanese painter looked to classical Hindu-Javanese art and to the *wayang* tradition as sources of healing. Then I will briefly discuss his work.

Aspects of Javanese mysticism, variously called *kebatinan* (mysticism, spiritualism) or *kejawen* (Javanism), at times glossed as "Javanese science" or "philosophy," have been studied by Dutch and other Western scholars since the colonial era.[1] *Kebatinan*—"all the beliefs that concern potency and the imperceptible world"[2]—has also been the subject of Javanese and Indonesian-language studies, the latter especially in the last two decades.[3] Because those who study and practice *kebatinan* lack formal organizations *kebatinan* is seen as poten-

This article is based on research carried out in Java, primarily Yogyakarta, Jakarta, and Bandung between August 1987 and February 1989. I am grateful to Stanley J. O'Connor, Umar Kayam, Mary-Ann Lutzker, Gigi Weix, Suzanne Brenner, and Mike Bosler for valuable comments on this essay when it was first presented as a paper in March 1991.

[1] Studies such as Douwe Adolf Rinkes, *Abdoerraoef van Singkel: Bijdrage tot de kennis van de mystiek op Sumatra en Java* (Heerenveen: Hepkema, 1909), and Louis A. Bachler, *Gadadara inggih Rama Kresna: kepetik saking serat-serat ingkang kawedalaken dateng* (Jakarta: Lodji, 1921), are examples of biographical and literary approaches to indigenous mysticism. See the sociological discussion of mysticism and mystical sects, with interesting passages of informants explaining their history and personal experiences, in Clifford Geertz, *The Religion of Java* (Chicago: University of Chicago Press, 1960), p. 309–52. Other sources on the subject will be found in the footnotes below.

[2] Ward Keeler, *Javanese Shadow Plays, Javanese Selves* (Princeton: Princeton University Press, 1987), p. 109.

[3] For the sake of simplicity, and because an in-depth discussion of the complexities of the subject is not my aim here, I will continue to use the term *kebatinan*.

tially uncontrollable and has become a subject of scrutiny for the Indonesian government.[4] It has been argued that *kebatinan* involves ideas and practices that carry back to pre-Indic influence. Stange writes that mosques, like the Hindu-Buddhist temples before them, "were erected on a landscape already profoundly infused with spiritual tradition."[5] Today *kebatinan* is a syncretic mix of Hindu-Buddhist, Islamic, and indigenous animist beliefs and practices, based on a belief in "the essential oneness of all existence."[6] It is practiced both by individuals and in groups and may involve meditation, ascetic exercises, fasting, study, and discussion—all directed towards embracing life in all its minute details as a total religious experience.

Like any "living thing," *kebatinan* is practiced in many different ways by different groups, who tie their specific approach to person-centered histories or genealogies—in some cases leading right back to Mohammed.[7] These groups center on a *guru*, who commands the loyalty of followers numbering anything from a few individuals to thousands of people on a regional, national, and even international basis.[8] Although these groups vary in practice and use of terminology, the essential content of their teachings is similar. Far from being a strictly codified, dogmatic belief system, *kebatinan*, as do many other cultural creations of Java, illustrates the idea of syncretism—the combining of elements from different religions or cultures which, from an external, logical perspective, appear to contradict each other.

In the practice of *kebatinan*, Geertz writes, "the final appeal is always to (emotional) experience which carries its own meaning. God, forms of worship, and views of the nature of man, are always validated on these grounds—never on grounds of logic or essential rationality, ... [or] social consequences . . ." It is always "the quality of experience" itself which validates one's spiritual insights.[9]

During both meditation and question-and-answer sessions with the *guru*, it is thought necessary to make the transition from "thought-centered" to "feeling-centered" awareness, so that one can "experience rather than simply understand what is meant"—only in this way does one retain the insight, without it just going "right through one."[10]

Life is seen as a mystical journey, proceeding in four stages from the outer to the inner realms. Rather than being a passive victim of fate, man has the power to direct his own spiritual progress.[11] The first stage in the mystical journey consists in correct living, according to

---

[4] In 1978 a separate branch of the Ministry of Religious Affairs was established called the Directorate of Local Beliefs, under the Directorate General of Culture, which is under the Department of Education and Culture; see Haryati Soebadio, *Cultural Policy in Indonesia* (Paris: Unesco, Studies and Documents on Cultural Policy, 1985), p. 21.

[5] Paul Stange, "The Sumarah movement in Javanese mysticism" (Ph.D. Dissertation, University of Wisconsin, Madison, 1980), p. 33.

[6] Geertz, *Religion of Java*, p. 20.

[7] Ibid., p. 331.

[8] For example, the headquarters of Subud, one of the biggest groups, is in London. In the Jakarta *asrama*, numerous foreigners reside on a semi- or permanent basis. There have been several studies of Sumarah, another large group counting many members internationally. See, for example, Paul D. Stange, *Sumarah, Javanese Mysticism in the Revolutionary Period* (Madison: University of Wisconsin Press, 1975).

[9] Geertz, *Religion of Java*, p. 318.

[10] Paul Stange, "The Logic of Rasa in Java," *Indonesia* 38 (October 1984): 113–34; p. 119.

[11] Niels Mulder, *Mysticism and Everyday Life in Contemporary Java: Cultural Persistence and Change* (Singapore: Singapore University Press, 1978), p. 15.

social and religious etiquette and laws. At this stage, man is still living in his outer aspects.[12] The second stage constitutes the first step towards a fuller inner life: this stage implies perfecting and reflecting upon behavior and ethics in the outer world. In the third stage of the mystical journey, man begins to confront truth; at this point the differences between various forms of religious ritual and expressions appear meaningless. Finally at the fourth stage, the goal of complete insight and "eternal unity between Master and servant" is reached.[13]

Meditation is considered an important way to gain insight and strength. It may involve getting in touch with the spirits of ancestors or other powerful beings. In one form of meditation, one's mind-spirit is guided step by step through the stages outlined above, duplicating the mystical journey. The first step, removing oneself from the outer world, is initiated by the act of withdrawing into silence to meditate. A student of meditation described the process like this:

> The first part [of the meditation] represents the Micro-level; the next represents the Macro-level; the third is the Cosmic/Universal. To grasp this, it is easier for me to think in terms of first concentrating on and understanding the Self, then the world and all of nature around the Self, then finally the Universal Principle itself. The specific symbols and colors that appear during meditation have different meanings depending upon in which of the three stages they occur.[14]

A Case of Art and Healing

A Hindu-Javanese temple, *wayang* puppets, Javanese mysticism, and contemporary painting all connected with each other in an interesting way during my fieldwork in Indonesia. Jono, a painter who practiced *kebatinan*,[15] had been asked to meditate on the health of someone just diagnosed by one of Yogyakarta's most famous Western-trained medical doctors as suffering from a "fist-size, probably malignant tumor, requiring immediate operation."[16]

Meditating around midnight, after first purifying the room with holy water, incense, and flowers bought at the market the same morning, Jono had a vision which consisted of two images. The first was a *wayang* shadow-puppet figure passing across the sky, heading South. The sky in front of the figure was black and behind it, white. Then the light turned, the sky became green, and the shape of a *candi* emerged—a temple consisting of three towers, the central one taller than the two which flanked it.

---

[12] Mystical practices have often intersected with politics in Indonesian history, as in the faith in the invulnerability rendered by the use of spells and the wearing of amulets and allegiance to certain spiritual leaders. In the early 1970s, *malam tirakatan* (night of meditation) preceded important rallies or demonstrations during student protest movements; see Rendra, *The Struggle of the Naga Tribe*, translated and introduced by Max Lane (St. Lucia: University of Queensland Press, 1979) p. 51, translator's note 65.

[13] Ibid., pp. 22–23.

[14] From my fieldnotes.

[15] The painter, his artist-partner, and the patient requested anonymity and therefore fictional names have been used. Both the artist partner and the patient were foreign women familiar with Javanese culture. Clearly the presence of foreigners in the present story may have influenced interactions in ways that an all-Javanese cast would not have—such is the nature of field-work.

[16] From interview with the painter's artist-partner, Yogyakarta, November 1987.

The role of the visionary does not necessarily include elaborating on his visions.[17] This meditation vision was at first described only briefly to the patient, without further explication. Appropriate to such interactions in Java, the patient received it gratefully, without comment, and the small party lapsed into silence. In my own experience this silence rarely seemed comfortable in Java. It was as if no-one knows what to say and fears saying something inappropriate. Rules of etiquette prevent spontaneity from lightening the situation.[18]

Following this period of strained silence, then, the patient timidly started to question the painter about the meaning of the images through a mutual friend present, a woman who had been practicing both art and meditation with him for several years. According to Javanese etiquette, which prohibits direct and intense questioning of a person to whom you owe respect, this woman played the role of intermediary and interpreter.[19]

At first Jono answered, eyes averted, that the meaning of the vision was not entirely clear to him. While he continued to sit immobile, gaze withdrawn, his helper explained that he was also reticent because he did not want to hurt the patient's feelings by communicating too directly that she would have to consider rearranging the priorities of her life.[20]

Was the *wayang* figure a specific one, a recognizable character? Jono said that it was not: there had been no details with which to identify it. It was a *wayang* figure in the general sense. After a long time of circling around the issue it became clear that what was important were the black and white areas in the sky. In Javanese mysticism, Jono said, black symbolizes one's worldly (self-serving material and physical) desires (*nafsu*), while white symbolizes one's objective context (*kenyataan*). The two colors together symbolize the direction one's outer and inner life takes, when one's choices are in harmony with one's personality and the outer circumstances of one's life.

The problem with the image in the vision was that the black was in front of the white, leading it, rather than the other way around. This order indicated that the patient's ideals led her more strongly than did a realistic evaluation of her concrete life-situation. This tendency had led to a spiritual imbalance which could lead not only to further spiritual sickness but also to physical disease.

---

17 There are many types of visionaries in Indonesia, from the ordinary man or woman who claims some psychic abilities, to the village *dukun*, and the *guru*, traditionally with ties to the courts. The visionaries rely more on their own experience with meditation, asceticism, and visions than on any written body of doctrine. Since most of the literature (Mangkunegara, Mulder, Geertz, Stange) deals more with general aspects of various *kebatinan* groups than with instances of specific meditations or visions, complete with symbolic interpretations, I do not know how generally acceptable the "reading" given by the painter here would be.

18 The atmosphere experienced by the author contrasts to that described by Mulder as typical during *latihan*—spiritual exercise sessions. Mulder, *Mysticism and Everyday Life*, pp. 29–30. This may be due to the fact that the incident at which I was present was not a regular *latihan* session, but a private interview, and the fact that the patient was not one of the regular students/followers of the painter, who had not yet established himself as a *guru* and only practiced informally. For a discussion of rules of language and etiquette governing Javanese interaction, see Ward Keeler, *Javanese: A Cultural Approach* (Athens: Ohio University Center for International Studies, 1984), p. xxvii–xxiv, and the notes to each lesson; James Siegel, *Solo in the New Order* (Princeton: Princeton University Press, 1986), pp. 15–33. For a vivid description of two similar encounters, see Mulder, *Mysticism and Everyday Life*, p. 66.

19 Maya, the painter's partner in the small *batik* business they had established in part of the family household, is an American woman who had been studying meditation and Javanese mysticism with Jono and his father for several years.

20 I want to point out that the pattern of deference to the *guru* figure would not have been qualitatively different if the patient had been a male.

Next, the image of the *candi*. The painter said that this was a picture of the structure of the patient's personality: she was basically oriented towards god. That was one image to which he felt he could give a definite interpretation. Furthermore, the temple was clearly Hindu, Hinduism being a religion "based on the knowledge and insight we get from nature—not like Middle Eastern or Western religions which are based on laws." The patient was told that the temple-image was like the Prambanan temple near Yogyakarta, and that indeed she should go there and study it in order to find a functional model for her life. The patient was told to study the reliefs, to find out what they symbolize and what message there might be in them for her.

"The *wayang* image was heading in the southern direction," Jono said to the patient. "Find out what the southern side of Prambanan symbolizes. South is the direction of the worldly life. You should find a way to harmonize your worldly orientation with your personality (*kepribadian*), which is oriented towards god."

"But you don't have to worry about the tumor itself," Jono said in conclusion: "It is not fatal—it is only a signal, a warning. But if you don't take care of the problem and correct the imbalance, after a long time with more signs, there could be more serious effects. For now you need not worry about your immediate health: the green light in the image is the color of god. If it had been red, that would have been a sign of danger."

The *Wayang* Figure

To interpret the *wayang* figure in the vision, we must look briefly at what *wayang* means in the context of Javanese culture. *Wayang* means "shadow" and is used to denote dramatic performances of various kinds, with either human or puppet actors. On its own, the word stands either for a shadow play performance or for a *wayang* puppet, the latter being the most relevant in our context. The *wayang* shadow puppet performance complex, through which stories from the Hindu and various Javanese folk-epics have been made familiar to the Javanese for centuries, can be seen as the most elaborate and popular visual expression of *kebatinan*.[21]

The history of this art form is unclear. It may have originated in India, where "shadow play" is referred to in the Pali canon of the first century B.C.E.[22] In Java, *wayang* is first mentioned in an inscription found at Prambanan, issued by King Balitung in 907 C.E., where mention is also made of both the *Mahabharata* and the *Ramayana*. This inscription documents that the fascination with the Hindu epics in Javanese art, still apparent in the ongoing tradition of *wayang*, has survived for at least eleven hundred years. It is interesting to note the possibility that the historical prototypes for both the image of the temple and the *wayang* figure in the painter's meditation-vision date from the same historically distant era, which Javanese today see as a golden age, spiritually, culturally, and politically.

---

21 "In the *wayang* lies hidden the secret Javanese knowledge concerning the deepest significance of life . . ." wrote Mangkunegara VII of Surakarta. See his essay *On the Wayang Kulit (Purwa) and its Symbolic and Mystical Elements* trans. Claire Holt (Ithaca: Cornell University Southeast Asia Program, 1957), p. 1. One of Mangkunegara's motivations for writing about the *wayang*, he said, was to teach both foreigners and Javanese about a part of the traditional culture in the face of rapid change. The ways in which *wayang* performances and meaning have been changing in the modern era is an important area of investigation which I will not touch upon here, as I am concerned with *wayang* in its broadest sense.

22 Claire Holt, *Art in Indonesia* (Ithaca: Cornell University Press, 1967), p. 128–29. The earliest mention of shadow puppet plays in China is during the Sung dynasty, when in the eleventhth century, stories from the Three Kingdoms were performed. The earliest mention of Thai shadow puppet plays is in 1458; ibid., p. 130.

The *wayang*—as art-form, philosophy, and frame of reference—still has a variety of functions in Javanese culture: it is placed in the group of "refined" art forms along with *batik*, *gamelan* music, the making of *keris* daggers, court-dances, and court-poetry.[23] Furthermore, it is still, although in changing form, one of the most popular types of village entertainment.[24] A *wayang* performance is believed to have the power to protect, cure, and exorcise. It also lends to Javanese a vocabulary for the classification of personality and provides cosmic analogies to characters and events within the realm of earthly politics.[25] *Wayang* represents both the philosophical and the spiritual-magical aspects of *kebatinan*. In Central Java, the most frequently used source for *wayang* performances, at least during the hundred years or so of Dutch and Javanese writing about *wayang*, has been the *Mahabharata*, in which the five Pandawa brothers are pitted against their large group of cousins, the Korawa. The world is divided into two, represented by Pandawa (right) and Korawa (left); the conniving, competing, and final fullscale war between the two, is frequently simplified into a battle between "good" and "bad." At its most sophisticated level, however, *wayang* expresses the full range of thought of Javanese mysticism, in which god is seen in everything. According to this view, apparent dualities played out in the stories are only resolved temporarily; the perspective of ultimate reality or truth is amoral and timeless and cannot be fathomed by men.[26]

Every Javanese, except perhaps some members of the urban generation under thirty years old for whom TV and movies have largely replaced *wayang*, recognizes the figures of Arjuna, Bhima, Kreshna, Durna, and others, not to speak of the beloved figures of Semar and the clown-retainers—Javanese additions to the Indian epic. Everyone recognizes Srikandhi as the beautiful but somewhat too active and courageous female archer, second wife of Arjuna—another Javanization of the original *Mahabharata*.[27] Javanese discourse is

---

[23] Geertz, *Religion of Java*, p. 261; Mulder, *Mysticism and Everyday Life*, p. 81.

[24] James Siegel attests to the fact that *wayang* continues to be an important source of imagery in Java.

[25] B. R. O'G. Anderson, *Mythology and the Tolerance of the Javanese* (Ithaca, N.Y.: Cornell Modern Indonesia Project, 1965; 4th printing 1982); G. J. Resink, "From the Old *Mahabharata* to the New *Ramayana* Order," in *Bijdragen van het Koninklijk Instituut voor Taal-, Land- en Volkenkunde* 131 (1975): 214–35. See also Mulder, *Mysticism and Everyday Life*, p. 32 for stories of how Sukarno used *wayang* for his political ends, and in turn was almost undone by the power of one of the stories which, according to the Javanese view, turned on him. See Willard A. Hanna, *The Magical-Mystical Syndrome in the Indonesian Mentality*, Southeast Asia Series, Vol.XV, nos. 5–9, for a discussion of how both Sukarno and Suharto have used *dukun* for advice and guidance and legitimation of their power, with sketches of some of the central mystics involved.

[26] Geertz, *Religion of Java*, p. 270. On the notion of paired opposites, see below. Here I would just like to point out how the lack of simplistically opposed values is illustrated in the way in which qualities of nobility, loyalty, and divine insight are also associated with characters fighting on the Korawa side. Furthermore, the opposition of "right" and "left" refers to the *dalang*'s perspective, whereas the audience on the other side of the screen sees the inversion of this. Here lie intriguing possibilities for interpretations relating to esoteric knowledge, social hierarchy, and gender which must be pursued elsewhere.

[27] Not having read any literature concerning the specifics of these changes of the original text in the course of Javanization, I was surprised, while traveling to Ajanta in central India with a Brahmin university rector in the summer of 1988, to be told that Srikandhi—a female figure in Javanese *wayang*—is a male in the Indian version of the *Mahabharata*: prince Sikhandi [sic] is the reincarnation of Amba, daughter of the king of Kási, whose revenge for failure in love can only be wreaked on Bhisma in a later lifetime if she is reborn a man. With my self-appointed brahmin teacher I tried to pursue a discussion of the fascinating process of cultural assimilation and native psychology that must lie behind this kind of rewriting, but he was so shocked and, it seemed, disgusted at this bastardization of the text that he would not discuss it further. (For a synopsis of the Indian version, see Narasimhan, *The Mahabharata* [New York and London: Columbia University Press, 1965], p. xvi).

To further convolute the question of Srikandhi, Benedict Anderson related the following: When he himself asked about this difference between the Indian and the Indonesian versions in the mid-1960s, Mas Purnadi, pro-

filled with references to *wayang* figures and their characters, likening people to this one or that one, or choosing one as a model to emulate. Questions concerning a person's favorite *wayang* figure are not answered lightly, yet every major person in Indonesian cultural or political life does seem to have a favorite.

Given the specific characteristics of the individual *wayang* figures, identified by differences in facial expression, bodily proportions, bearing of the head, as well as by details of clothing, jewelry, and hairstyle, how should one read a *wayang* figure, in the generic sense, such as the one seen in the painter's vision?

In its most generic sense, a Javanese *wayang* figure, with its high degree of stylized reference to the human body, is an image or shadow of that aspect of a human being which is itself immaterial; thus the projection of its shadow on the screen by the use of light, may be seen as the shadow of a shadow.[28] This two-steps-remove from any notion of realistic portrayal, in itself indicates that a *wayang* figure represents something invisible to the physical eye, which merely records the optical illusions of which the material world, in *kebatinan* philosophy, is thought to consist. The *wayang* figure represents that part of man which, though invisible, is not illusory, but real: the soul or spirit (*batin*). And since *batin* is also that part of man which is divine, its "form" (visualized as a fluttering shadow) is simultaneously an image of the gods. Thus the *wayang* figure links man directly to the divine principle.

In contrast to a specific *wayang* character, the generic *wayang* figure calls to mind *all* the battles, struggles, victories, and losses, in the realms of love and of power, experienced by the numerous characters in the Indian epics. Gathering all these references into a single symbolic figure, the *wayang* comes to represent a perception of the self which is not only imbued with infinite potential but also embodies a duality: it is a self in which desires and illusions war with the "real"; a self torn between that which is *not* universal and divine in every human being and that which *is*.

This duality fits in with other paired opposites in the system of *kebatinan* thought. These opposites—ultimately, at the deepest levels of mystical insight, seen as connected and identical—are, when translated into values as they operate in the material world, nonetheless ranked hierarchically; a Javanese expression of how all things are equal, but how (in practice) "some are more equal than others."[29] Among such opposites may be found, aside from "outward, corporeal aspect < inner aspect" (*lahir < batin*), also such pairs as "microcosmos < cosmos" (*Jagad cilik < Jagad gede*); "material reality < ultimate reality" (*realitas < kenyataan*); "rational understanding < intuitive insight" (*ratio < rasa*); "coarse < refined" (*kasar < halus*).[30]

---

fessor at the Law Faculty at University of Indonesia and son of Purbatjaraka, "laughed and said that of course people in the kraton knew quite well that Srikandhi was a man, a man who liked to dress up as a woman, and with whom Arjuna had a homosexual relationship—'That's why Srikandhi is the only woman in *wayang* who doesn't have any children, heh-heh!'" But this, Mas Purnadi said, would be difficult for the people to understand or deal with, so the popular *wayang* treats 'him' as an ordinary woman." Personal communication with Benedict Anderson, August 1990.

[28] Holt, *Art in Indonesia*, p. 123.

[29] This contrasts to the ideal model of binary opposites, as illustrated in the Taoist symbol of yin and yang. It may also contrast to an originally Hindu ideal of the unity of equal pairs, as illustrated in the *lingga-yoni* symbol. Wendy Doniger O'Flaherty discusses the bias towards the male aspect, and all those that are grouped with it; see *Women, Androgynes and Other Mythical Beasts* (Chicago: University of Chicago Press, 1980).

[30] Mulder, *Mysticism and Everyday Life*, pp. 13–18. Such binary opposites are usually in the literature placed on either side of a colon (:). More attention needs to be paid to the meaning of this third factor in what is described as systems of dualities, which indicates the nature of the relationship between them. It is interesting to note that

In this system of unequal complementary opposites, it appears from the horizontal perspective of a single lifetime that some men are inferior to others. This inequality is mirrored in the social hierarchy, which is based on both birth and differing abilities, the two being ultimately connected.[31] In the same way, as one man appears inferior to another, all men appear inferior to the gods. However, the idea that the lesser of the pairs shadows the greater is an idea imbued with potential power. Man may be an imperfect image; he is nonetheless an image of god, and his personal battles are shadows of universal ones. Thus the tensions played out between the Korawa and the Pandawa may be seen as an allegory of the struggles of a single human being between his earthly, physical, and material desires and his longing for spiritual development—between the self and the soul.

The image of a generic *wayang* figure traveling across the sky comes to mean the self on its mystical journey through the world of material illusions and inequalities, in search of unification with the divine. In the vision, the *wayang* figure was led by its ideals, reluctantly trailing the circumstantial realities of its life. The image of a soul in imbalance, it was trapped in a physical body now growing tumors from the burden of skewed perception and misdirected action. The idea that each person's way to god must be suited to his/her personality and outer life-circumstances, learning to live in harmony with both their inherent challenges and limitations, is what the image is conveying to the patient.

Seeking at the Temple

As background to the second part of the meditation-vision—the image of the *candi*—we note that the building of Javanese *candi* in stone probably dates to the beginning of the eighth century.[32] The *candi* are believed to have been erected to commemorate and possibly to hold the ashes of deceased royalty, deposited in a casket under a statue of the dead king or queen depicted in the form of a Hindu or Buddhist deity.[33] As the two religions coexisted in Central Java from the eighth century on, each inspired uniquely Javanese architectural and sculptural styles and iconographies in numerous temple structures throughout Central and East Java.

The structure of the *candi* as a whole was understood to symbolize Mahameru, the Cosmic Mountain. Its base (*bhurloka*) represented the sphere of mortals, the temple-body (*bhuvarloka*) the sphere of the purified, and the superstructure (*svarloka*) the sphere of the gods.[34]

These temples served as focal points for the rituals of the new religions, imported with their highly developed cosmologies, fully visualized in architectural and iconographical detail. The temples also provided focus for the cult of kings, as represented by the idealized

---

the lesser of these pairs often are named with Western loan-words. It makes one wonder what words were originally used in texts or by *guru* to denote these qualities and how their meanings and relative status have subsequently been changed.

31 Ibid., p. 16.

32 According to Dumarcay, there were probably wooden *candi* several centuries earlier, as the fifth century inscription of King Purnavarman of Taruma (near Jakarta) demonstrates; Jacques Dumarcay, *The Temples of Java* (Oxford: Oxford University Press, 1986), p. 9.

33 Holt, *Art in Indonesia*, p. 39. The exact function of the *candi* is not clear and is still under debate. It is possible that, in the same way that stupas were non-functional, purely symbolic structures, with no usable interior spaces, the *candi* were symbolic or commemorative markers or products of merit-making activity; see Adrian Snodgrass, *The Symbolism of the Stupa* (Ithaca: Cornell University Southeast Asia Program Studies on Southeast Asia, 1985).

34 Soekmono, "Notes on the Monuments of Ancient Indonesia," in *Ancient Indonesian Art of the Central and Eastern Javanese Periods*, ed. Fontein, Soekmono and Suleiman (New York: The Asia Society, 1971), p. 14.

figure of a historical human being—a Javanese development of the Indian tradition of the god-king. The temples thus functioned as metaphors in stone for both macrocosm and microcosm, mirroring the cosmic order and the political realm at its most ideal.[35]

The Prambanan, a Hindu-Javanese temple complex built by the Sanjayas of Central Java in the latter part of the ninth century C.E., has been called "the most magnificent of all Shivaite monuments in Indonesia."[36] As the largest of the Shivaite temples in Java, it exemplifies the ideal arrangement which was adhered to from the eighth to the thirteenth century. Its plan is cruciform and the four main statues are placed correctly in their various chambers in the central structure.[37] The three main temples all face East: the central temple is dedicated to Shiva, the flanking ones to Vishnu (North) and Brahma (South). Facing these three temples are three structures which once housed the mounts of the gods: Shiva's bull Nandi, Vishnu's bird Garuda, and Brahma's goose Hamsa.[38] Probably the most well known feature of the Shiva temple are the reliefs running on the inside of the balustrade of the gallery, depicting scenes from the Ramayana.

* * *

At this point we return to the narrative of the patient with the tumor and the meditation vision. The patient had been to Prambanan several times, but never with the specific focus of seeking clues to her life in the images and reliefs. She now went there with a Javanese girl-friend (a young woman rarely goes anywhere alone in Central Java) at six-thirty in the morning to avoid the throngs of school children and tourists who every day swarm around the temple area from eight in the morning till sundown. They first climbed the Shiva temple, paid quick obeisance to the Shiva-statue in the central chamber (semi-facetiously, as the young in Java often behave vis-a-vis the unfamiliar rituals and beliefs of older generations). Then they sought the subsidiary chambers: in the northern one they found Durga, stepping victoriously on the bull, her sword above her head; in the western one they found Ganesha seated—plump, rich, and worldly-wise. Then, with a certain amount of excitement, they sought the south chamber—and found a potbellied elder with a long beard: Agastya.

The patient and her friend walked round the gallery looking at the Ramayana-reliefs on the southern wall: here was depicted the figure of Rama after the awakening of Vishnu (Rama being an incarnation of that deity); Rama and Laksmana fighting demons; Rama winning the hand of Sita in the archery contest, and the departure of Rama, Laksmana, and Sita to exile in the forest.

The Vishnu temple to the north, still in process of reconstruction, was hidden under scaffolding, and as south was the main direction of concern, the patient and her friend went directly to the southern temple, dedicated to Brahma, architect of the universe. Gods and goddesses graced all the outside walls of the temple. On the south, was found, again, the figure of Agastya.

Clearly Agastya was of special importance.The meaning of this figure in Indonesia, however, is complex and unresolved. Statues of a potbellied bearded man of mature age,

---

[35] Dumarcay, *Temples of Java*, p. 5. For a discussion of the political realm and the meaning of the king-figure, see Soemarsaid Moertono, *State and Statecraft in Old Java: A Study of the Later Mataram Period* (Ithaca: Cornell Modern Indonesia Project, 1968).

[36] Holt, *Art in Indonesia*, p. 54.

[37] Dumarcay, *Temples of Java*, p. 45.

[38] Ibid.

with certain Shivaite attributes, are variously referred to in the archeological literature as Bhatara Guru (the Javanese name for the Supreme god), Divine Teacher, or Agastya.[39]

Agastya is connected with the cardinal direction South, which, according to the painter, represents the worldly, secular life. This is a simplification of the meaning of South in Hindu symbolism. On various Indian *mandala* depicting the organization of the universe, South, represented by the color yellow, is the region of human habitation. Within the human realm, South is the region attributed to the Vaisyas caste. South is the region of Yama, God of Death, who is clothed in red;[40] it is the region of night, of demons, and the dark feminine force, in Java represented above all by the beautiful but dangerous Nyai Lara Kidul, Queen of the Southern Sea. South is the direction from which come all personifications of things belonging to the worldly dimension as opposed to the divine—which, essentially, once one sees beyond the illusory divisions of things into separate entities, are one.[41]

The consensus is that the figure of Agastya represents, at the very least, a *rishi* (holy teacher)who acts as a spiritual guide, showing the devotee the way to Lord Shiva himself. Another possible interpretation is that he is an aspect of Shiva—Shiva as teacher.[42] In both cases, however, the figure of the teacher, whether as the historical saint or as Shiva, plays an important role. The cult of Agastya was prevalent in Java, as demonstrated by the number of statues and inscriptions relating to it that have been found. There is a work named after him in both Javanese and Sanskrit. Furthermore, a Javanese poem dating to about 1150 C.E. acclaims a court poet as Agastya reincarnated.[43]

Besides being a teacher, Agastya is also believed to have played an important role as a cultural mediator between two different peoples in India: the Aryans of the north and the non-Aryans of the south.[44] He also acts as a facilitator in times of cosmic trouble and as conciliator between quarreling gods.[45] He stands for truth, purity, and power—once within the walls of his hermit abode, "no liar, no cruel person, nor a rogue, nor a sinful person" can remain alive.[46]

After studying the south-facing reliefs on the Shiva temple which depict Rama in struggles pertaining to love, exile, survival, and the combat of evil—illustrating the qualities of faith, courage, and perseverance—and after dwelling on the various meanings of the sage

---

39 See the discussion in Bernet Kempers, *Ancient Indonesian Art* (Amsterdam: van der Peet, 1959), p. 36, plates 39 and 41; and p. 61, plates 157–58; and in Albert le Bonheur, *La Sculpture Indonésienne au Musée Guimet* (Paris: Presses Universitaires de France, 1971), pp. 272–76, which also has further bibliographical references. See also Purbatjaraka's *Agastya in den Archipel* (Leiden: Brill, 1926).

40 John Dowson, *A Classical Dictionary of Hindu Mythology* (New Delhi: Oriental Books Reprint Corporation, 1973), p. 374.

41 See Heinrich Zimmer, *Myths and Symbols in Indian Art and Civilization* (Princeton: Princeton University Press 1946, 1972); Snodgrass, *Symbolism of the Stupa*, p. 39; J. C. Cooper, *An Illustrated Encyclopaedia of Traditional Symbols* (London: Thames and Hudson, 1978), p. 155. In Java, Agastya is always found in the south chamber, or to Shiva's right. This is not always so in India; see G. S. Ghurye, *Indian Acculturation: Agastya and Skanda* (Bombay: Popular Prakashan, 1977), footnote 49, and le Bonheur, *La Sculpture Indonésienne*, p. 274, notes.

42 This would be another version than the one known as Mahaguru; Agastya is a standing *guru*-figure as opposed to the seated Mahaguru figure known in other depictions.

43 Ghurye, *Indian Acculturation*, p.77.

44 Kempers, *Ancient Indonesian Art*, p.37; Ghurye, *Indian Acculturation*, p. 20–21.

45 Ghurye, *Indian Acculturation*, p. 24.

46 Ibid., p. 6.

Agastya, the patient began to feel formulating in her mind a personal message about her life's direction. For many years, she said, she had been vacillating between choosing a secular and a religious life, drawn to both but unable to choose. At the same time, despite encouragement and training, she had been avoiding becoming a teacher because of shyness and an unwillingness to place herself before other people in a position of authority. Thus she had found herself stuck, unable to move one way or another. Yet all the clues at Prambanan seemed to highlight the importance of leaving the insecure ego behind and pursuing with courage a path of service, specifically a path of teaching. In her mind the voices of the images in the meditation-vision and on the temple seemed to be saying: "The contradictions you perceive yourself caught between exist only on the surface. The challenges, struggles, and insights of the secular and the religious life are the same; teaching true knowledge—attempting to bridge the gap between the divine and the worldly, the known and the unknown, the foreign and the familiar. This is your duty."

When the patient returned to the painter to discuss what she had seen and thought in relation to the vision, he only gave a small, non-committal smile and did not comment further. Neither did his helper. This, as it turned out, is in accord with the *kebatinan* view that, in the final analysis, it is personal experience that is the ultimate teacher.

Batik and Painting

Although some Javanese painters create canvases that are connected directly with the iconography of Javanese *candi* and Javanese mysticism, Jono (then 30) had worked with more personal images and symbols since, after graduating from highschool, he started devoting his energies to painting. Although he must have received some art education in school, he started painting in oils as an amateur: he did not study with anyone, whether within or outside an art educational institution.[47] In his painting he uses the imagery of women and children in harmonious, mysterious unity with nature, and his work is filled

---

47 There is in modern Indonesian painting (which is centered mainly in Java and Bali) a certain aura to the label "self-taught" (*otodidak*) which, I think, ties in with wanting to claim or demonstrate innate creative talent and power in an idiom which comes close to the Javanese idea of spiritual potency. On the institutional level, *otodidak* is used in opposition to "graduate" (*lulus*) or "holding an academic degree" (*sarjana*) and today denotes someone who is an outsider to the increasingly important structure of modern educational institutions and degrees. The deeper implications of *otodidak*, however, tie into older patterns, relationships, and beliefs. According to a pattern of education much older and more fraught with personal, familial, emotional, and spiritual overtones than modern, institutionalized education, artists who are *otodidak* have often studied extensively with individual artists, who play the role of "father" or "*guru*." When finished with this apprenticeship, the younger artist is thought to have imbibed some of the older artist's power and insight which will increase with time. Even within the educational institutions the student's relationship to his or her teacher carries resonances of this older system. (For a discussion of how Islamic *pesantren* education approximates such a model of personalized initiation into the mysteries of life, see Benedict Anderson, "The Idea of Power in Javanese Culture," in *Culture and Politics* ed. Claire Holt et al (Ithaca: Cornell University Press, 1972), pp. 17–77, especially p. 55.) How *otodidak* may imply being in possession of superior spiritual insight can be seen in the other attributes that are cultivated by many artists who use that label, such as long hair (traditionally a sign of holy men, or of people who have demonstrated the ability to mediate between the living and the ancestors, or have demonstrated their spiritual power in other ways, such as a *dalang*) and an irregular lifestyle without regular wages. The "self-taught" painters I met had in most cases either greater originality in their work or greater conformity to traditional spiritual symbolism than academically trained painters. As most of the first generation of Indonesian painters were *otodidak*, by using this term today a painter identifies his spiritual connection with men like Affandi and Hendra. These artists, it could be argued, hold the same powerful position in the minds of the later generations as ancestors have held and still hold in the minds of Indonesians.

with details that hold significance according to *kebatinan*, such as water, plants, animals, seashells, and so on.[48]

Jono had great difficulty in giving titles to his paintings or talking about them. When asked about such matters, he usually answered *"terserah"*—it depends on/ it's up to you. He was reluctant to sign, date, and exhibit his work; at times he even destroyed it. Yet he kept on painting fairly diligently, often late at night when the noise of traffic and people had died down and the commercial *batik* studio was quiet. The process of trying to capture the images in his innermost mind and the frustration of not succeeding was the focus of much of his conversation. At the same time, there was little overt sense that he might learn anything of importance from an art teacher, other painters, or even his artistic partner. The *kebatinan* idea that spiritual progress depends on one's own search and experiences finds here its equivalent in the artistic journey.

Jono would never have labeled himself or his focus in life "artistic." He felt he was only at the very beginning of a total spiritual process, and the paintings themselves were less important than the process they signified. From what I gathered, he saw it as a process of searching between form and no-form, between that which *is* but which cannot be spoken *of*, and that which might be grasped and formulated, given a deep level of spiritual insight. Feeling the urge to paint while experiencing that he could not capture what he "saw"/felt, was extremely painful to him. Lao Tzu's verse "The Tao which can be spoken is not the true Tao" expresses the dilemma Jono felt. In accord with these feelings, he refused to call himself an "artist." By the same logic, he refused to fill out any of my questionnaires or to be interviewed formally about his art, although we talked in informal group situations frequently.

In the last four years, Jono has been painting more abstract pictures in oils, trying to grasp the form and meaning of the moon, symbol of the feminine principle, both during the day and at night, and trying to capture the immaterial, swirling presence of ether—symbol of the masculine and the most elevated of the five elements. His realistic selfportrait (1988; **Plate 1**), painted in monochromes, shows him prostrate before the rising full moon, against a background of swirling air (ether), punctuated by occasional flame-like shapes. The painter's hand is resting on his chest, in a way that might be interpreted as gripping his heart; his visage is enigmatic, hovering between being overwhelmed by the ferment of inner and outer turmoil and willingly yielding, submitting to it.

The painting is composed with a strong diagonal division, marked by the line of the painter's body going from lower right to upper left. The light of the moon fills the upper right triangle thus created; the darkness of the earth on which the painter lies fills the lower left triangle—a use of triangles and color which triggers associations to the polarities in the universe, where darkness and the downward-pointing triangle represents female, earth, the material dimension, death, and light and the upward-pointing triangle represents male, heaven, the spiritual dimension and eternal life. The brightest part of the painting is in the center of the canvas, at the transition point between the dark and the light half: Jono's left eye gleams in the reflection of the moon.

During these last few years Jono has also increasingly been turning his attention to *batik*-painting. The art of *batik* was often passed down from one generation to the next in both noble and village families. As Jono's family had been involved with *batik* in the past, and his

---

[48] Because of time constraints and difficulties in communication, I was unfortunately unable to obtain a more detailed explanation of these symbols during my initial period of research in Indonesia.

Plate 1: Jono (pseud.), "Selfportrait" (1988), no dimensions, oil on canvas.
Photo: Astri Wright

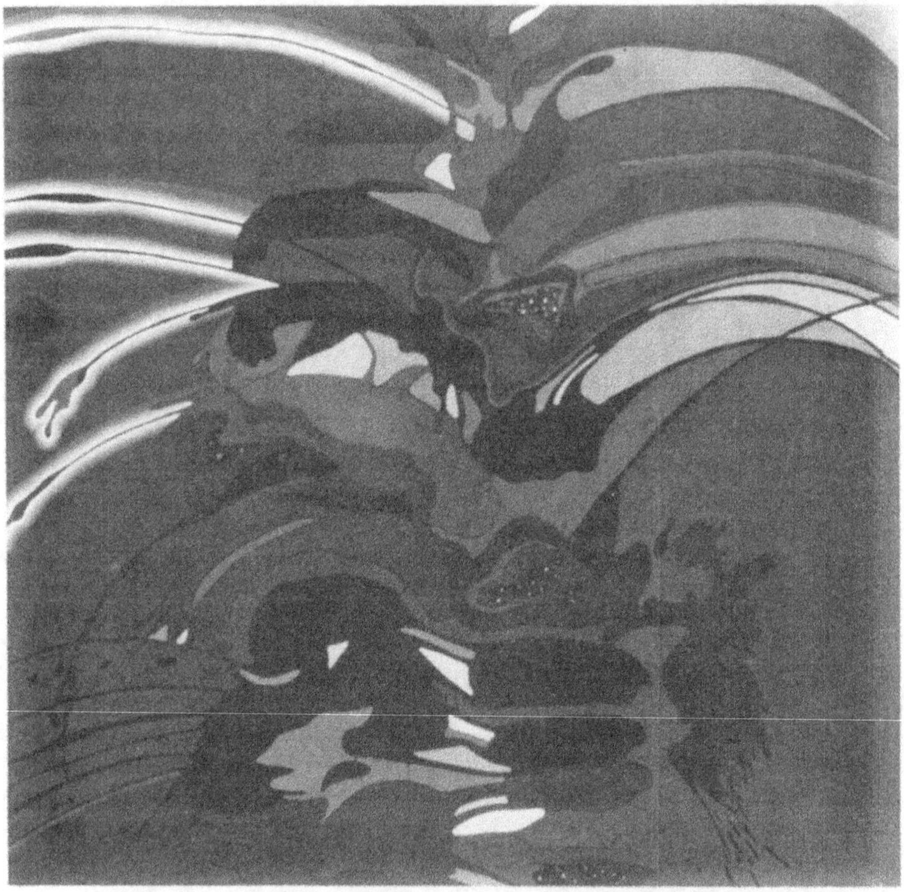

Plate 2: AMRI YAHYA, no title, (1988), 36 x 36, batik painting.
Photo: Astri Wright

father was something of a local *guru* in Yogyakarta, it was perhaps natural for his interest to incline in that direction. No doubt his meeting and artistic collaboration with Maya, a textile artist from New York who had come to Java to study traditional *batik* and meditation, further triggered Jono's interest in *batik*.

Convinced that the motifs and designs used in traditional *batik* had originally been imbued with explicit spiritual meaning, the two artists started studying the ancient patterns. *Kawung*, for example, is a pattern derived from the shape of a fruit stylized into four ovals within a square. The cross-design in the center is thought to represent a "universal source of energy," the whole representing the structure of the universe. *Semen*, meaning "sprout" or "grow," is a pattern with various motifs that represent the gods, holy places, animals, Heaven and Earth—the sum of which is thought to refer to fertility worship.[49]

On a formal level, Central Javanese *batik* are patterned with repeated motifs which cover the entire cloth more or less densely, either with geometric patterns or motifs derived from nature. In the geometric designs, negative and positive spaces interlock in a balanced design where both have equal value. There is no attempt to break out of two-dimensionality and to introduce spatial depth. This approach to a pictorial surface echoes throughout Balinese traditional or neo-traditional painting and much of modern Indonesian painting.[50]

In their spiritual research, Maya and Jono interviewed old artists still living in the Yogyakarta courts. They meditated for insights into the original, symbolic meanings of specific motifs, and they sought explanations in the archaeological literature on motifs found on the ancient monuments scattered throughout the region.

Jono's interest in *batik* as it was practiced in ancient times and its spiritual symbolism has resulted in work that is strikingly different from that of the leading abstract *batik* painters who have come to the fore as innovators of the art in Indonesia in the last twenty-five years, such as Amri Yahya and Tulus Warsito, who claim no direct connection with the *kebatinan* culture.[51] Amri Yahya's designs (see **Plate 2**) are abstract plays of color in which a flat silk-

---

49 Inger McCabe Elliot, *Batik: Fabled Cloth of Java* (New York: Potter, 1984), p. 68.

50 Another illustration of such continuity in approaching two-dimensional arts, which I refer to as aesthetic affinity (keeping in mind that the term "aesthetic" here does not preclude a ritual dimension) was given in the summer of 1988, when a group of Aboriginal artists from various northern and western Australian settlements came to study *batik* with Maya and Jono. As ideas about pattern, symbol, meaning, composition, and color were exchanged between the Javanese-American and the Aboriginal contingents, an immediate rapport was established. After ten days, they parted with the feeling that their various views had been greatly enriched in ways that were immediately accessible and even familiar, and that the spiritual and aesthetic links between Javanese *batik* and Aboriginal sand-painting were deep and real, and that the medium of *batik* could easily be adapted to the contemporary expressive demands of the latter. This initial meeting has resulted in annual workshops given to white and Aboriginal Australians by the Javanese-American artist team at various locations in Australia, ranging from art institutes to Aboriginal settlements.

51 Because of the different technical and historical dimensions that inform it, *batik* painting is not discussed at length here, although, as the only true hybrid form between indigenous two-dimensional textile arts and a modern, painterly expression, it deserves attention. One of the many aspects of *batik* painting that in most cases distinguishes it from oil painting is that most *batik* painters employ craftspeople to do the actual waxing and dying, based on their drawn and painted specifications. One difference between Amri Yahya and Maya/Jono would be that the latter would tend to do more of the actual work on the cloth themselves, so the possibility of the presence of "signature" in their work would be greater. An in-depth study of the modern form called "*batik* painting" has yet to be made, despite the fact that some very interesting *batik* paintings exist in Malaysia, Singapore, and Indonesia. The relationship of this painting to traditional *batik*, which in Indonesia achieved such a great diversity of beautifully conceived, designed, and executed patterns and styles ranking in quality with any two-dimensional art, should also be studied. For excellent plates that support this statement, see N. Tirtaamidjaja SH, *BATIK, pola & tjorak—Pattern & Motif*, trans. Benedict Anderson (Jakarta: Penerbit Djambatan, n.d.).

Plate 3: "Jomaya" (pseud.), "Wave Breaking" (1988), ca 150 x 65 cm, batik painting.
Photo: Astri Wright

screen-like character alternates with areas that signify *batik,* where one can feel the presence of hot wax dripped or painted on the cloth before dye was added. Amri Yahya (b. 1939), who came originally from Padang, West Sumatra, has an enormous output, employs the very best *batik*-workers who translate his painted sketches onto the cloth, runs his personal gallery successfully, leads the Islamic prayers which initiate formal artist gatherings, and in jest calls himself the king of Yogya.[52]

Living, working, and meditating with another artist caused another shift in Jono's approach to art. Deciding to work collaboratively and create the design for each piece together, the artist-team worked on the same piece of cloth with wax-brushes and *canting* (wax-pens), placing their individual "signature" styles side by side with pattern areas on which they had both worked. Thus, on a single surface, the work of each artist is in some places identifiable, such as Jono's flame-like shapes and repeated outlines and Maya's more watery shapes, often created with folding-and-dyeing techniques used in African *batik.* At other times the individual contribution is not identifiable. Even when it is, the other artist may have done the covering, scraping, or dyeing work which constitutes one of the several stages in bringing out the individual patterns. In this way, the Javanese painter and the American textile artist took their artistic process yet a further step away from Western notions of the individual self or individualistic creativity.[53] The art works were not signed; the commercial products—simplified versions of the patterns in their art works, sewn into clothing—were labeled "JOMAYA."

"Jomaya" created two of their strongest works in 1987–1988. "Wave Breaking" **(Plate 3)** is in part a quote and a tribute to Hokusai's famous wave, here transformed into a broad and powerful upward sweep of water. The top and bottom of the wave are decoratively translated into a flat ochre area with no detailing. This contrasts with the rest of the surface, which is densely treated with repeated waxing and dyeing, in a crisscrossing of turquoise and dark indigo areas and lines over a dominant ground in shades of purple. The white foam is delineated both by crackling, darker color-areas, and lines. Above it a delicate turqoise-blue sky punctuated by starry dots provides a sense of depth. It is a densely conceived and executed work, filled with surge and movement.

"Red Fire" **(Plate 4)** is dense in a different way: rather than attempting to depict burning flames, it is more conceptual and speaks to the nature of fire as symbol. Flickering, sparking, licking, darting flamelike shapes fill the work with hues of red, mauve, ochre, and yellow against darker areas of brown and indigo, all interlocking as a negative-positive so that there is no "empty" background space; each part of the two-dimensional design is a complete and equal statement in itself.

The surface treatment of each body of flame is different—some are delineated with repeated, concentric or dotted lines, other areas are dotted with large, medium, or small points, some in contrasting colors, others in shades of the same color. Yet others are crackled in a number of different ways. The work displays the variety of ways a surface can be

[52] Personal communication, August 1987. Amri Yahya also paints oil paintings, with similar compositions and colors to his *batik* paintings, but without their clarity and sharpness.

[53] As their artistic process developed, they had to start up a more commercial line of production to try to support their costly and time-consuming art work, and *batik* workers were hired on a regular basis to do the waxing, scraping, and dyeing. These workers worked on both the commercial products and on certain parts of the art products, thus introducing yet another factor which removed the creative process from the control of the individual artist.

Plate 4: "Jomaya" (pseud.) "Api Merah" (Red Fire) (1988), 120 x 90 cm, batik painting.
Photo: Astri Wright

treated, and many of the techniques used are traditional ones. The choice of water as the subject of the previous work (symbolizing fecundity and the unification of polarities, coming as it does from the heavens to penetrate the earth, producing life) and of fire as the subject of the present predominantly red work, illustrate the artists' preoccupation with *kebatinan*. On the most basic level, according to Jono, fire and the color red represent youth, the passions, desire for wealth, and madness. They represent the earthly, material dimension. But fire also consumes earthly matter, transforming and conveying it into the ethereal. In addition to this interpretation of red, Jono interpreted other colors as follows: blue is the color of balance, equilibrium; green is the color of God; violet is the color of compatibility (as between partners or lovers); yellow is the color of love (greenish yellow represents divine love); and black is the color of one's behavior and actions. We heard previously that, according to Jono, black represents worldly desires and white symbolizes objective reality.[54]

Only a detailed account of the entire *batik*-process—making the design, drawing it on the cloth, applying the first round of wax and color, then reapplying more wax in some areas and scraping it off others, before dyeing it again, a third and fourth and possibly a fifth time—can make one fully appreciate the process that carries the artists from creative idea to end result. This process is completely different from painting in oils. To paint on a canvas is to work "in the positive," adding the forms and colors you want to see in the end result; to work in *batik* entails working "in the negative," blocking out the forms you want to appear as positive, keeping in mind at every stage what the final aim is, and allowing for the inevitable departures from this aim caused by the materials themselves, in processes involving wax, chemicals, water, sunlight, and temperatures ranging from hot to cold.

In "JOMAYA's" art is applied a notion of self similar to the *kebatinan* idea of a soul or spirit, separated from but journeying towards reintegration with the absolute, universal soul. In this perspective, the making of a work of art becomes equivalent to the mystical journey. The artist attempts to overcome the limitations of the individual self through meditating on and manipulating the materials, uniting mind with action and matter. Transforming matter becomes a metaphor for transforming the soul. By working with another artist on every step of a long and complex process, mind is united with mind—a metaphor for overcoming the illusion of separation between individuals.

Jono's father, a local *guru* in Yogyakarta whose mantle Jono has been taught since boyhood that he will inherit someday, says that, in *kebatinan*, human beings are ranked into five levels of spiritual attainment. The second highest level is held by artists.[55] Artists are per-

---

[54] Personal communication, October 1988. It is interesting to compare this color-symbolism with a passage in Holt: "Although the use of colors may be becoming more arbitrary, there is still considerable consensus about their meaning. Black is supposed to indicate inner maturity, adulthood, virtue, including calmness. Red, on the other hand, denotes uncontrolled passions, desires. Gold has a double function: it may denote beauty (of the hero), royal or princely status, glory, but may also reflect the desire of the maker or owner of the puppet to make the wayang itself as beautiful as possible. White is said to indicate noble descent, youth and beauty too, but its use is ambiguous. Some say that beings with blue faces are cowardly.... The prevalent facial colors are black, red, and gold. In the course of one play the same character may appear at one time with a golden face and at another with a black face to indicate different aspects of the hero or stages in his life." Holt, *Art in Indonesia*, pp. 142–43. Between these two systems of color-symbolism, only the color red seems to hold similar meaning. The fact that the other colors are given differing interpretations may illustrate differences in place, time, and medium (Holt is speaking about dramatic make-up). It may also indicate the fluid nature of a tradition which is oral rather than based on the authority of a written text.

[55] From handout prepared for the Prakarti Foundation, Yogyakarta, October 1987. As Benedict Anderson has pointed out to me, there is no mention of artists as a separate or special group in Javanese mystical literature; this is probably therefore a recent re-writing of older ideas. To me, rather than invalidating the point, this only makes the inclusion of artists into Javanese cosmology all the more interesting, illustrating that it is not based on a static

ceived as people whose gift of seeing goes beyond the world of appearances; artists are people whose faculty of sight signifies insight.

Although many painters cited mysticism as a source of inspiration, only a few of those I encountered in Java were as active in practicing *kebatinan* techniques as Jono.[56] Whether Moslems, Protestants, or Catholics, many older as well as younger artists nonetheless draw on ideas and symbols rooted in the cultural matrix in which *kebatinan* plays a central role.

With the varying depths of personal involvement and degrees to which mystical ideas are accepted or rejected by the younger, emerging generations of artists, even the form rejection takes is shaped by what is being rejected. And since *kebatinan* still flourishes as a part of Javanese culture, some knowledge of it is essential to any scholar of Javanese art, whether traditional or modern.

---

formula; indeed, that it is transforming in ways that take account of modern life. The reference to "tradition" is thus a commonly performed claim to legitimacy. In this instance, the high status given to artists may reflect Ismoyo's father's preparing his small spiritual following to accept his son as his legitimate heir.

56 The most extreme version I heard of a painter-mystic was a painter living in or near Jakarta, who could only paint, naked, on an island off the coast. When inspired, it was said, he would throw off his clothes, jump in a row-boat and go to the island to paint. Naturally I could not find out the name or whereabouts of this painter and it is impossible to say how many feathers originated this particular chicken [cf. Norwegian proverb: "The story about the five feathers that became two chickens"]. The point is, again, the way the Indonesian imagination works with respect to the image of artists.

Vivere Pericolosamente

Tjalie Robinson

Translated by Winniefred Anthonio

Translator's Note:

Jan Boon (1911-1974), better known under his pseudonyms Tjalie Robinson or Vincent Mahieu, was born in Nijmegen, the Netherlands, but grew up in the former Dutch East Indies in the city of Batavia. He began work as a journalist and became famous for his *piekerans* (ponderings) for Dutch newspapers in the Indies. These pieces were later published as *Ponderings of a Streetloafer* (1953). Like many Dutch Eurasians, he left Indonesia after the country gained its independence and in 1954 settled in the Netherlands. He there became well known for his Dutch Eurasian magazine *Tont-tong*. Unwillingly, he became the spokesman for the Indo refugees who tried to start a new life in a cold and hostile environment. Proud of his dual heritage, he sharply criticized the Dutch for their treatment of Indos and Indo culture. He encouraged Indos to preserve their unique culture, even though many felt that the only possible way to survive in the Netherlands was by total assimilation. This controversial stand brought him many enemies and divided the Indo community. Nevertheless, he stood firm in this conviction until his death of a heart attack in 1974.

Tjies (1958), in which "Vivere Pericolosamente" appears, was his first collection of short stories published under the name Vincent Mahieu. He received the literary prize of the city of Amsterdam for the collection. On the back cover of the 1978 edition, Robinson explained the hunting term *"tjies"* as follows (my translation):

> *Tjies* is the nickname and pet-name given to the first firearm full-blooded Eurasians received upon finishing elementary school and entering society as "first-class citizens." Even though this *Tjies*, the cal. 22, is the smallest firearm, it is a deadly weapon. Holding life and death in his hand, to the maturing youth, from this time on, life does not consist of "sweet talk" any more, and however unbelievable it might seem to the ethic-embracing city person, life becomes indeed even more subtle. Toughness makes way for hardness, cruelty for mercy; with the power to kill, the young man learns to spare life. There is an extremely profound difference in character between the young man living in the city, with libraries and slaughterhouses, and the young man in nature, a vulnerable

individual with scanty needs, scanty demands, but with the highest physical and moral efficiency.

With the *Tjies*, the consciously awakening human being learns what life is really about.

VIVERE PERICOLOSAMENTE

Tjalie Robinson

How many people lead double lives? For how long. When do these lives clash? How do they begin? Sometimes from the two lives of the European house itself. Something one would never guess. Indeed such living structures exist; their respectable facades faced a respectable street, but their backdoors vile slums. How many affairs erupted through these little backdoors? And how much misery and ruin caused in return! In the old Indies, those things usually remained secret. To be European carried status. The annexes built in the back of the houses and anything beyond remained, as a matter of fact, "terra incognita." Affairs, referred to as "naughty little things," were kept a secret, tucked away or at the most whispered about over drinks. Like *yarns*. But how was it still possible for the most concealed secret to come out in the open even if no European had seen it? Ah. One hears about it by snooping around and beyond the annexes. Eyes see, ears hear and thus mouths speak.

Along the Tjiliwoeng,[1] in the center of the city of Batavia, existed such houses leading two lives. Naturally, those houses did not officially stand along the Tjiliwoeng. The Tjiliwoeng flowed behind them. No one saw anything of the river except by crossing her bridges, even then one would only notice tiny little chunks in such short units of time. And since Europeans never row in the Tjiliwoeng—don't even mention swim—no one knew what the other life of the houses would be like. Their fronts were inhabited by refendaries,[2] government officials, and academicians, while the other life in the rear of these houses was as obscure and unknown as it ought to be. From the river, one would only see the stern, soiled, and dusty enclosures of the annexes with their stiff, round, eye-shaped ventilation holes, with vicious pieces of glass on the top of the walls; sometimes even a weathered and half way mouldered door, with a corroded lock. Behind the doors, narrow passages were so cluttered up with piles of trash, that an intruder could not come in even by forcing the door. Occasionally, brittle pieces of soil covered with weeds leading a deprived life in the midst of smashed bottles, broken china, and rusted cans tossed over the wall in anger, extended from those walls to the river bank. The only people who occasionally set foot on these little pieces

---

This story is printed in *Tjies*, pp. 56–70. The footnotes are the translator's.

[1] Flowing through the city, the Tjiliwoeng river was and still is the most important source of water for the people living in Jakarta.

[2] A refendary (*referendaris*) is a department head of a specific branch of the colonial government.

of soil were fishermen who cleaned out their casting-nets. But too many thorns, pieces of broken glass, and too much filth prevented one from having a good time there. Also, there were often snakes. Once in a great while, a naughty boy would climb over the wall to nose around there, but after those vicious pieces of broken glass cut his bare feet his Mom definitely put an end to those wanderings. Perhaps, at one time, a long time ago in fact, people really made use of those pieces of soil. Otherwise, how could one explain the presence of barbed wire marking the compounds' boundaries, extending at times even deep down into the river? Nobody asked questions because nobody noticed it.

Except *one*. That was Mister Barkey. Actually Mister Barkey was an *Indo*, a Dutch Eurasian, evident from his name, according to insiders. But he was indeed of a conspicuous kind. He belonged to the type endowed with all the necessary characteristics to be successful: a white one. With his blond hair, blue eyes, and fair skin, many Europeans regarded him a *totok*, a native Dutchman. Perhaps that's why his career had been so successful, because, in spite of his 34 years and only fourteen years of service, he was a department head. He didn't associate much with his brown-skinned colleagues who envied his success and accused him for denouncing his own race.

Mister Barkey was childless. He had a sociable, corpulent wife whom he early on called Moesje,[3] because of her motherly appearance and nature. But also Pompelmoesje,[4] because she was so fat. They led a contented life. Mrs. Barkey was four years older than her husband and well on her way to turning into a matron. Mister Barkey, who had married when he was only nineteen, quite early on lost interest in being a ladies' man and *amant* ("lover"). That always happens when "you get a day older." You don't long for anything extraordinary, anyway nothing that requires energy.

Mister and Mrs. Barkey, unacquainted with anybody in the neighborhood except by appearance, quietly consumed the flame of the candles that measured their lives. To keep themselves occupied like contented children, they had their novels, their book-dispatch box,[5] their petty daily tasks at home, and their trivial hobbies without getting in each other's way. Mrs. Barkey had the habit of reading in bed long beyond midnight, which she compensated for by sleeping for a considerable long stretch in the afternoon like a water buffalo, like an ox; starting at one thirty, immediately after the usually abundant *rijsttafel*,[6] until five o'clock. Mister Barkey, on the other hand, never slept during the afternoon hours. Perhaps because he always slept in his office. Indeed proof that he wasn't at all a man driven by ambition. When his wife was asleep, he rummaged through the house; his ready hands always found something to do, such as fixing the chicken coop, the electric wiring, working

---

[3] Moes, Moesje, Ma, or Maatje are all Indo equivalents for Moeder in Dutch.

[4] The Dutch *pompelmoes* stands for "grape-fruit." The nick-name Pompelmoesje is a play on words.

[5] To keep up with the events in the West, many Europeans had a subscription for a book-dispatch box containing Western journals, magazines, and newspapers. Some of the magazines were the *Wereld Kroniek* [World Chronicle] comparable with *Life Magazine; De Lach* [The Smile] which focused on movies and lives of movie stars; *Sports in Beeld* [Sport Images] which gave an account of sports events in Europe; *d'Orient*, another news magazine; and *La Vie Parisienne*, a cultural magazine, which was written in Dutch in spite of its French name. Because a subscription to a book-dispatch box was rather costly, many Indo families shared one subscription. One usually kept the book-dispatch box for a week or two; then it was picked up and replaced with a new supply. All this information comes from my father and my mother's cousin.

[6] To Europeans, the highlight of the day was the *rijsttafel*, an abundant meal served after the man of the house came home from work. The *rijsttafel* is in fact a colonial fabrication out of the *selamatan*, the indigenous ritual meal consisting of cooked rice and lots of side dishes. A complete Dutch *rijsttafel* consists of cooked rice with side dishes including beef, fish, shrimp, and poultry besides vegetable dishes.

in the garden, the *goedang* ("storage room") all kinds of petty, insignificant repairs of petty useless things.

One day he repaired the corroded lock of the useless rear door. With a bundle of keys, coconut oil, and a screwdriver, he managed to get the lock in perfect working condition without paying any attention to the *kali*, the river, behind the house. After all there was indeed nothing unusual about the river. He became quickly aware of this when, after finishing the job, he took a well-deserved break, and looked out over the river smoking a cigarette. He did not see anyone either on his or on the other side of the river, where a desolate banana tree garden seemed to be. Further on, down the stream at the curve was a *kampong* ("village") invisible through the dense growth of trees, but evident from the bamboo raft in the river, where women washed clothes. But that was indeed far away. Therefore, Mister Barkey could stand in his underwear without getting embarrassed.

He was always dressed in underwear[7] of a really ridiculously old-fashioned cut. But Pompelmoesje was still old-fashioned and thus made old-fashioned clothes. Underpants made of strong cotton with a delicate red stripe running through, and with tight legs reaching below the knees. And with a *kolor*, a cotton string, that's one of those cords to draw pyjamas tight before the invention of the elastic rubber band. Mister Barkey wore undershirts with short sleeves, a high round neck, two buttons, and a pocket on the stomach[8] to keep *tepak*,[9] his tobacco, and a lighter. Mister Barkey in underwear was in fact Mister Barkey "sec-and-clean" ("the real Mister Barkey"). The dressed up office-Mister Barkey was a gentleman, a civil servant, a kind of office-upholstery. That's why Mister Barkey felt most comfortable in his undergarments.

Leaning against the door-post, Mister Barkey looked at the river drifting by brown and lazy and cool. The filthy *kali*, in which rubbish floated around and bodies of dead animals and lumps of human feces. To Mister Barkey the *kali* was also the symbol of everything that was low and vulgar in the Indies. Not that Mister Barkey was conscious of it at that moment. The *kali* was just the *kali*. He sat down and looked contentedly at the *kali*. He really had nothing to do with it. Perhaps because of her contrast to Mister Barkey's backyard that demonstrated such perpetual indifference with dead things, the active *kali* became actually attractive, even lovely. Perhaps also because of the primitive clutter of crumbly edges and wild vegetation on the river banks in contrast to all the civil neatness inside Mister Barkey's house, that made him look with interest at the river. In any case, Mister Barkey became captivated by the *kali*, even intrigued in an unexplainable way. Drawn by something incomprehensible, he carefully walked over to the river bank on his wooden slippers. He took off a slipper and put his foot in the water which was not brownish-yellow at the edge but almost clear, yet hazy and romantically transparent.

Standing solidly on one leg like a heron, Mister Barkey played with his toes of the other with the cool water. There were *djoeloeng-djoeloeng*, little fishes with pike-like little pointed

7 Europeans would not walk around in their underwear at home but in their pyjamas.

8 Mr. Barkey's underwear resembled both the pyjama and the *tjelana monjet*, literally "monkey suit," also called *hansop*, the traditional playsuit for Indo children. Usually made out of sturdy cotton, the *tjelana monjet* was a kind of jumpsuit, but without sleeves or long legs. Based on Robinson's description, Mr. Barkey's underpants were a variation of those of a pair of pyjamas, but the legs were shorter; they reached below the knees. Similar to pyjama pants, a *kolor*, cotton string tied around the waist, kept his pants from falling. The top of his underwear had, like the *tjelana monjet*, a round collar, two buttons, and a pocket sewn on the front at the height of his stomach to keep his tobacco and his lighter.

9 *Tepak* is the Indo jargon for the Dutch word *tabak*, tobacco in English.

heads, swimming in the water. And tiny, golden flat-headed fishes with bright stars on their heads. Weeds and algae twirled and whirled gracefully in the soft current. Myriads of tiny golden *ting-a-ling-a-ling*[10] sailed through the water. Mister Barkey proceeded to stand with both legs in the shallow water. Immediately his legs looked shorter, yet whiter but nevertheless more beautiful. It was very odd. He noticed a kind of sand bank with small, smooth, round stones, and smoothly polished white pieces of glass and small chunks of red brick. Gradually the sand bank declined but dropped sharply towards the middle. So he noticed. In spite of the afternoon heat, the water was cool beyond description and refreshing. She was in fact cleaner than one would assume. The water snuggled up against his legs, refreshingly tinkled against the hollows of his knees and smelt pleasant like fresh dirt. All of a sudden Mister Barkey sat down.

It wasn't until an hour later that he went back inside the house, after a whole hour of playing like a child, acting like a rascal, swimming like a man. This was still during the time that there were no swimming pools in the city of Batavia. Thus Mister Barkey never swam. He didn't even have a bathing-suit. But it didn't matter whether he swam in his underwear. Here was no one anyway. The game in the *kali* had all the sweetness of something forbidden and the spell of something completely private. Who of the department heads would swim in the *kali?* Not even a third *commies.*[11] It was so exquisite and so private, that Mister Barkey didn't tell his wife about it. He bathed thoroughly using lots of soap to get rid of the *kali*-smell. He succeeded in keeping his secret for months.

Every afternoon when Pompelmoesje was asleep,[12] Mister Barkey plunged into the *kali.* He denied the impurity of the water based on evidence that water only in very close proximity to filth—up to one centimeter at the most-- was contaminated by that filth. He rejected the insanitary state of the river based on medical doctors' evidence that the enormous radiation of the sun's heat completely decontaminated the upper layer of the water. And even if that wasn't true, so what? During the following weeks, Mister Barkey changed into an unbelievable *branie,* dare-devil. He swam to all the protruding points of the *kali* bank that drew his attention. At the other side of the river, he sank deeply into the slimy muddy banks, went ashore between bramble-bushes, kept on swimming when a snake crossed the *kali,* even plunged into the water when the *kali,* swollen by rain, flowed faster. For a whole hour even in the midst of swiftly flowing water, he would fight the current by swimming vigorously without giving in one inch. Swiftly swimming in the strongest current, he could get ten meters ahead. He could dive minutes at a time. He purposely played with danger and loved it. Mister Barkey was well on his way to becoming a different person. It was only so slow because for the rest of the remaining twenty-four hours he successfully managed to force himself into the hypocritical strait jacket of the typical government official.

Mister Barkey had only *one* fear. That *one* time would be the last. Like any other seemingly infinite daily pursuits, above all the pleasant ones, one would be the last. It wasn't that Mister Barkey was afraid of the possibility of a sudden accident; therefore he had become too intimate with the *kali.* Mister Barkey was not afraid of the cause for such a loss, but of

---

[10] *Ting-a-ling-a-ling* is onomatopoeic, imitating the sounds of little bells. In this context it means all kinds of little nothings.

[11] The rank of third *commies* was the lowest among clerks.

[12] Mister Barkey acted like many Indo children when their parents were asleep in the afternoon. After lunch, people usually took a nap, including the children. But as children, we often could not sleep and sneaked out to play outside. Even though we were punished if our parents caught us, often with a week's house arrest, we took the risk.

the loss itself. It also seemed as if the *kali* gradually was getting to know him and to love him. Time and time again, she smiled cheerfully welcoming him. Also the *kampong* inhabitants further along the river had become used to that queer, swimming *blanda,* the white man. The first couple of weeks children had gathered together on the bamboo raft, but that curiosity quickly wore off. Also the European Barkey had become a *kali*-phenomenon, similar to other bathing people, similar to floating garbage, dead animals, and lumps of human excretion.

Also the last time, Mister Barkey cheerfully plunged into the water without any hesitation. It had rained heavily for the last two days, apparently also in the mountains. The swollen *kali* had even washed away the tiny pieces of the river bank behind the annexes. Nevertheless, Mister Barkey plunged into the water like a white sea lion, for whom the water could not present any possible danger but only delight. This time the *kali* was heavy with mud and dull brown with whirlpools that were almost black and rapids full of slime. Now even huge tree trunks floated along. Thus Mister Barkey enjoyed himself like never before. Roaring like a lion, he propelled through the water, unwilling to give the current one inch, even in the middle of the *kali* where the current was the strongest. He paid close attention to the filth drifting in his direction, skillfully avoiding branches and banana-trunks. But the danger took him by surprise in a humiliating way.

His *kolor* ("cotton string" to hold up his pants) suddenly broke and the strong current immediately stripped down his pants from his rear end. All of a sudden Mister Barkey became overwhelmed by a turmoil of sensations and by the water itself. Even under the transparently brown water, he felt himself shamefully naked, but in addition the crotch prevented him, particularly at the knees, from producing a powerful kick with his legs and at last he lost both direction and speed, because frightened he had grabbed his pants. He went head down, came up and went down again, swallowed enormous amounts of *kali* water and spun helplessly around. However, virtuousness always gets rewarded. Mister Barkey's struggle to pull his pants up prevented him from drowning. His mind stayed alert and his arms and legs automatically made movements, even though small, but just enough to stay above water. He got a hold of his pants when he was close to the curve and with a few powerful strokes managed to reach the bamboo raft.

Puffing and spitting he pulled himself up on the raft in a sitting position, with one hand he supported himself, with the other he kept his pants together. There were three women on the raft busy washing clothes and rinsing rice. They hadn't seen the swimmer and (thus) were completely taken by surprise when the white man suddenly rose out of the brown waters like in a spectacle. Unable to control themselves, they screamed and cackled like chickens, so Mister Barkey was forced to use his most stern authoritarian voice: "Shut up, damn it, shut up!" The women fell silent, trembled, calmed down, and giggled. Agitated, Mister Barkey pulled the *kolor* out of its seam, tied the ends together, strapped it around over the pants and wrapped the upper seam of his pants around the cord as tightly as possible. While he was doing this, he realized once more, but this time greatly alarmed, that his white underwear was quite transparent. He couldn't possibly get up like this without sending the women into fits of laughter. So his initial intention to stroll up-stream along the river and then to swim across to the other side, could not be carried out.

There was no alternative but to swim across starting at this point and to stroll back at the other side. It was true that some spots had pieces of barbed wire, but he could just swim around them. Mister Barkey plunged back into the water, lying in the spindle of the current, and swimming both slantwise and sideways to the other side. Again and again, he felt the *kali* boldly pulling at his pants and again and again he had to grab them quickly in order to save his modesty. It was a tremendously tiring crossing and Mister Barkey was almost totally exhausted when he reached the other side, just at the spot before the barbed wire, so he thought. Then with dismay and anguish, he noticed that the wire also continued under the water. Somewhere his pants tore open and he got a nasty scratch on his leg. Furthermore, he had suddenly lost so much speed, that he drifted away and it wasn't until he reached the new curve that he was finally able to scramble ashore.

Just one look around him convinced Mister Barkey of the worst possible. Anyone on the bridge with its heavy traffic could see him. He did not even think twice and stumbled as fast as he could to the rear wall of the house and knocked on the back door. For Heaven's sake, I have to ask these servants to go to my house and get my clothes. Anyway no European would be awake at this hour of the day. He would get home regardless. And servants—who would talk to servants? While he was knocking on the door he prepared his short speech: I fell into the water and was dragged away (oh, what is "to be dragged away" in Malay?—gesture); please help me.

The door opened and there stood the widow, Mrs. Aubrey. Mister Barkey looked at her with his mouth wide open. He only knew her by her name on the door-plate, had only seen her occasionally and had heard some things about her. Mrs. Aubrey looked at him with her mouth wide open too. But only for one moment. Startled she asked:

"Did you have an accident? Please come in, come in, come in." Mister Barkey stepped forward closing the door behind him.

"No," he said stupidly, "I was swimming in the *kali* and then, then. . . ." Mrs. Aubrey slyly smiled her famous seductive smile and twinkled her famous flirting eyes.

"And then you thought, I'll just go and pay Mrs. Aubrey a visit. Shame on you. And above all in your undershirt and underpants!"

Crushed Mister Barkey cast down his eyes, became aware of his transparent pants, turned quickly around, discovered the hole in the seat of his pants and turned back half way.

"In God's name, Mrs. Aubrey, this is not a laughing matter!"

"Eeee! You're turning it into a laughing matter, hahaha. You're so naughty, Mister Barkey!" She kept her hand in front of her face, and only shook her index finger disapprovingly.

"What are you going to do now! I can see *everything!*"

Mister Barkey turned as red as a steamed lobster, he licked his lips and rolled his eyes. With both hands covering *himself*, he said urgently:

"Madam. Madam. Would you please help me!"

She could not help laughing. Again and again she folded double laughing. Keeping her kimono half closed with her left hand, she slapped herself on the thigh with the other. She walked away, saying between bursts of laughter: "Just come along." He walked behind her, bewildered, humiliated, and confused. She reached the bathroom and Mister Barkey quickly hopped right behind her into the bathroom and closed the door.

"What am I supposed to do with a man in my bathroom!" Mrs. Aubrey laughed, "a poor widow protecting her honor and virtue all by herself. And what's more, a man visiting in his underwear during the afternoon hours! I wouldn't even dare to call the police!"

Once hidden behind the bathroom door from those immodest female glances, Mister Barkey quickly regained his self-confidence.

"Mrs. Aubrey, I beg you. Please control yourself and help me. Would you please be so kind to go to my house - "

"I won't even think of it. Your wife will scratch my eyes out!"

"My wife is asleep. She will sleep for several hours more. If you go through the side-gate, which is always open, you'll see on the rear verandah, precisely at the end of the corridor of the main building ("Yeees," she said mockingly interested, catching her breath coyly), an ironing board ("Yeees") and on it a pair of underpants and an undershirt ("Yeees"). In the yard, on the clothes-line hangs a pair of pyjamas and by the corridor's staircase are my slippers ("Yeees"). Would you please get those for me?"

"Is that all?"

"Yes. Ooo! Yes, Mrs. Aubrey. I beg you, Mrs. Aubrey!"

"If I get caught?!"

"Oh, God! No, Mrs. Aubrey, nobody will catch you. After all nobody is up?"

"Well, alright. But it will take a while. First I have to change. And I still have to make you a cup of coffee to recuperate." Mister Barkey moaned.

"Madam. Madam."

She giggled and went away with her flying kimono, rustling in the corridor. She returned for just a moment.

"In the meantime, please feel free to take a bath, Mister Barkey."

"Yes, madam."

"Otherwise your clean clothes will get dirty again."

"Yes, madam (Oh, my God!)."

"Feel free to use my soap."

"Yes-yes-yes madam, please madam—eh. . . ."

"I'm going. I'm going!"

Out of misery Mister Barkey's knees almost gave up. But he quickly got a hold of himself. Hurry, hurry. Wildly, he looked around the bathroom, saw a few pieces of intimate underwear dangling from the clothes rack and embarrassed, quickly turned his eyes away. He took his sticky clothes off. Fortunately the scratch on his thigh wasn't too bad. Diligently, he began to pour the water over himself,[13] then took a piece of soap out of the soap-dish. It smelled unbelievably delicate and seductive. It would be such a pleasure to use it. But suddenly he realized with awe that Pompelmoesje would smell it too. No soap. There was a

---

[13] During this time, most European houses did not have running water, showers, or bathtubs. Built in the annexes, the bathroom often had a tiled floor and a tiled basin, a *mandi-bak*, filled with water. Usually one of the servants was in charge of filling the basin twice a day with water from the well, located also in the back of the house. To take a bath, one would simply throw water over oneself with a scoop made out of a coconut shell.

knock on the bathroom door. Already? She was a perfect sweetheart.—What?! She was—he cracked the bathroom door and got a glass of Dutch gin pushed against his nose.

"Drink this," Mrs. Aubrey said firmly, "against catching a cold."

"Oh, my God!" Mister Barkey groaned closing the door, but her small high-heeled shoe was stuck in-between.

"Drink this, Mister Barkey. And stop hurting me."

"Madam," Mister Barkey pleaded, "Madam."

"Sir," Mrs. Aubrey said, while standing outside the door, "if I help my fellow-men, I like to do that well. I won't allow you to get sick in my house. You—drink—this—first."

"But I never drink!" Mister Barkey argued.

"You drink this now," she said resolutely.

"And above all a cognac-glass!" Mister Barkey shrieked.

"Aaaah. You indeed recognize a good drink, don't you, Mister Barkey. *Ajo*, to your health!"

Blindly Mister Barkey grabbed the glass, took a swallow and gagged, almost choked, coughed and heard Mrs. Aubrey say:

"Don't you dare to throw that away! Drink it!"

Mister Barkey drank like Socrates. He pushed the glass into her hands and shoved the door closed, staggered backwards and sat down on the edge of the *mandibak*, almost slipped over it, regained his balance and his somewhat hazy consciousness.

However, that consciousness was so shaken that he hardly recognized himself. The fact that he was alive at this very moment, was totally absurd. But his living, naked body was the evidence. He started to bathe again. The cold water refreshed him and calmed down his nerves. No soap, but certainly Mrs. Aubrey's towel. It was a soft, lavender-colored thing, unlike the well-known large, rough, white pieces of cloth with the small stripe, he and Pompelmoesje always used. It smelled pleasantly of light perfume and was confusingly scented with something completely different. Fiercely, Mister Barkey began to rub himself dry with his back facing the clothes rack. Suddenly at the left of him, he saw a huge mirror where he saw himself completely from head to toe. It embarrassed him a bit, but it also did him good. Quite pleased, he looked closely at his big, robust body, which undoubtedly had become broad and strong due to regular swimming. Close to his head he saw those two insignificant pieces of clothing hanging from the clothes rack. He sniffed at them. He looked at them. He touched them. They were silky and caressing and delicate, not at all like those coarse cotton jackets Moes used. Not with those big, wide pieces of trimmed lace, but with a very fine flimsy of spiderweb.

Mister Barkey closed his eyes and Mrs. Aubrey's image appeared before his eyes in the way men who knew her talked about her. Well, what would you expect of a merry widow, a jewel of only twenty-two carat gold. She hooked anybody she put her eyes on, whether young or old, of high or low status, married or unmarried. But without any serious intentions. She just took advantage of life, that was all. He thought of her the way he had seen her at times with that sudden twinkling flicker in those dark eyes and that sophisticated, evoking smile around the lips, that always shook Mister Barkey up, and made him look straight in front forgetting quickly. And he thought of her the way she had stood before him, just a short while ago, unable to control her laughter, that was true, but also with such open admiration in her eyes. Once more he looked in the mirror. He did what he hadn't done since he was eighteen. He tightened up his biceps and was satisfied. Suddenly, he saw a small sunspot in the *mandibak:* the sunrays penetrated at an angle through the air hole in the wall. What time was it? Mister Barkey was suddenly at his wit's end again. Where was she in God's name? Suddenly he heard her clicking heels in the corridor and opened the door half way.

Like a hungry animal, he grabbed his bundle of clothes. He slammed the bathroom door shut again and started to put them on, fumbling and muddling hurriedly, but still listening to Mrs. Aubrey's voice:

"Shaaame on you! To seduce me into sneaking in like a thief. To steal clothes, then to sneak out like a thief. Actually, I must have been really out of my mind to have done that."

"You are indeed very kind-hearted!" rebutted Mister Barkey full of fire, "I'll never forget you!"

"Neeever? Really neeever?" she asked him teasingly and naughty. There was an arousing, insinuating intonation in her voice. Confused, Mister Barkey remained silent.

"Please tell me, Mister Barkey, why is there a set of underwear ready waiting for you, over there in the back of the house?"

"I get dirty from swimming, don't I," Mister Barkey explained sheepishly. For a moment she remained quiet, thinking.

"So, you swim every day?"

"Yes," Mister Barkey said with boyish pride.

"In that dangerous *kali?*" He didn't hear the teasing undertone.

"Oh, what dangerous *kali!*" he grumbled proudly.

"You know, Mister Barkey, I think you're really magnificent!"

"Ach," he said and stepped outside.

She looked at him with unfeigned admiration. Suddenly he felt awkward and loutish. He was getting ready to walk away quickly through the side-gate.

"No, no," Mrs. Aubrey said, "first you'll drink a cup of warm coffee. I insist, really." Stubborn, he shook his head.

"No, Mrs. Aubrey, I really can't. I'm indeed very grateful to you, but *that's* impossible."

"What do you mean?" She asked surprised as if there should be a special reason. He blushed.

"There isn't any time left," he said hurriedly, "now, I still get home unnoticed. I mean, my wife won't notice a thing."

"So nobody is supposed to notice anything?"

"But of course not, isn't that true? But not you, not you."

"But I don't mind that at all. I find it tremendously interesting and indeed quite a funny joke. I certainly don't mind telling it to everybody! Really! Well, anyway, I'll go back to bed.

Good-bye, Mister Barkey!" She said good-bye affectingly and seductively. Gracefully, she turned around and stepped lightly down the corridor, leaving Mister Barkey in anguish.

All of a sudden he trotted behind her.

"Mrs., Mrs. Aubrey! Please don't do that. No, please don't!"

Over her shoulder:

"Why not? Why shouldn't I tell about such a clumsy gentleman, who doesn't even want to sit down just for a little while ("I will sit down!") to drink a cup of coffee ("I will drink coffee!") while it will do him so much good."

"It is good for me!"

"So, that's better."

He sat in the little cozy verandah (it was just a pavilion where she lived) with the shutters intimately pulled down. It was cool but still comfortable. He blew on his steaming hot coffee and was aware of the sophisticated, exquisite surrounding. The chairs, the curtains, the mats, the gorgeous objects, the paintings with the provocative, proud nudes. These were all things from foreign illustrations. The center of this subtle but exquisite display was now lying on the sofa, enrobed yet simultaneously unrobed in a delicately thin, black dress, which confusingly contrasted against her ivory skin. Underneath that thin dress was that silky underwear from the bathroom with that dreamy fragrance. Mister Barkey forgot the coffee. He forgot the time. He was afraid and felt drawn to that object of his fear. Something about her was like swimming in the *kali*.

They sat silently for quite a while. Then she said:

"I'll promise I won't tell anyone, because I think you're very sweet." Confused, he searched for an answer.

"I think that's very nice of you."

"Just nice? Or also sweet?"

"Y—yes."

"Then give me a little kiss before you leave."

He couldn't get out of this situation and he didn't want to either. He walked over to her and hesitantly bent over. Her eyes were closed. She was so innocent, harmless, so serene and so lovely like the *kali* in the dry season. He kissed her lightly and trembled. He pulled his lips back, but her lips followed and he lost ground. He. . . .

In short, he returned home a quarter of an hour later. Although nobody saw him, he had the feeling that everyone had seen him, was pointing at him. He felt even more absurd than a while ago in the bathroom. His head and body were completely in turmoil. He entered his house through the side-gate and went straight to the back verandah. He stood in front of the side-passage leading to the back door between bathroom and kitchen. He saw a small strip of the *kali*, brown, powerful, irresistible, enchanting, and gigantic. Behind him he sensed the dull lifeless things of the house, the passage leading to the main building, the peaceful back verandah, the rustling tranquility of the sleeping Moes, the quiet front room with the desk and all kinds of petty paperwork.

He walked over to the back door carefully closing it. He turned the key in the lock then pushed it out underneath the door. He went to the *goedang* and pulled out two large top shelves from a packing-case. He took hammer and nails. Then with calm, well-aimed blows, he hammered the nails into the doorposts through the wooden shelves. Four at the left and four at the right. He shook the dust of his hands, slowly turned around, and went inside the house.

Why I Didn't Set Up My Own Business

Idrus

Translated by A. L. Reber

I am an employee of the Indonesian "Import-Export" Company. My office is a newly painted garage. My desk is the size of a pocket handkerchief and my chair, an aged rocking chair.

When I come to the office in the morning, I open a cabinet—almost empty—and take out last month's newspapers and put them on my desk. All these are the acts of a man eager to start in on heaps of accumulated work. After this, I sit on that rocking chair and read the papers until my head droops onto my chest.

One time I even had a dream while asleep in that chair. It seemed to me that the Head Director of the company came.

"Why aren't you working?" said he, talking through his nose.

"Why do I have to work?" I answered.

"You're my employee, aren't you?" he responded.

"No," I replied, "I'm an angel."

Hearing this, he opened his wallet and gave me five hundred rupiah, while saying:

"Go back to being an ordinary human being," and he jumped into his sedan.

After two months of being treated like an angel—a being that doesn't need to eat or drink—one Sunday I was invited to the Company Director's home.

His house was beautiful and modern and located on a main road. The grounds were so large that my Director considered it necessary to have separate entrance and exit gates for

From "Mengapa Saya Ta' Jadi Dirikan Perusahaan Sendiri," *Dengan Mata Terbuka* (Kuala Lumpur: Pustaka Antara, 1961). The capitalization is the author's own.

his car and the cars of cabinet ministers. That he was certain ministers of state would come to visit the house, he had mentioned to me one or two times.

Because I came on foot, I didn't have to worry about which was the entrance and which the exit to get to the house.

I was welcomed warmly by the Director of my firm and by two other people, a pretty woman who turned out to be his new wife, while the other, a man of middle age, happened to be the Vice President of a small bank.

After inviting me to sit down on a comfortable chair, my Director said:

"All of you probably already know about the new import regulations. Gentlemen, we have to pay forty percent in advance before we can import anything. Where can we get that kind of cash? Besides, it's certain that nobody wants to use his own money for such a purpose." Because the Director was looking at me, I felt obliged to offer my opinion. So I said:

"But these regulations absolutely don't apply to our company. . . ."

I would have continued but my Director's face turned red with anger at my first sentence. So I just looked down at my shoes again and listened to his words, which seemed sure to be a reprimand.

"How can they not apply to our enterprise? We are an Import-Export Company, aren't we?" he said, laying special stress on the word 'import'.

After that, the Director did not look in my direction again. He talked on and on with the Vice President of the little bank, and finally reached an agreement that the bank Director would be appointed as a Director of our Import-Export Company.

Then, quite unexpectedly, my Director said to me:

"Beginning now, I appoint you as Deputy Director."

My face blanched, and it was only after I arrived home, that I realized that from that day on I had become a person of very great importance for the national economy.

Almost every day now, my Director came to the office. Each time he came, he asked me if there was a letter for him. And each day I had to spread my empty hands wide and shake my head regretfully.

But one day a letter really did come. Just as my Director's car stopped in front of the office, I waved the letter at him from inside the office. He jumped out of his car and like a small child snatched the letter from my hand.

With great attention, he opened the letter, read it, and suddenly he shouted like a mad man:

"Got it, got it."

From inside his car he still had time to yell to me:

"Come to the house tomorrow and get your pay."

And this was the first joy that I ever felt during my stint as Deputy Director.

Even though I only got one month's salary paid—or maybe he thought the 750 rupiah I received was pay for five months' work?—I began to have real hopes for this firm. The Director had been able to borrow four hundred thousand—because that was the total permitted by the credit bank. Now surely the Company would move ahead as it ought.

In my imaginings, I received piles of letters each day from both inside the country and abroad. I happily sought tenders from overseas and gradually formed a staff of assistants.

But not one of these things actually happened. Our Import-Export Company didn't import or export anything at all, while the firm's Director never even stuck his nose inside the door. Eventually word came that my Director was buying rice fields and houses and land all over the place. From being the Director of a certain Company he had become a well-known landlord.

As for me, I went back to being an angel. I had long since thrown away the necktie of a Deputy Director—who knows where—and each day, I did nothing but play chess with a friend of mine who happened to be out of work.

But since my friend couldn't tell castles from knights, he made the same moves with both, so that finally we stopped playing and just swapped stories all day long.

One day my friend said:

"You already have lots of experience in this Company. Why not set up one of your own? I can help you get credit from a bank. If you like, you can become Head Director and I'll be a member of the board. You'll be able to live in comfort and won't have to work here any more." I at once clasped my friend's hand and said earnestly:

"Yes, I agree. Try to arrange it," and the two of us danced for joy in the garage.

The next day my friend came again. Happily he told me that he had called on the Minister of Justice to explain why he was setting up a Company. The Minister of Justice agreed in principle, he said. But he needed one hundred rupiah to cover various expenses. And this one hundred rupiah had to come from me, he said.

But before he could finish, I interrupted and said:

"Apparently my Director found out about our plan to set up this new firm. Because yesterday he paid me two month's salary all at once."

"So you won't go on with setting up our Company?" asked my friend.

"Right now, there's no more reason to," I answered. "My Director promised to pay my salary regularly from now on."

"You don't have the guts," he said angrily. "And to hell with the guy who calls himself a Company Director but is afraid to compete with us."

I didn't say anything else and just looked at my shoes that were already getting holes in the toe. But meanwhile my friend's attitude had changed completely and like a man begging, he said:

"If you really got two months' pay, surely you won't mind lending me a hundred rupiah. We're in a real mess at home right now."

With some reluctance, I lent him twenty-five rupiah and in my heart of hearts, I hoped that with twenty-five rupiah as capital he would, with luck, be able to set up a Company that was 100% national.

Malay Manuscripts and Early Printed Books at the Library of Congress

A. Kohar Rony

I

This article has two purposes.Its primary purpose is to describe the Library of Congress holdings of Malay manuscripts and early printed books in terms of their provenance and contents and to highlight the role played by the nineteenth-century missionary Alfred North in acquiring most of the collection. The second purpose is to begin to suggest the significance of the documents for Malay studies. The Library's holdings of Malay manuscripts, although limited in extent, concern the history and literature of the Malay world in the first half of the nineteenth century. Unlike twentieth-century imprints, which are generally accessible in North America and elsewhere, these early volumes may be the only copies extant.

Before describing the provenance and contents of the collection, it is important to clarify the special way in which the terms "Arabic script" and "Malay" will be used throughout this article. The term "Arabic script" here denotes the Arabic writing system adapted to the Malay phonetical system. In Indonesia, such a writing system is referred to simply as *huruf Arab,* in Brunei, Malaysia, and Singapore, as *huruf jawi.* The term "Malay" will be used to refer to the name of the language as opposed to the scripts in which the above texts were written. Indigenous to the island of Sumatra, and in use long before the birth of the modern states of Brunei, Indonesia, Malaysia, and Singapore, the Malay language developed over

I wish to thank Miss Asma Ahmat of the National Library of Malaysia, who did her internship at the Library of Congress in 1989-1990, for sharing with me her knowledge of our Malay collections. While assigned to the Asian Division, she undertook a special project of listing and describing the Malay manuscripts and early printed materials. The data for the description of such materials discussed in this paper is derived from her report of the project, "Report on the Library of Congress Malay Manuscripts and Early Printed Books." I also want to thank Lou Jacob and Warren Tsuneishi, both of the Library of Congress, Annabel Teh Gallop of the British Library, Kent Mulliner of Ohio University, Dorothy Rony, Joseph Saunders, and Philip Lee Thomas for their invaluable criticism and suggestions.

the centuries from being the mother tongue of coastal Sumatrans to being the *lingua franca* of trade and the learned language of the entire Malay archipelago. The early Malay manuscripts and early printed books to be discussed in this article are part of the body of literature of the people who used the Malay language. In this sense they are the cultural heritage of the Malays of modern-day Malaysia, but also of those in Brunei, Indonesia, and Singapore.

II

The Malay manuscipts and early printed books in the Library of Congress were not described until recent times. Although Horace Poleman reported four of the titles in *A Census of Indic Manuscripts in the United States and Canada,*[1] nobody seemed to take note of them. Perhaps the title of the census itself was a little misleading, and it may have been assumed that it concerned only Indian manuscripts.

It was not until Professor A. Teeuw came to visit the Library of Congress in 1966 that our Malay manuscripts were first brought to the attention of scholars. I remember how pleasantly surprised he was when I showed him the collection. In the following year, he published a brief article in the *Bijdragen tot de taal-, land-, and volkenkunde,* reporting the existence of eight of the Library's Malay manuscripts.[2] Soon thereafter, we began to receive inquiries about them, as well as requests for photocopies. A positive microfilm copy of the eight manuscripts can now be purchased from the Library of Congress Photoduplication Service.

Most of the Library of Congress Malay manuscripts, and a few of the early printed books, bear the so-called "Smithsonian Deposit" stamps, which are to indicate that they were first acquired by the Smithsonian Institution from the Wilkes Exploring Expedition (1838-1842). The expedition was so named because it was commanded by Captain Charles Wilkes, a US Naval Officer who had earlier explored the Antarctic region. Authorized by the Congress of the United States, the Wilkes Expedition included naturalists, botanists, mineralogists, taxidermists, and, most importantly from our profession's point of view, a philologist. I imagine one of the purposes of the mission was to collect and bring back examples of "native" culture, and the philologist was there to help identify and select Malay manuscripts and other publications. When the members of the expedition reached Singapore in February 1842, they were greeted by the US Consul, Joseph Balestier and his wife, Maria Revere Balestier, and also by an American missionary, Alfred North, who was stationed there. It was North who helped the expedition acquire not only the Malay manuscripts and early printed books, but also other manuscripts written in the Bugis script, the script of the Buginese people of South Sulawesi.

As part of an agreement worked out in 1865, the Smithsonian transferred major parts of its collections, including the Malay manuscripts and early printed materials acquired through the Wilkes Expedition, to the Library of Congress. By the close of the year 1866, Librarian of Congress Aisnworth Rand Spofford was happy to announce the transfer of "this large accession ... especially valuable in the range of scientific books, comprising by far

---

[1]Horace I. Poleman, *A Census of Indic Manuscirpts in the United States and Canada* (New Haven: American Oriental Society, 1938).

[2]A Teeuw, "Korte Mededelingen: Malay Manuscripts in the Library of Congress," *Bijdragen tot de taal-, land-, en volkenkunde* 123, 4 (1967): 517–20.

the largest collection of the journals and transactions of learned societies, foreign and domestic, which exists in America." This came to be called "The Smithsonian Deposit."

At the present time, these manuscripts and the printed books are in the custody of the Southern Asia Section of the Asian Division in the Library of Congress. They are housed in a secured area, although access is available to any legitimate researcher.

III

The Malay manuscripts consist of fourteen codices and a bound volume containing handwritten correspondence and letters with officials seals to the Chief British Resident in Singapore from heads of state in what are now Brunei, Cambodia, Malaysia, and Indonesia. As I have mentioned earlier, eight of the manuscripts were described briefly by Professor A. Teeuw in 1967. These were *Kinta Buhan, Isma Dewa Pakurma Raja, Kitab Khoja Maimun, Hikayat Amir Hamzah, Hikayat Johor, Hikayat Patani, Hikayat Muhammad Hanafiah,* and *Hikayat Abdullah.* Twenty years later, in 1987, Harun Mat Piah described them in greater detail in an article in *Sari.*[3]

The six additional codices are as follows:

1. *Hikayat Panca Tanderan,* also known as *Galila (or Kalila) dan Damina.* Four Indian tales translated by Abdullah bin Abdul Kadir with the help of one Tambi Matubar Fafatar. Malacca [handwritten by Abdullah bin Abdul Kadir] 1835. Folio. 67 p., 29.3 x 21.7 cm. Laid paper; 12 lines

Written in black ink with rubrication for chapter headings and punctuation words, the handwriting is neat and large. There is vowelization of names and of countries, etc., which are difficult to pronounce.

Binding: softboard, covered with marble paper, bound at the Singapore Free Press Office.

Contents: 1. Galila Damina Sakralaum. —2. Sendi Bikrawam. —3. Arta Nasam. —4. Sambi Tarica Kariwum.

2. *Kitab Tib: pengetahuan segala ubat-ubat adanya.* Singapore [Handcopied by Abdullah bin Abdul Kadir?] 1837. Quarto. 41 p. 19.7 x 16.5 cm., 13 lines.

Bluish white English laid paper. Watermarks: "Joseph Coles," "1836," and image of Britannia in a crowned circle.

Binding: softbound covered by marble paper, quarter binding.

Discusses medicinal values of honey, ginger, black pepper, etc.; medicines for coughs, constipation, sinus; Malay charms used to cure sickness caused by demons and spirits.

3. [*Four Tales*] Singapore [handcopied by Muhammad Arif] 1837. Quarto. 154 p. 18 x 15 cm., 11 lines.

Bluish white English laid paper. Watermarks: "J. Coles," "1834," 1835," "1835," "1836," and a mark of a lion in a crowned shield.

[3]Harun Mat Piah, "Manuskrip-manuskrip Melayu dalam Koleksi Library of Congress Amerika Syarikat," *Sari* 5 (1987): 3–15.

Written in black ink in a firm, neat hand, with certain words rubricated, e.g., punctuation words, names, and Arabic phrases.

Binding: soft cardboard covered by marble paper; quarter binding.

Contents: 1. *Hikayat Abu Sahmah.* A story about Abu Sahmah, the son of Umar and his sentencing by Umar according to Islamic laws. —2. *Hikayat bulan belah dua.* —3. *Hikayat Saerah dan Hadhri.* —4. *Hikayat Derma Taksiah.*

4. *Hikayat Syah Mardan.* Singapore [Handcopied by Muhammad Arif, a teacher in the Raffles Institution] 1837.

Quarto. 230 p., 19.5 x 14.7 cm; 13 lines.

Blue English laid paper. Watermarks: "Joseph Coles," "1836," and an image of Britannia in a crowned circle.

5. *Hikayat Isma Yatim.* Malacca [copied by Ismail, 1837?]

Quarto. 268 p., 22.5 x 18 cm., 17 lines. Woven paper, yellowish white. 23 gatherings numbered in Arabic in red ink.

Written in black ink in firm, neat handwriting, with rubrication of punctuation words and Arabic phrases.

Binding: bound in softboard covered with marble paper and quarter leather.

6. *Kitab Adat segala Raja-raja Melayu dalam segala negeri.* Singapore [copied by Abdullah bin Abdul Kadir, 1837]

Quarto. 90 p., 19.5 x 16 cm., 13 lines. Bluish white Egnlish laid paper. Watermarks: "Joseph Coles," "1835," and a mark in the shape of Britannia in a crowned circle.

Written in black ink with rubrication of punctuation words.

Binding: softboard covered with marble paper. Quarter binding.

An earlier copy dated 1819 belonged to Datuk Sulaiman of Kampung Melayu Malaka. Datuk Sulaiman was Abdullah's teacher mentioned in his *Hikayat Abdullah.* The original work was done in 1779 at the request of the Dutch Governor De Bruin.

The bound volume of correspondence contains early nineteenth-century official correspondence from heads of state in neighboring Southeast Asian countries to William Farquhar, British Resident in Singapore. This is an important source of information about the early period of British domination in Southeast Asia from the point of view of Southeast Asian political leaders. Altogether, the correspondence numbers forty-seven letters consisting of the following:

a. Three letters from Brunei to Colonel William Farquhar, British Resident of Singapore:

(1) From Sultan Muhammad Khan Zul Alam ibn Sultan Omar Ali Saifuddin, dated 5 Rejab 1236 (8 Apr. 1821);

(2) From Sultan Muhammad Khan Zul Alam ibn Sultan Omar Ali Saifuddin, dated 6 Syaaban 1237 (28 Apr. 1822);

(3) From Pangeran Muda Muhammad Alam ibn Sultan Muhammad Khan Zul Alam to Tambi Muhammad ibn Arsyad of Malacca, dated 7 Syaaban 1237 (29 Apr. 1822);

b. A letter from Tuan Syed Abdul Hamid bearing the title of "Nak Cu Pa of Rapadi?" Kambuja to Colonel William Farquhar, British Resident of Singapore, dated 4 Jamadil Akhir 1235 (18 Feb. 1820);

c. Seven letters from Raja Bendahara of Johor-Pahang to Colonel William Farquhar, British Resident of Singapore:

(1) Undated;

(2) Dated 30 Syaaban 1234 (24 Jun. 1819);

(3) Dated 1 Zulkaedah 1234 (22 Aug. 1819);

(4) Dated 10 Ramadhan 1235 (21 Jun. 1820);

(5) Dated 24 Ramadhan 1236 (25 Jun. 1821);

(6) Dated 10 Zulhijjah 1236 (8 Sept. 1821);

(7) Dated 10 Syaaban 1237 (2 May 1822);

d. A letter from Dato Bendahara of Johore-Pahang to Syed Syarif Umar Jamid of Singapore;

e. A letter from Yang Di Pertuan Kelantan and Tengku Syed Abdul Rahman bin al-Habib Hussein Aidid to Colonel William Farquhar, British Resident of Singapore, dated 3 Syaaban 1237 (25 Apr. 1822);

f. A letter from Dato Penghulu Naning to Colonel William Farquhar, British Resident of Singapore, undated;

g. Three letters of Pengeran Dipati from Palembang:

(1) addressed to Colonel William Farquhar, British Resident of Malacca, dated 7 Jamadil Akhir 1234 (3. Apr.1819);

(2) addressed to Colonel William Farquhar, dated 7 Jamadil Akhir 1234 (3 Apr. 1819);

(3) addressed to "Tuan Besar of Singapore," dated 13 Zulkaedah 1236 (12 Aug. 1821);

h. A letter from Sultana Siti Fatimah binti Jamaluddin Abdul Rahman of Pamanah to Colonel William Farquhar, British Resident of Singapore, dated 13 Zulkaedah 1237 (1 Aug. 1822);

i. Letters on Riau:

(1) A letter from Yang Di Pertuan Muda Riau to Colonel William Farquhar, British Resident of Malacca, dated 24 Zulkaedah 1233 (25 Sept. 1818);

(2) Twenty-two letters addressed to Major or Colonel William Farquhar, British Resident of Singapore:

(a) from the Shabandar of Riau

(i) dated 25 Zulkaedah 1233 (26 Sept. 1818)

(ii) dated 25 Zulkaedah 1233 (26 Sept 1818)

(iii) dated 3 Safar 1236 (10 Nov. 1820);

(b) A letter from Yang di Pertuan Muda of Pulau Penyengat, dated 5 Rabiulthani (Jumadil Akhir?) 1234 (1 Feb. 1819);

(c) Four letters from Tengku Pengeran of Siak [Sri Indrapura]:

(i) dated 11 Rejab 1234 (6 May 1819)

(ii) dated 19 Jumadil Akhir 1236 (22 Feb. 1821)

(iii) undated

(iv) dated 23 Rabiul Ackhir 1237 (17 Jan 1822);

(d) Two letters from the Acting Yang di Pertuan Muda of Riau:

(i) dated [1819?]

(ii) dated 10 Ramadhan 1234 (3 Jul. 1819);

(e) A letter from Tengku Besar of Kampar Pulau Daun, dated 1235 A.H. (8 Oct. 1820)

(f) A letter Dato' Seri Pikrama Raja of Siak Sri Indrapura, dated 18 Muharram 1235 (6 Nov. 1819);

(g) Two letters from Egku Syed al-Syarif Muhammad Zain ibn almar-hum al-Habib al-syed Abdul Rahman al-Kudsi of Lingga:

(i) dated 17 Ramadhan 1235 (28 Jun. 1820);

(ii) dated 4 Maulid (Rabiul Awal) 1236 (1820);

(h) A letter from Engku Syed Muhammad Zain ibn al-marhum al-Habib Abdul Rahman al-Qudsi of Riau, dated 9 Jamadil Awal 1236 (12 Feb. 1821);

(i) A letter from Sultan Syed al-Syarif Abdul Jalil al-marhum Saifuddin Yang Di Pertuan Besar Siak Indrapura, dated 20 Jamadil Akhir 1236 (23 Feb. 1821);

(j) A letter from Tengku Long of Riau, dated 17 Safar 1227 (20 Feb. 1812);

(k) Two letters from Yang Di Pertuan Muda Riau:

(i) dated 10 Rabiul Awal 1231 (9 Feb. 1821)

(ii) dated 8 Syawal 1237 (28 Jun 1822);

(l) A letter from Colonel William Farquhar, British Resident of Singapore to Yang Di Pertuan Muda Riau, dated 25 Rabiul Awal 1237 (20 Dec. 1821);

(m) A letter from Dato' Syahbandar of Lingga to Baba Hock Kee of Singapore, dated 23 Syawal 1236 (24 Jul. 1821);

(n) letters from Trengganu:

(1) from Sultan Ahmad ibn Sultan Zainal Abidin to Colonel Farquhar, British Resident of Malacca, dated 1 Zulhijjah 1234 (21 Sept. 1819);

(2) from Sultan Ahmad ibn Sultan Zainal Abidin to Colonel William Farquhar, British Resident of Singapore

(i) dated 29 Rejab 1234 (24 May 1819)

(ii) dated 5 Syaaban 1237 (1822);

(3) From Sultan Abdul Rahman ibn Sultan Zainal Abidin, Yang Di Pertuan Muda, Acting Sultan of Trengganu, to Colonel William Farquhar, British Resident of Singapore:

(i) dated 27 Muharram 1235 (15 Nov. 1819);

(ii) dated 12 Muharram 1236 (20 Oct. 1820).

IV

The early printed books in this collection, although few in number, nevertheless represent a body of literature which is important both for the study of the historical development of the Malay language and for the history of printing in the Malay archipelago. As noted earlier, all but one are in the Arabic or *jawi* script and were printed in various places: Great Britain, India, Malaysia, the Netherlands, and Singapore. The earliest title in the collection is in the roman script and was printed at Oxford, England, in 1677. Only a few printed books bear the "Smithsonian Deposit" stamps. It may therefore be assumed that not all of the books came to the Library in the Smithsonian Deposit of 1865, but most were acquired separately over the years.

Those books printed by the Mission Press serve as examples of the early printing presses in the region. In Malaysia and Singapore, for example, the first printing press was started on Prince of Wales Island, Penang, in 1806, followed by missionary presses in Malacca in 1815 and in Singapore in 1822. It was the Mission Press that brought out early imprints in the Arabic script in 1817 bearing the titles "The Ten Commandments" with "The Lord's Prayer" appended, and "Dr. Watts' First Catechism."

The early printed books in the collections can be described as follows:

1. Bibles:

a. *The Bible: Old and New Testament* or *Al-Kitab iaitu segala Surat Perjanian Lama dan Baharu;* tersalin kepada Bahasa Melayu atas titah segala tuan pemerintah Kompani Wolanda Tentera di Bandar Betawi pada tahun 1758. Rev. ed. Calcutta: R.S. Hutchings, 1821. 1453 p.

b. *Songs of David with Prayers or Puji2an yaitu segala Zabur Daud lagipun beberapa doa yang dipakai sehari, pagi dan petang.* 2nd ed. Singapore [s.n.] 1831. 273 p.

c. *The Bible: Old and New Testament* or *Al Kitab iaitu segala Surat Perjanjian Lama dan Baharu;* tersalin kepada Bahasa Melayu atas titah dan belanja kerapatan al-kitab di Wolanda iaitu tuan2 yang ada rapat akan memberita firman Allah daripada banyak kesalahan bahasa tesuci dan tertera pula. Harlem: Johannes Enschede, 1824. 778 p.

d. *The Bible: Old Testament or Al-qul ul-utif iaitu segala Surat Perjanjian Lama.*

[Tersalin] atas titah dan belanja kerapatan al-kitab di Wolanda iaitu tuan2 yang ada rapat memberita firman tersuci dan tertera pula. Harlem: Johannes Eschede, 1824. v. 2 (p.779-1304)

c. *The Bible: New Testament* or *Wasiat yang Baharu iaitu segala Kitab Perjanjian Baharuu atau Injil tuhan kami Isa a-Masih.*. Tersalin kepada Bahasa Melayu pada kedua kalinya dan lagi dicap atas belanja Netherlands Bible Genootschap [S.I.: s.n.]. 1889. 683 p. Lithograph.

f. *The Bible: New Testament* or *Injil al-Kudus Isa al-Masih iaitu segala Surat Perjanjian Baharu.* [Tersalin] atas titah dan belanja kerapatan al-kitab di Wolanda iaitu tuan yang ada rapat akan memberi firman Allah daripada banyak kesalahan bahasa tersuci dan tertera pula. Harlem: Johannes Enschede, 1820. 423 p.

g. *The Bible: New Testament* or *Kitab al-Kudus iaitu Injil Isa al-Masih atas segala Surat Testament Baharu.* Rev. ed. Singapore: The Mission Press for the British and Foreign Bible Society, 1831. 2 v. (953 p.) v.2 bound with v. 1.

2. Malay Textbooks.

a. Keasberry, B.P. *Ini kitab teki2 terbang iaitu pada menyatakan daripada permulaan belajar alif ba ta sampai boleh membaca dan mengarang surat2 Melayu.* Singapore: Malay Missionary Singapore [1872] 165 p.

Also contains *Ceritera ilmu kepandaian orang puteh.* 165 p.

Lithograph.

b. *Hikayat Jaya Asmara.* Singapore [s.n.] 1899. 3 v. LC has v. 2 (p.101-270); v. 3 (p.271-356).

"Akan menjadi pergunaan kepada kanak2 yang belajar dalam sekolah2 Melayu supaya mengetahui jalan Bahasa Melayu yang betul."

Lithograph.

c. Nuruddin ar-Raniri, Sheikh. *Bustan as-salatin.* Bab Yang Kedua. Singapore: American Mission Press, 1900. 128 p.

d. A collection of four titles:

(i) *Karangan perkataan pendek.* 3rd ed. Singapore [s.n.] 1836. 11 p.

(2) *Ibarat perkataan.* 3rd ed. Singapore [s.n.] 1836. 16 p.

(3) *Beberapa hal kelahiran orang* 3rd. ed. Singapore [s.n.] 1836. 20 p.

(4) *Ibarat pelayaran kehidupan* 3rd. ed. Singapore [s.n.] 1836. 28 p.

3. The Works of Munshi Abdullah bin Abdul Kadir

a. *Hikayat Abdullah.* (The Story of Abdullah)

(1) *Hikayat Abdullah.* Bahawa inilah jilid yang kedua begi *Hikayat Abdullah bin Abdul Kadir Munshi.* Singapore: Matbaah Government, 1888. v. 2 (p.243-487).

(2) *Hikayat Abdullah bin Abdul Kadir Munshi.* Singapore: Sidang Methodist, 1915-1917. v. 1 (165 p.); v. 2 (p. 166-339). Bound with v.1.

b. North, Alfred, and Abdullah bin Abdul Kadir.

Bahwa ini ceritera kapal asap [An Account of the Steam Ships] (Singapore: Mission Press, 184?). 86 p.

The first nineteen pages contain an account from Abdullah of his visit to the steamship *Sesostris* which lay at anchor at Singapore in 1841. An account of this visit is also related by Abdullah in his *Hikayat Abdullah.* The rest of the pages are written by Alfred North, relating the power and uses of steam. In the last pages, 67-86, North urges Malays to move away from the Arab sphere of influence.

4. Two publications of *Sejarah Melayu*:

a. North Publications:

(1) 1st ed. Preface by Alfred North. Singapore: Mission Press [1840] 5, 368 p.

According to a note found in the cover, the *Sejarah* existed only in manuscript until 1841 when it was printed in Singapore at the expense of Thomas MacMicking Esq. under the careful supervision of Mr. Alfred North, assisted by Abdullah. The work is said to have been collated from six manuscripts.

(2) 2nd ed. Preface by Alfred North. Singapore: Mission Press [1840] 5, 368 p.

According to a note found inside the cover, the work was collated from various manuscripts with the help of a "learned native" (i.e. Abdullah bin Abdulkadir Munshi) and was first printed in 1840.

This edition contains thirty-four chapters and ends with the death of Tun Ali Hati.

b. Shellabear Publication. Singapore: Mission Press [1896] 7, 345 p.

"Segala perkataannya dibandingkan dengan beberapa kitab tulisan tangan dan kitab-kitab yang tercap dahulu maka barang perkatannya yang salah telah dibetulkan oleh tuan W. J. Shellabear."

5. A collection of religious tracts published by a Christian missionary in Singapore in the 1830s.

The Library of Congress has only one roman script title in this collection: *Jang Ampat Evangelia derri Tuan Kita Jesu Christi, daan Berboatan derri Jang Apostoli Bersacti.* Bersalin dallam bassa Malayo; that is *The Four Gospels of Our Lord Jesus Christ, and the Acts of the Holy Apostles,* translated into the Malayan tongue. Oxford: Printed by H. Hall, 1677. 14, 215 p.

This translated work is unique because of its written testimony to the use of the Malay language—the percursor of the present Bahasa Indonesia and Bahasa Melayu spoken in Malaysia, Brunei, and Singapore—as the *lingua franca* of the Malay world in the seventeenth century. The introduction contains some information about other early translations into Malay of books of the Bible, as well as information about dictionaries by the translator.

V

This collection of Malay manuscripts and early printed books constitutes a unique source of material for historical and comparative philological studies. For research purposes, the volume containing official correspondence consisting of forty-six letters by heads of governments in Southeast Asia is a real find, enriching resources available for the study of early nineteenth-century history in Indonesia, Malaysia, and Singapore. Almost all of the letters concern the establishment of friendly relations with the British power seated in Singapore. It is quite evident from reading the correspondence that British supremacy in the area was so respected that even a ruler of Palembang felt compelled to send a letter of greetings to *Tuan Besar* ("big boss").

While the correspondence casts light on the nature of the political relationship between the British power and Malay rulers, *Hikayat Abdullah,* one of the Malay manuscripts in the collection, provides a most colorful description of social changes in the Malay world under the newly imposed British rule. Abdullah noted, for example, how the Dutch Eurasians in Malacca eagerly adapted themselves to the British way of life, in clothing, customs, and language.

Kitab Adat segala Raja-raja Melayu dalam segala negeri [Customs of the Malay Kings] is another significant source for historical research. It provides insights into the royal life and customs of a Malay ruler from the time of his birth to his death, and contains rules of conduct for every aspect of royal life.

For philological purposes, the Library of Congress holdings can be compared with those in the collections described by Ricklefs and Voorhoeve in *Indonesian Manuscripts in Great Britain* (1977). The Library of Congress *Hikayat Abdullah*, though copied by a Bugis scribe, Ismail bin Hussein, should be close to Abdullah's original work since it was copied under the close superivison of Alfred North and completed in about five months. When the text of this manuscript is compared with the lithographic text in the Shellabear edition (1915), which purports to be close to Abdullah's original, differences in words and paragraph order alter the interpretation of the events described. Consider the following:

1. Shellabear (p.4): "Kemudian belajar bahasa dan belajar kira. . . ."

LC Manuscript (p.4): "Kemudian belajar bahasa Keling dan belajar kira. . . ."

2. Shellabear (p.7): "pada hijrah nabi sanat 1231 tahun maka bapakupun kembalilah ke rahmattullah kemudian. . . ."

LC Manuscript (p.6): "pada hijrah nabi sanat 1239 tahun bapakupun kembali ke rahmatullah taala. . . ."

3. Shellabear (p.7): "Sebermula adapun negeri yang tempat aku tumpah darah yaitu negeri Melaka yang dipeliharakan Allah daripada segala bala' dan aniaya maka pada masa itu Inggeris memegang perintah dalam Melaka. . . ."

LC Manuscript (p.6): "Sebermula adapun negeri yang tempatku tumpah darah itu yaitu negeri Melaka yang dipeliharakan Allah . . . dan aniaya kepada tarikh 1211 sanat tahun kepada tujuh. . . ."

VI

Let me now turn to what this Malay manuscripts collection means for the library profession in terms of acquiring publications from Southeast Asia. It is quite clear that, in retrospect, the successful acquisition of the manuscripts and early printed books was the product of fortuitous timing and circumstances. Congress authorized and funded the Wilkes Expedition; the expedition was commanded by a naval captain interested in acquiring recorded culture—handwritten or printed materials. However, even more crucial for the success of the mission was the role of an American missionary residing in Singapore by the name of Alfred North, who was known as a Malay expert, a practical printer, and, above all, a Malay bibliophile.

No matter how well the expedition was funded or how keen the interest shown in acquiring research materials from Southeast Asia, success would have been far less likely in the absence of a cultural go-between; someone with a mastery of the local language and the book trade in the region. When the expedition arrived in Singapore in 1842, there were neither national bibliographies nor book publishers, nor bookshops to turn to for acquisitions. It was indeed fortunate that Alfred North was around. He knew the country well: its people, culture, language, and, above all, where important materials were to be purchased.

Being a bibliophile, he had apparently cultivated a friendship with Malay authors and scribes and could identify those he thought to be the best among them. Not only did he encourage them to write or copy works wanted by the expedition, but he also published their works with his missionary printing press. Thanks chiefly to his efforts, significant records of the cultural heritage of the ethnic Malay population of Brunei, Indonesia, Malaysia, and Singapore, was preserved for many generations to come.

Alfred North was born on March 19, 1807 in Exeter, New Hampshire. His family having moved to two different states before he reached the age of twelve, he attended schools in West Windsor, Vermont, and in Boonville, New York. Finally, in 1823, he attended a denominational school in Utica, New York, where he received instruction in religious subjects, including religious music. In addition, he was tutored in music as well as trained in printing by Thomas Hastings, a noted composer and publisher of *The Western Recorder.*

In 1832, Alfred North moved to New York City and worked as a printer. There he regularly attended a Protestant religious revival where he met his future wife, Minerva Bryan, who shared his vision of spreading Christianity throughout the world. Not long after he "professed" religion as his way of life in 1833, he married Minerva Bryan. In 1835, both husband and wife received appointments as assistant missionaries by the American Board of Commissioners for Foreign Missions and were sent overseas to Singapore.

A question might arise as to why the newly married young couple wanted to go to that distant land. The answer seemed to be that at the time there was a widespread belief that the millennium was fast approaching. In fact, one minister had even fixed the date for its imminent arrival as 1999 and had suggested that the time had come to save the world for Christ. According to Geoffrey Ward in a recent article,[4] it was the Rev. Timothy Dwight, President of Yale College, who set the ambitious agenda of the American Board's special mission: that is, to hasten the time "when the Romish cathedral, the mosque, and the pagoda, shall not have one stone left upon another which shall not be thrown down...."

Whatever the case may be, the Norths arrived in Singapore on February 7, 1836 on board the *Sachem*. In Singapore, North took up studying the Malay language with the famous Munshi Abdullah Kadir. In his article "The 'Lost' Manuscript of Hikayat Abdullah,"[5] H.F.O'B. Traill wrote that in Singapore North studied Malay with Abdullah, who thought of him as one "who has bathed in the waters of the Malay language and drunk his fill of them." When North completed his assignment in Singapore, he was given another missionary assignment. This time it was in India. He, along with his family, left Singapore for India on board the *Shah Alam* on November 20, 1843. In 1847, two years after his wife had died of cholera, he was summoned home by the Commissioners for Foreign Missions. Although he was asked to return to India, North decided to stay home and entered Auburn Theological Seminary to qualify for Presbyterian ministry. He died on March 3, 1869, in Chilton, Wisconsin.

VII

In this article I have attempted to describe the provenance and contents of the Library of Congress holdings of Malay manuscripts and early printed books, highlighting the role played by Alfred North in acquiring the materials for the Wilkes Expedition. I have argued that this collection represents a body of literature which is important for the study of the historical development of Malay language and society and also for the history of printing in insular Southeast Asia. No other library institutions, except the British Library, appear to

[4]Geoffrey C. Ward, "Two Missionaries' Ordeal by Faith in a Distant Clime," *Smithsonian* 21, 5 (1990): 118–32

[5]Dato H.F.O'B. Traill, "The 'Lost'Manuscript of Hikayat Abdullah Munshi," *Journal of the Malaysian Branch of the Royal Asiatic Society* 15, 2 (1982): 126–34.

have examples of the Malay manuscripts and early printed books at the Library of Congress. Indeed, two copies of the *Sejarah Melayu* held at the Library of Congress are the only copies extant: neither the British Library nor the National Library of Malaysia have copies of them in their holdings. More importantly, they represent the first acquisition of research materials from Southeast Asia by the United States Government. It was not until 120 years later that the acquisition of research materials was resumed in earnest with the establishment of the Library of Congress National Program for Acquisitions and Cataloging in 1963.

APPENDIX

List of Library of Congress Malay manuscripts:

1. *Kinta Buhan*
2. *Isma Dewa Pakurma Raja* or *Hikayat Isma Dewa Pekerma Raja*
3. *Khoja Maimon* or *Hikayat Khoja Maimon*
4. *Amir Hamzah* or *Hikayat Amir Hamzah*
5. *Hikayat Johor* or *Salasilah Raja-Raja Johor.*
6. *Hikayat Patani.*
7. *Hikayat Muhammad Hanafiah.*
8. *Hikayat Abdullah.*
9. *Hikayat Panca Tanderan.*
10. *Kitab Tib.*
11. [*Four Tales*]
12. *Hikayat Syah Mardan.*
13. *Hikayat Isma Yatim.*
14. *Adat segala Raja-raja.*

SOUTHEAST ASIA PROGRAM PUBLICATIONS

Cornell University

East Hill Plaza
Ithaca, New York 14850

Studies on Southeast Asia

Number 1 *The Symbolism of the Stupa,* Adrian Snodgrass. 1985. Rep. with index, 1988. 469 pp. $16.00.

Number 4 *In the Center of Authority: The Malay Merong Mahawangsa,* Hendrik M. J. Maier. 1988. 210 pp. $14.00.

Number 5 *Southeast Asian Ephemeris: Solar and Planetary Positions, A.D. 638–2000,* J. C. Eade. 1989. 171 pp. $15.00.

Number 6 *Trends in Khmer Art,* Jean Boisselier. Ed. Natasha Eilenberg. Trans. Natasha Eilenberg and Melvin Elliott. 1989. 124 pp. $15.00.

Number 7 *A Malay Frontier: Unity and Duality in a Sumatran Kingdom,* Jane Drakard. 1990. 215 pp. $15.00.

SEAP Series

Number 2 *The Dobama Movement in Burma (1930–1938),* Khin Yi. 1988. 160 pp. $9.00.

Number 2A *The Dobama Movement in Burma: Appendix (Documents in Burmese).* 1988. 140 pp. $16.00.

Number 3 *Postwar Vietnam: Dilemmas in Socialist Development,* ed. Christine White and David Marr. 1988. 264 pp. $12.00.

Number 4 *Independent Burma at Forty Years,* ed. Josef Silverstein. 1989. 118 pp. $10.00

Number 5 *Japanese Relations with Vietnam: 1951–1987,* Masaya Shiraishi. 1990. 174 pp. $12.00.

Number 6 *The Rise and Fall of the Communist Party of Burma (CPB),* Bertil Lintner. 1990. 124 pp. $10.00.

Number 7 *Intellectual Property and US Relations with Indonesia, Malaysia, Singapore, and Thailand,* Elisabeth Uphoff. 1991. 67 pp. $8.00.

Translation Series

Volume 1 *Reading Southeast Asia.* 1990. 188 pp. $12.00.

* * *

In the Mirror, Literature and Politics in Siam in the American Era, ed. and trans. Benedict R. Anderson and Ruchira Mendiones. 1985. Reprint 1991. 303 pp. Paperback $12.00.

Data Papers

In Print

Number 18 *Conceptions of State and Kingship in Southeast Asia,* Robert Heine-Geldern. 1956. 6th printing, 1987. 14 pp. $3.50.

Number 75 *White Hmong-English Dictionary,* comp. Ernest E. Heimbach. Linguistics Ser. 4. 1969. 3rd printing, 1991. 497 pp. $12.00.

Number 92 *Feasting and Social Oscillation: A Working Paper on Religion and Society in Upland Southeast Asia,* A. Thomas Kirsch. 1973. 4th printing, 1990. 67 pp. $5.00.

Number 102 *No Other Road to Take,* Memoir of Mrs. Nguyen Thi Dinh, trans. Mai Elliott. 1976. 77 pp. $6.00.

Indonesia

Indonesia, a semiannual journal, devoted to Indonesia's culture, history, and social and political problems. The following issues still available:

No. 16, October 1973, No. 17, April 1974, No. 20, October 1975, $4.50 each
No. 21, April 1976, No. 22, October 1976, No. 23, April 1977, $5.00 each
No. 32, October 1981, No. 34, October 1982, $6.50 each
No. 37, April 1984, No. 40, October 1985, $7.50 each
No. 41, April 1986, No. 42, October 1986, $7.50 each, $14.00 both
No. 43, April 1987, No. 44, October 1987, $8.50 each, $16.00 both
No. 45, April 1988, No. 46, October 1988, $8.50 each, $16.00 both
No. 47, April 1989, No. 48, October 1989, $8.50 each, $16.00 both
No. 49, April 1990, No. 50, October 1990, $9.50 each, $18.00 both
No. 51, April 1991, No. 52, October 1991, $9.50 each, $18.00 both

Special Issue of *Indonesia* (1991):

The Role of the Indonesian Chinese in Shaping Modern Indonesian Life $10

STUDY AND TEACHING MATERIALS

Obtain from Southeast Asia Program Publications
Cornell University, East Hill Plaza, Ithaca, New York 14850

Thai

A.U.A. Language Center Thai Course, J. Marvin Brown, Book 1, $12.00; Book 2, $9.00; Book 3, $9.00. Tape supplement for books 1, 2, 3, $4.00. Small Talk (dialog book A), $12.00. Getting Help (dialog book B), $12.00. Book R (reading), $12.00. Book W (writing), $12.00.

Indonesian

Beginning Indonesian through Self-Instruction, John U. Wolff, Dédé Oetomo, and Daniel Fietkiewicz. 1984. 900 pp. 3 vols. $27.00/set.

Indonesian Readings, John U. Wolff. 1978. (3d printing, 1988). 468 pp. $16.00.

Indonesian Conversations, John U. Wolff. 1978. 2d printing, 1981. 297 pp. $14.00.

Formal Indonesian, John U. Wolff. 1980. 2d printing, 1986. 446 pp. $16.00.

Vietnamese

Intermediate Spoken Vietnamese, Franklin Huffman and Tran Trong Hai. 1980. 401 pp. $12.00.

Khmer

Cambodian System of Writing and Beginning Reader, Franklin E. Huffman. Originally published by Yale University Press, 1970. Reissued by Cornell Southeast Asia Program, 1987. 365 pp. $14.00.

Modern Spoken Cambodian, Franklin E. Huffman, assist. Charan Promchan and Chhom-Rak Thong Lambert. Originally published by Yale University Press, 1970. Reissued by Cornell Southeast Asia Program, 1984, 1987, 1991. 451 pp. $16.00.

Intermediate Cambodian Reader, ed. Franklin E. Huffman, assist. Im Proum. Originally published by Yale University Press, 1972. Reissued by Cornell Southeast Asia Program, 1988. 499 pp. $16.00.

Cambodian Literary Reader and Glossary, Franklin E. Huffman and Im Proum. Originally issued by Yale University Press, 1977. Reprinted with permission by Cornell Southeast Asia Program, 1988. 494 pp. $16.00.

Tagalog

Pilipino through Self-Instruction by John U. Wolff with Ma. Theresa C. Centano and Der-Hwa U. Rau. 1991. Series, 1,493 pp. 4 vols. $50.00/set. Vol. 1, 362 pp., $15.00; Vol. 2, 384 pp., $15.00; Vol. 3, 436 pp., $15.00; Vol. 4, 308 pp., $15.00. Vol. 4 contains the answer key, glossary, and index for all four volumes.

Accessions List of the John M. Echols Collection on Southeast Asia, ed. John H. Badgley. Compiled monthly. Annual subscription $20.00.

Language Tapes

Order tapes from The Language Laboratory, Dept. of Modern Languages,
Morrill Hall, Cornell University, Ithaca, NY 14853-4701. Tel: (607) 255-7394.
(Write checks to "Cornell University.")

A.U.A. tapes: Institutions should order a master set directly from the A.U.A. Language Center, 17 Rajadamri Road, Bangkok 5, Thailand. Cassettes sold in sets only.

A.U.A. books: Books 1, 2, 3, $56.00 per set (8 cassettes/book).

Beginning Indonesian through Self-Instruction: Lessons 1–12, $210.00; lessons 13–25, $196.00; complete set $348.00; individual cassette, $7.50.

Indonesian Conversations: Complete set of 20 cassettes, $140.00.

Modern Spoken Cambodian: Set of 26 tapes, $189.00; individual tape, $7.50.

Pilipino through Self-Instruction: Book 1, $217; Book 2, $224; Book 3, $210; Book 4, $63; individual cassette, $7.50.

CORNELL UNIVERSITY
MODERN INDONESIA PROJECT PUBLICATIONS

102 West Avenue
Ithaca, New York 14850-3982

In Print

Number 6 *The Indonesian Elections of 1955,* Herbert Feith. 1957. 2d printing, 1971. 91 pp. $3.50. Interim report.

Number 7 *The Soviet View of the Indonesian Revolution,* Ruth T. McVey. 1957. 3d printing, 1969. 90 pp. $2.50. Interim report.

Number 25 *The Communist Uprisings of 1926–1927 in Indonesia: Key Documents,* ed. and intro. Harry J. Benda and Ruth T. McVey. 1960. 2d printing, 1969. 177 pp. $5.50. Translation.

Number 37 *Mythology and the Tolerance of the Javanese,* Benedict R. Anderson. 1965. 6th printing, 1988. 77 pp. $6.00. Monograph.

Number 43 *State and Statecraft in Old Java: A Study of the Later Mataram Period, 16th to 19th Century,* Soemarsaid Moertono. 1968. Rev. ed., 1981. 180 pp. $9.00. Monograph.

Number 45 *Indonesia Abandons Confrontation,* Franklin B. Weinstein. 1969. 94 pp. $3.00. Interim report.

Number 48 *Nationalism, Islam and Marxism,* Soekarno. Intro. by Ruth T. McVey. 1970. 2d printing, 1984. 62 pp. $4.00. Translation.

Number 49 *The Foundation of the Partai Muslimin Indonesia,* K. E. Ward. 1970. 75 pp. $3.00. Interim report

Number 50 *Schools and Politics: The Kaum Muda Movement in West Sumatra (1927–1933),* Taufik Abdullah. 1971. 257 pp. $6.00. Monograph.

Number 51 *The Putera Reports: Problems in Indonesian-Javanese War-Time Cooperation,* Mohammad Hatta. Trans. and intro. William H. Frederick. 1971. 114 pp. $4.00. Translation.

Number 52 *A Preliminary Analysis of the October 1, 1965, Coup in Indonesia* (Prepared in January 1966), Benedict R. Anderson, Ruth T. McVey, assist. Frederick P. Bunnell. 1971. 174 pp. $9.00. Interim report.

Number 55 *Report from Banaran: The Story of the Experiences of a Soldier during the War of Independence,* Maj. Gen. T. B. Simatupang. 1972. 186 pp. $6.50. Translation.

Number 56 *Golkar and the Indonesian Elections of 1971,* Masashi Nishihara. 1972. 56 pp. $3.50. Monograph.

Number 57 *Permesta: Half a Rebellion,* Barbara S. Harvey. 1977. 174 pp. $5.00. Monograph.

Number 58 *Administration of Islam in Indonesia,* Deliar Noer. 1978. 82 pp. $4.50. Monograph.

Number 59 *Breaking the Chains of Oppression of the Indonesian People: Defense Statement at His Trial on Charges of Insulting the Head of State, Bandung, June 7–10, 1979,* Heri Akhmadi. 1981. 201 pp. $8.75. Translation.

Number 60 *The Minangkabau Response to Dutch Colonial Rule in the Nineteenth Century,* Elizabeth E. Graves. 1981. 157 pp. $7.50. Monograph.

Number 61 *Sickle and Crescent: The Communist Revolt of 1926 in Banten,* Michael C. Williams. 1982. 81 pp. $6.00. Monograph.

Number 62 *Interpreting Indonesian Politics: Thirteen Contributions to the Debate, 1964–1981.* Ed. Benedict Anderson and Audrey Kahin, intro. Daniel S. Lev. 1982. 172 pp. $9.00. Interim report.

Number 63 *Dynamics of Dissent in Indonesia: Sawito and the Phantom Coup,* David Bourchier. 1984. 128 pp. $9.00. Interim report.

Number 64 *Suharto and His Generals: Indonesia's Military Politics, 1975–1983,* David Jenkins. 1984. 300 pp. $12.50. Monograph.

Number 65 *The Kenpeitai in Java and Sumatra.* Trans. from the Japanese by Barbara G. Shimer and Guy Hobbs, intro. Theodore Friend. 1986. 80 pp. $8.00. Translation.

Number 66 *Prisoners at Kota Cane,* Leon Salim. Trans. Audrey Kahin. 1986. 112 pp. $9.00. Translation.

Number 67 *Indonesia Free: A Biography of Mohammad Hatta,* Mavis Rose. 1987. 252 pp. $10.50. Monograph.

Number 68 *Intellectuals and Nationalism in Indonesia: A Study of the Following Recruited by Sutan Sjahrir in Occupation Jakarta,* J. D. Legge. 1988. 159 pp. $8.00. Monograph.

Number 69 *The Road to Madiun: The Indonesian Communist Uprising of 1948,* Elizabeth Ann Swift. 1989. 120 pp. $9.00. Monograph.

Number 70 *East Kalimantan: The Decline of a Commercial Aristocracy,* Burhan Magenda. 1991. 120 pp. $11.00. Monograph.

CONTRIBUTORS

Winniefred Anthonio teaches Minority Literature at Eastern Michigan University

Suzanne Brenner is Assistant Professor of Anthropology at the University of California at San Diego

Jan Wisseman Christie teaches in the Centre for South-East Asian Studies at the University of Hull

Hermann Kulke is Professor of Asian History at Kiel University

Pierre-Yves Manguin is with the École Française d'Extrême Orient

A. L. Reber is Research Bibliographer in the Southeast Asia Collection of the Ohio University Libraries in Athens, Ohio

A. Kohar Rony is Southeast Asia Area Specialist in the Asian Division of the Library of Congress, Washington, D.C.

K. W. Taylor is Associate Professor of Vietnamese Studies at Cornell University

Astri Wright is Assistant Professor of South and Southeast Asian Art at the University of Victoria

www.ingramcontent.com/pod-product-compliance
Lightning Source LLC
Chambersburg PA
CBHW080636230426
43663CB00016B/2894
* 9 7 8 0 8 7 7 2 7 8 5 3 5 *